A BIRD

— in the —

HAND

A BIRD

-in the-

HAND

And the Stories Behind
250 Other Common Expressions

Leonard Mann

Prentice Hall General Reference
New York   London   Toronto   Sydney   Tokyo   Singapore

PRENTICE HALL GENERAL REFERENCE
15 Columbus Circle
New York, NY 10023

Contact Library of Congress for full CIP data.

ISBN: 0-671-88995-8 (hardcover)

ISBN: 0-671-88994-X (paperback)

Manufactured in the United States of America

10 9 8 7 6 5 4 3 2 1

Contents

Introduction

This is a book of stories, both serious and humorous, some quite familiar and some little known. They have not previously appeared in the company of one another as they do here, nor have they been told with the intent and interpretation they are given in these pages.

These stories have this in common: Each has made a contribution to our language; from each has come an expression that found its way into our common speech. Altogether, offering both entertainment and enrichment, they stand as a literary family well worth knowing.

Sometimes a story is so powerful in its portrayal of an idea, image, or concept that its very phrasing enters permanently into our language, becoming a new and vivid means of expression: for example, "pound of flesh," "good samaritan," and "wolf in sheep's clothing." Sometimes a person, historical or fictional, has such singular qualities of character that his or her very name becomes a synonym for those qualities or for any individual possessing them: for example, *Uriah Heep, Don Juan, Jezebel,* and *Bluebeard.*

On occasion, someone is said to have "an Achilles' heel" or a "dog in the manger" attitude. Or it may be said that the "handwriting is on the wall" or that the "piper must be paid." These word combinations, in themselves, say nothing, or almost nothing. But each has a history, and because of its history, it forcefully portrays a concept that is both specific and graphic.

There was, in fact, a time when these word combinations did not mean what they mean now. Somewhere along the way, however, something happened to change that. More often than not, that happening was an event in history or a narrative in literature. These stories, whether factual or fictional, contain representations of life and experience so vivid that their language, in each instance, became an enduring part of the English vocabulary. It would be logical to suppose that a story that contributed so lastingly to our language would be a tale of some interest, and so it usually is.

In this family of stories, two salient features prevail. The first is insight. These stories have much to say about life, that is, what human life is and how it works. They are quite vocal concerning the dynamics of personal behavior and interpersonal relationships. The second feature is humor. Included here are a lot of the whimsical, the ridiculous, and the improbable, the sort that occurs notably in myths and fables. There is also a great deal of human interest and much having to do with the absurdities of human nature.

For me delving into this has been both entertaining and exciting, as I hope it is for you. So I offer this book of story sources of common expressions as they come to us from literature and history. This is not meant to be a "scholarly" piece of work; it is informal and designed for easy reading. It is not a dictionary or encyclopedia; it is a reading book, intended for enjoyment and enrichment.

Insofar as these stories relate to history, they are historically accurate. In a few instances, however, there are two or more possible sources for the expression, and in these instances I have developed the one story that appears most plausible or seems most appealing. In other instances, there exist multiple versions of the same story, such as in the legends of classical mythology. Here also it has been necessary to choose among the alternatives.

Especially when dealing with stories from ancient times, it is often difficult, and sometimes impossible, to distinguish between the historical and the mythological. This is a distinction I have not attempted to make. It has been my purpose to let the story be the story, without dissection or analysis.

In a small number of cases, some limited use of an expression may predate the story; nevertheless, these expressions were popularized by a particular story. Attempting to maintain a reasonable level of quality, I have omitted a few stories that otherwise might have been included, insisting rather that the stories comprising this book offer certain qualities of human interest, humor, insight, uniqueness, moral or aesthetic value, or some combination of these.

All are notable, though, for having added colorfully to the vigor and force of our everyday speech, giving us dramatic alternatives as we look for the more effective and the more exciting ways of saying things.

– A –

Achilles' Heel   Thetis, the mother of Achilles, was overly protective of her son. From the beginning she tried to prepare her child for the brutal bludgeonings of the world. In the daytime she rubbed his body with ambrosia, the elixir of the gods, and at night she laid him on the fire to toughen him against any future injury. She took him down to the dark valley of the River Styx, and there she dipped him in the magic water that divided the living from the dead.

Thetis believed that the water of the Styx would make her baby immune to all harm, so no arrow could ever wound him, no wild beast could tear him, and no spear could bring him pain. Moved by a mother's deep yearning, Thetis braved the perils of the desolate River Styx.

When she dipped her baby, though, Thetis made one mistake that years afterward would prove fatal to him. She failed to get the child's entire body under the water; the heel by which she held him was not immunized.

As the baby grew, his mother feared that some day he might have to fight in a war, for in those days there were many wars. She undertook to spare him this by rearing him as a girl. She dressed him in girls' clothes, put him to girls' tasks, and taught him girls' skills.

But one day a peddler came selling his wares. The sisters of Achilles were agog over the jewelry and fine linens, but Achilles showed interest only in the implements and weapons, handling them most skillfully, more skillfully than any female ever would. Thus it became known to all that Achilles was a boy.

Years later came the Trojan War, and Achilles was called to join in the siege of Troy. The struggle continued for ten years, and Achilles was involved in almost all of that conflict.

Agamemnon, a much older man, was commander-in-chief of the Greek forces, and there was bad blood between him and the impulsive young Achilles. At one time, Achilles withdrew completely from the fighting; but when Trojan prince Hector killed Achilles' best friend, he rejoined the struggle, soon afterward killing Hector in hand-to-hand combat.

A truce was arranged for the funeral of Hector, and during this interlude, Achilles saw and fell in love with a Trojan princess named Polyxena. Promising the Trojans that he would use his influence to persuade the Greeks to withdraw, he was given permission to marry the princess.

Going then into the temple of Apollo to arrange for the wedding, Achilles was ambushed and murdered by Paris, a son of King Priam of Troy and brother of Polyxena. (It was this Paris who had earlier taken a woman named Helen away from her husband and brought her to Troy, and it was for the purpose of "rescuing" Helen that the war was being fought.)

Anyway, in a cowardly act, from some hiding place, Paris fired the arrow that killed Achilles. And where did that arrow strike? Of course, in the heel, the very one by which his mother had held him when she dipped him in the Styx. An Achilles' heel, then, is any point of weakness, either physical or emotional, usually the latter, where there is susceptibility to harm or hurt. The expression is also used impersonally, as in reference to military, business, or social entities.

Aladdin's Lamp   Coming to us from a dim antiquity, *One Thousand and One Arabian Nights* is a collection of adventure tales from the Muslim culture of Persia, Arabia, India, and related areas. The story of Aladdin is one of these tales.

Aladdin was the son of an impoverished tailor who died early, leaving the young man and his mother in dire circumstances. Soon afterward, a stranger showed up in their city, a man claiming to be Aladdin's father's brother. Actually he was an imposter, an evil man, an African magician, and a practitioner of sorcery.

Under a nearby mountain in a treasure-filled crypt was a lamp the magician had located by his sorcery. He wanted that lamp; but an ancient wisdom had decreed that it could be brought out only by a young man of Aladdin's exact description.

Promising vast riches and placing a magic ring on Aladdin's finger, the imposter sent him down into the treasure cavern, where Aladdin secured the lamp and filled his pockets so full of precious stones that he was unable to climb out. This angered the magician so much that he sealed Aladdin in the cavern and went back to Africa.

Rubbing his hands together in despair, Aladdin accidentally rubbed the magic ring, and a powerful genie appeared, offering to help Aladdin in any way. Asking to be gotten out of the pit, the youth was immediately transported to the surface, the ring and the lamp in his possession, and his pockets bulging with priceless gems. At this moment, however, Aladdin had no idea of their worth.

Returning to his home, he and his mother continued to exist in poverty and hunger, until one day Aladdin decided to take the lamp to the dealers and try selling it to obtain a little money for food. To improve the appearance of the old relic, Aladdin's mother began to polish it, when instantly another genie, the Genie of the Lamp, stood before them, offering to do anything they wished. Their wish was for food, and it appeared, the very best and in enormous quantity. Now the two had a convenient way of supplying all their needs; the friendly genie stood always ready to act at their command.

One day, Aladdin sneaked a look at the young princess of the realm, the sultan's daughter, and was instantly in love. A huge dowry would be required to obtain the girl's hand in marriage; but the genie supplied what was needed, and the wedding was set for four months later. Within three months, though, the sultan changed his mind, and arranged to have his daughter marry the grand wazir's son.

Aladdin really messed up this arrangement, though, by asking the lamp's genie to transport the couple, bed and all, to his own house early on their wedding night, very early, frustratingly early! This happened two consecutive nights, and both times Aladdin's friendly genie threw out the bridegroom until sometime the following day. The fracas finally ended with the marriage of Aladdin to the princess, with the genie providing the most lavish of wedding embellishments, and in one night erecting a magnificent palace for the newlyweds.

All went well until the evil magician returned seeking revenge against Aladdin, and by trickery was able to make off with the lamp. In Aladdin's absence, by commanding the lamp's genie, he had the whole palace and all its occupants lifted up and transported from China to Africa. Aladdin's bride, his lamp, and everything else was now gone, mysteriously, as though they had never existed.

Deeply distressed, but having forgotten the long unused ring on his finger, Aladdin again accidentally rubbed it, and the ring's genie appeared. This genie, however, didn't have the power to undo the actions of the magician. He could not bring back the palace, but he could transport Aladdin to Africa, which he did. Here, Aladdin was able to kill the magician and recover the lamp. Then, by means of the lamp, his palace was moved back to its place in China.

There's more to the tale, but this much is enough, too much really. It's wholly preposterous, obviously. Nevertheless, Aladdin and his lamp are widely known and well remembered. They appear often in our speech and literature. To wish for Aladdin's lamp is to wish for some miraculous power. One who is expected to accomplish some extremely difficult task may very well respond, "You know, I don't have an Aladdin's lamp."

Albatross Around Your Neck   An albatross around your neck is the excessive burden you put on yourself by your own ill-advised action or by having blundered into difficulties.

The expression comes, of course, from that exquisite, mystical poem of Samuel Taylor Coleridge, *The Rime of the Ancient Mariner*. As narrative poems go, this is one of the great ones. An aged and wizened seaman, whose years of seafaring are now long past, seizes compulsively upon a certain guest at a wedding, compelling him to listen to the story of a strange, strange voyage. A bare-bones version of these events goes as follows.

The ancient wind-driven ship sails south, but encounters such mountainous icebergs that it is totally immobilized. The albatross appears, that great white seabird; for all seamen it is the best of omens. As the great bird circles above, the ice is broken up and the ship passes through. But the ship is haunted by the bird, following insidiously, perching sometimes among the rigging and seeming to view the ship with a certain uncanny, supernatural air.

Able to endure the eerie circumstance no longer, with his crossbow the ancient mariner shoots and kills the bird. Doing so, he has violated a cardinal code of the sea: Never slay an albatross, for to do so always brings the worst of ill fortune. Ill fortune now comes, immediately. A deep depression settles upon the crew, the wind ceases and the ship is becalmed, there is no rain and no fresh water, and a slimy sea crawls with slimy creatures.

Putting the blame on him, the crew secures the body of the dead albatross around the ancient mariner's neck, its long, slender wings almost touching the deck in front of him. They take the cross he has worn there, and in its place they put this accursed thing, and as though it were one of the chains of hell, he cannot be rid of it.

Out of the mists, a ghost ship then appears, its skeletal hull and phantom sails, and on its deck a pale woman and her mate, Death. Soon, every member of the 200-man crew is dead, their glazed eyes glistening in the moonlight, and staring at the mariner from everywhere. He is left alone, that horrible thing about his neck.

At last, though, he is able to shake off the spell that holds him and find his way to God in prayer. The albatross dislodges from his body, dropping like a stone into the sea. Some strange undersea force impels the ship homeward; the dead men stand up, although still dead, taking their assigned places and doing their normal work.

The ship arrives in its home port at last, and the mariner is rescued by the hermit, a singular personage who appears to have knowledge of such alien goings-on. By the hermit, the ancient mariner's sin is expunged, and the ship abruptly disappears beneath the harbor waters with all its grisly cargo.

Amazon   This story is not about a river, but it is convenient to begin with one. In 1541, Spanish adventurer Francisco de Orellana made the first exploration of the world's mightiest watercourse—the Amazon. Draining most of the northern half of South America, it flows eastward almost 4,000 miles to the Atlantic Ocean. One may suppose the river was named for its size and strength. Not so; it was named for a group of women. Orellana reported having found the river's banks populated by tribes of warlike women. They were the Amazons.

A powerful nation, the Amazons played a major role in Greek mythology and, to some degree, Greek history—maybe. Their land was somewhere in the Black Sea area, their primary occupation was war, and their culture and traditions were unusual. Descended from Ares, the god of war, his genes were clearly in their blood. To facilitate archery, the right breast of each newborn was surgically treated so that it would never develop. Hence the name *Amazon*, Greek for "those having no breasts." (Male infants were usually killed, sometimes maimed for life, or, on rare occasions, given to the fathers.)

How could a race made up of one sex hope to perpetuate itself? These women detested men and would tolerate them only in the most menial roles as servants and slaves. But the Amazons were dependent on men for one thing, procreation. But under their law, no woman was permitted to mate with a man until she had killed at least one.

Many of the Greek heroes, at one time or another, had the harrowing experience of fighting against these women—Bellerophon, Theseus, Heracles, and Achilles. The ninth of Heracles' twelve labors entailed a fight with them. His taskmaster, Eurystheus, required him to get the girdle worn by Amazon queen Hippolyte and return with it—a rather risky undertaking to make off with any woman's girdle, especially a queen's, and even more dangerous, an Amazon queen's. The mighty Heracles did it, however, and in the process killed Hippolyte.

Accompanying Heracles on this expedition was Theseus, one of the more important of the Greeks. As they left the Amazons' country, Theseus took with him an Amazon princess named Antiope, sister of the slain queen. At home in Athens the highly improbable came to pass: He married the woman.

Predictably, the marriage was troubled from the start. When Theseus left this wife for another woman, the Amazons swore vengeance against all Greeks and marched into Athens. They made their camp on the hilltop where their ancestor, the war god Ares, once fought a crucial battle. Named in honor of him, the hill was called the Areopagus (later known also as Mars Hill, *Mars* being the Roman name for the same god). They fought fiercely, but at last the Amazons were compelled to go home in defeat, and in the fracas Antiope was killed.

At another time, when Agamemnon and his Greeks were at Troy attempting to rescue Helen, the Amazons showed up to help the Trojans defend their city. Fierce and skillful warriors, they proved to be a major problem for the Greeks.

The Amazons worshipped Artemis, the virgin goddess and goddess of women, whose magnificent temple at Ephesus was one of the seven wonders of the ancient world. They lived to fight and their name has long been synonymous with immense size, strength, and fierceness, especially as applied to women. So as a warning to all gentlemen: Think at least twice before calling a woman an Amazon, for you may find out the hard way that she is!

Annie Oakley   Phoebe Ann Moses was born August 13, 1860, in a rural community at the western edge of Ohio, and in this same community she died in 1926. In the sixty-six intervening years, this quiet woman made a name for herself in markmanship, an arena usually reserved for rough and rugged men. Annie Oakley, as she became known, had an uncanny ability with guns; in precision and trick shooting she was a celebrity without peer.

Three years after her father died, when she was five, Annie began shooting and bringing home small game for the family table. Her older brother loaded the rifle for her, as she was too small to do this herself. (She never grew over five feet tall or weighed more than 100 pounds.)

Soon Annie was hunting commercially, supplying Cincinnati hotels with pheasant and other small game. Instead of a shotgun she used a rifle, always killing her quarry with one shot to the head, thus leaving the edible flesh undamaged and so obtaining a higher price for it.

Annie's fame as a markswoman began to spread. When she was fourteen, one of her Cincinnati customers arranged a trapshooting contest between her and a renowned sharpshooter named Frank Butler. She beat him, and a year later she married him. The two became a team, putting on exhibitions of shooting skills in various locations.

Then in 1885, Buffalo Bill Cody persuaded Annie and Frank to join his Wild West Circus. A skillful showman with a flair for publicity, he gave Annie top billings countrywide. She traveled with the circus for seventeen seasons—much of this time drawing a salary greater than the president of the United States—and attracted hundreds of thousands of people.

In those days, good marksmanship was a coveted skill, and in many areas it was necessary for survival. Annie was one of the very best, and therefore greatly admired.

In one of her acts, as Frank held a playing card, Annie perforated it with rifle bullets at preselected spots. In those days complimentary tickets for events were usually punched at certain places for identification or to indicate use. Because both types of cards had holes in them, free passes or tickets came to be known as "Annie Oakleys." Sometimes the name is used for anything that is free; for example, in baseball a base-on-balls is sometimes called an Annie Oakley.

Although she left Buffalo Bill's circus in 1902, Annie continued shooting, traveling, giving exhibitions, and teaching others the fine points of marksmanship. During World War I, approaching sixty years old, Annie toured American military camps to entertain the troops.

Almost twenty years after Annie's death, and after four long, dark years of World War II, Irving Berlin authored a musical comedy, a 1946 Broadway production by Rodgers and Hammerstein, entitled *Annie Get Your Gun.*

Apple of Discord   Avid storytellers, the people of ancient Greece loved the tales of their gods and heroes. Thetis was a nature goddess who the great god Zeus once desired to have as his wife. That union, however, did not come about, and the beautiful Thetis eventually married Peleus, a mere mortal.

At the wedding feast the immortals and the great of the earth were gathered. One of the immortals, Eris, had not been invited. As the goddess of discord she was usually unwelcome on such occasions, as she stirred up trouble whenever possible.

Angry at being omitted from the guest list on this major social occasion, Eris showed up anyway, eager to cause dissention among the guests. She appeared for just a moment, glanced disdainfully upon the assembled crowd, and tossed into their midst a single golden apple. On that apple was written, "For the most beautiful"; it was to be given to the most beautiful woman present.

You can guess what happened next—this clever act of the scheming goddess precipitated an immediate beauty contest! Aphrodite claimed the apple, as she was the goddess of beauty. But Hera could think of no one more beautiful than she. And Athena refused to recognize the claim of either. Everyone began to take sides, and havoc ensued.

The three competing goddesses, though, did agree on one point: They would permit the handsome prince, Paris, to make the decision. But each tried a bit of bribery first.

If Paris would rule in Hera's favor, she promised him wealth and power. Athena offered the gift of everlasting wisdom. Aphrodite pledged that one day he would have the most beautiful woman in the world as his wife. Wealth, wisdom, and woman! Of these three, Paris chose the third and Aphrodite was given the apple.

(Later, Paris did indeed get his woman. She was a queen, Helen by name, and Paris got her by taking her away from the husband she already had and sailing away with her to Troy, where his father and mother were king and queen. It was this bit of perfidy that brought on the Trojan War, a ten-year attempt by the Greeks to rescue "fair Helen.")

All this because of an apple, albeit a golden one. It was a trifle really, but trifles sometimes have a way of sundering relationships and driving people apart. There we have it, the story behind the apple of discord. Such an apple, flung into any peaceful or happy scene, may send out shock waves that can take a long time to subside.

Armageddon   This expression comes from a story that stands as one of the towering summits on the landscape of history. With the career of Jesus of Nazareth, by his followers known as the Christ, a new faith was born into the world—the Christian faith. During the first three centuries of their history, the Christians were subjected to horrible persecution; to be a Christian was a violation of Roman law, and in those times Rome ruled the world.

In the latter part of that first century, a truly remarkable man named John was among those arrested and prosecuted for his faith (whether one of the twelve apostles of Jesus or some other by this name, we do not know). He was a person of maturity and wisdom as well as a trusted leader in the Christian movement. His stature was such that the authorities chose not to impose the death penalty, and instead banished him to a penal colony on the island Patmos in the Aegean Sea. As he languished in lonely isolation, he thought about his fellow Christians out there struggling against their awful trials and he had a passionate desire to help them.

But how? Under guard on a penal island, he could not go to them, nor could they come to him. He might write to them, but as a prisoner, John was deemed guilty of propagating a seditious notion that could very well subvert the power of Rome. Anything he might write would therefore be closely scrutinized before it got off the island. What he wanted to say to his people was something those Romans would never approve; he knew this, and so did the Romans.

So what did John do? He wrote in code. He put his message in the form of a report of a vision he had experienced. It was a vast panoramic drama, filled with subtle symbolism expressed in delicately expanded metaphors and amplified by elaborate descriptions of scenes and situations. The censors let the report pass (probably thinking it was gibberish), and John's suffering friends eagerly read and deeply pondered what John had written, got its message, and rejoiced.

The message was this: Rome will go down; God at last will win; evil will perish and righteousness will rule; the troubles of the day are temporary, but joy will be eternal. Among the many figures of speech John used to communicate his truth, two have found lasting places in our language.

One is *Armageddon*. John's vision pictured a colossal final conflict between the forces of good and evil, with good the victor. Because the battlefield was described as the plain of Megiddo (already an over-worked battleground), the final battle was called the battle of Armageddon. The word survives as a synonym for any critical, decisive, final sort of struggle.

The other figure of speech is *millennium*; the word means a period of 1,000 years, but in this use it's a time where there will be perfect peace and felicity, as all contradictory forces are utterly immobilized by the power of God and good.

Hence, the millennium is an expression denoting a peaceful and perfect time in the future. The word figures commonly in some of the jargon of our day. One may say, for example, of a certain social proposal, "The idea is good, but I don't think it will bring in the millennium," meaning the proposal may help, but it won't solve everything.

Asmodeus Flight   An Asmodeus flight would be one in which the flier, soaring above the rooftops, is able to look into each house as though the roof has been lifted away. What a revelation! To express uncertainty as to public feeling or opinion, one may say, "Do you think I have some Asmodeus vision to see everything that's going on out there?" Seeking a better knowledge of what is happening, one may say, "I wish an Asmodeus would appear and show me around." A tabloid reporter, probing for the sensational, might wish for the power to make an Asmodeus flight.

Well, there is a rather good story concerning such a flight, by Alain René LeSage (written in 1707) entitled *Le Diable Boiteux* or *The Devil on Two Sticks*. Although it was set in Spain, the novel was a commentary on French manners and morals, especially the Parisian ones. Many prominent French men and women felt the sting of LeSage's satire and sarcasm, their respective identities veiled, but clearly implied.

The story begins as young Don Cleophas Zambullo is set upon one October night by a gang of hired thugs. Fleeing across the rooftops of Madrid, he came upon a lighted attic window, entered, and found himself in the quarters of a powerful magician. Hearing a moan of distress, he discovered a demon imprisoned in a bottle. The prisoner identified himself as Asmodeus, a demon with one redeeming quality: He always befriended troubled lovers.

Being at the moment one of these, Don Cleophas set the prisoner free. Tumbling from the bottle, he took the form of a misshapen, crippled, and ugly dwarf who walked with two crutches.

But Asmodeus could fly, and fly he did. As a reward for his freedom, he took Don Cleophas on a flight of exploration above the city of Madrid, and the dwarfish demon proved an informed and competent tour guide. Although he did a lot of talking and told a lot of stories, he enthusiastically pointed out the scenery, always knowing, it seemed, which rooftops concealed the more interesting scenes. There were many of these, and widely varied, both ugly and beautiful.

At one point along the way, the two looked in upon Donna Thomasa, a woman whose double-dealing shenanigans had made Don Cleophas a troubled lover in the first place. They found her entertaining the ruffians she had hired to chase him across the rooftops. At the request of Don Cleophas, Asmodeus cast a spell upon the scene, resulting in two deaths, several arrests, and Thomasa's eventual expulsion to the colonies.

At another point, the two discovered the home of Don Pedro de Escolano being destroyed by fire. Inside, his daughter, the beautiful Donna Seraphina, was trapped in a room. Again, Don Cleophas begged Asmodeus to intervene, and again he did. Changing himself into the form of Don Cleophas, he rescued the girl. Eventually, Asmodeus returned to the service of the master magician and Don Cleophas was married to Donna Seraphina. End of story—naturally.

Atalantian Apples   A woman who chooses not to marry sometimes has difficulty fending off the men who feel otherwise about her decision. To protect her singleness, she may develop all sorts of strategies.

The all-time prizewinner among such strategies, though, was the one developed by an Arcadian maiden named Atalanta.

She was a beauty, athletic, agile, skilled, and fleet-footed. Her father, Iasius, wished for grandchildren and urged her to accept one of the many hopeful fellows who stood in line. But Atalanta had been warned by the Delphian Oracle that marriage would be unwise for her, and in those days the Peloponnesian people put much stock in the word of that all-seeing prophet. For a long time, therefore, Atalanta steadfastly resisted all offers of marriage.

However, caught in the strong crosscurrents between her father's wish and the Oracle's warning, Atalanta eventually yielded—somewhat. She announced that any man wishing to marry her would have to run against her in a race; if the man won, she would marry him; and if the man lost, she would kill him; and the man must agree to these terms in advance.

Well, believe it or not, a lot of fellows took her on. Not one of them ever won; Atalanta outran every challenger and then dispatched them according to previous agreement. This ongoing show attracted countrywide attention, and many people came to watch it.

One who came was Hippomenes, a handsome, strong, intelligent citizen who had no intention of putting his life on the line for any woman. But when he saw Atalanta, he was so impressed by her grace and beauty that he decided to enter the competition.

When Atalanta saw him, she was as impressed with him as he was with her, and she cringed at the thought of having to kill him. But a deal was a deal; she was committed, and so was he.

As he prepared for the race, Hippomenes approached Aphrodite, the goddess of love, saying to her, "You stuck me with love for this woman; you got me into this; I expect you now to get me out of it." Responding favorably, Aphrodite gave Hippomenes three golden apples with instructions for using them.

At the critical moment the signal was given, and the strangest of all races began. At the beginning, Hippomenes pulled out ahead of Atalanta, but she soon came up beside him. As she was passing, he threw out in front of her one of those golden apples. Atalanta hesitated, then stopped, and picked up the apple—and in so doing lost the lead to Hippomenes. Later, as she was passing him, another of the golden apples was flung out; again she picked it up, and again

Hippomenes took the lead. And yet a third time it happened precisely as before.

The result? Hippomenes won the race and Atalanta married him. One further outcome: An expression sometimes heard in English speech meaning to create a distraction or a diversion is to "toss a golden apple." One who would stay on course and keep at it should beware of Atalantian apples that may appear along the way. On occasion, the advice is good: "Don't stop to pick up the apples."

For Atalanta, though, it didn't work out badly at all; Hippomenes was a fine gentleman.

Attila the Hun   *Flagellum Dei,* "Scourge of God"—by this name fifth-century Romans knew Attila, king of the Huns. The Romans held the man in low esteem, and because they did, so do we. Attila the Hun is the name we give to an aggressive, ruthless, barbarous person who goes about rudely running over everybody and everything. A person who is uncouth or rude, thoughtless or abusive of others, may be spoken of as an Attila the Hun.

Actually, the name *Attila* meant "little father"; and if the name suggests a gentle and loving parent, then this leader of the Huns was grossly misnamed. The Huns were a rugged Germanic people of north-central Europe. Beginning in 434, they were ruled by two brothers, Attila and Bleda, who shared the kingship.

In those times, the Roman empire existed in two divisions, the Western at Rome and the Eastern (often known as the Byzantine Empire) at Constantinople. Early in their reign, the Hun brothers moved against the Eastern empire, exacting annual "tributes." When the people could not pay the outrageous sums, the Huns repeatedly marched against them and increased their demands.

Throughout all of this, Attila maintained friendly relations with Roman general Aetius, the actual ruling authority in the West. (By 445, Atilla had murdered his brother to gain sole command of the kingdom.)

Then in 450 a freakish development complicated things immensely. Roman Emperor Valentinian III had a sister, Honoria, who had been committed to a marriage with which she was very displeased. She sent her ring to Attila with the request that he assist her in avoiding the marriage. Interpreting this as an offer to marry him, he claimed her as his wife and demanded half of the Western empire as her dowry.

The dowry not being immediately forthcoming, Attila prepared to attack Rome, but the Romans and the Visigoths combined their forces and dealt him the only real defeat he ever experienced. Later, however, he rebounded to invade Italy and sack several cities; but because of famine and disease, his forces were compelled to withdraw. The following year, 453, as he was preparing for another foray into the Eastern empire, he died in his sleep. His body was taken by a few of his men to a secret place and buried. These men were then put to death, so that the location of Attila's grave would never be known. It isn't; but his name and his reputation have not been forgotten.

Axe to Grind   The oldtime grindstone was a wheel-shaped piece of sandstone, two or three feet in diameter, mounted in a rigid frame and turned by a hand crank. Turning the stone was hard work; it was much less strenuous to hold an axe in place on the wheel than it was to keep that wheel spinning.

Early in the nineteenth century, Pennsylvanian Charles Miner wrote of a childhood experience involving a grindstone. One cold winter morning, as the boy was about to leave for school, he was approached by a man carrying an axe. The man spoke very kindly to the child, calling him "my pretty boy," and inquired, "Does your father have a grindstone?" The boy politely answered, "Yes, sir," and the man replied, "Will you let me grind my axe upon it?" As the boy led the man to the grindstone, the man kept up a constant stream of flattery, telling the lad what a fine fellow he was.

Since two people were required to grind an axe, the man put the boy to turning the crank, all the while chattering about the boy's strength and skill. Long before the grinding was completed, the boy's hands were blistered and bleeding; also, the school bell rang.

Finally, the axe finished to a fine edge, the man took it from the stone, sternly saying to the boy, "You little rascal, you're late for school; get going." No word of thanks, no apology, no more praise or pleasantry, only an abrupt, harsh dismissal that said, "My axe is sharp; I got what I wanted from you, kid; now get lost."

The writer of this story, which comes from an essay entitled "Who Will Turn the Grindstone," said that afterward when he observed one heaping excessive praise upon another, he always thought: That man wants something; he has an axe to grind.

The phrase very early made a place for itself in our language, and there it stands, firmly fixed. Adulation or praise given insincerely may arouse suspicion about the motive behind it; to express that suspicion, we may say, "That person has an axe to grind." Most flattery is not free; an instrument of barter, it is often given with an ulterior motive.

– B –

Babbittry   In the quest for life, George Follansbee Babbitt got lost along the way and never really found himself. Getting stuck at a point of mediocrity, he never reached self-realization or fulfillment. For him there was always an awareness of what might have been.

A middle-age real estate broker in the mythical midwestern city of Zenith, Babbitt stood about midway on the scale of business stature. In his personal development he was also at about midpoint, knowledgeable, disciplined, industrious, but utterly without savvy concerning cultural, social, and human values.

On Sundays, he sometimes attended church with his family, but through the week his view of God was almost totally eclipsed by dollar signs. At home he was usually bossy and grumpy, at work harddriving and efficient. His wife, Myra, was a rather bland woman who he had married mostly to avoid hurting her feelings. While he lived for success, Myra lived only for him and their children, a daughter and a son now in early adulthood.

Babbitt was proud of his modern house located in a better part of town. Almost exclusively, he socialized within the business community. With these folk he could drink Prohibition-era gin at a party at his lavish house and consider the morning-after hangover a normal cost of doing business. He was an insider in the local Booster Club and could sell real estate at double its value.

But all was not smooth in the life of George Babbitt. His best friend, dating from college days, Paul Reisling, who should have been a violinist but was a roofing contractor instead, was married to Zilla, a demanding, vicious, and nagging woman. To provide Paul a few days respite, the two men went on vacation to the lakes and woodlands of Maine. While there, Babbitt concluded his life wasn't all it should be, resolving to make it more simple and less hectic—but nothing came of it.

Once he happened upon his friend Reisling at dinner alone with a beautiful woman. Later he promised Paul he would keep the secret, and secretly he envied his friend's independence and initiative. At that moment, he thought of himself as stodgy and dull, although he didn't understand why.

Seneca Doane, a brilliant young attorney, ran for mayor of Zenith. Doane was a liberal, and Babbitt worked hard on the campaign against him. After Doane's defeat, the Booster Club rewarded Babbitt by selecting him as their vice president. By this expression of esteem, his pride was puffed to the bragging point.

But his moment of glory proved brief. Paul Reisling shot his insufferable wife, but didn't succeed in killing her. Reisling was sent to prison, and Babbitt's world collapsed around him. He began to doubt the power of money and, engulfed in a cloud of loneliness, he began to drink far more heavily than was his custom.

He became involved with Tanis Judique, an attractive widow, and for a while he found solace in her liberal, bohemian circle of friends. He even made peace with Seneca Doane. He felt a vague inkling of freedom, as though for the first time in his life he was really alive, although he wasn't altogether sure of it.

Then came the inevitable reaction to his affair and heavy drinking by his business associates and cronies. He was suddenly unpopular, uninvited, left out, and even snubbed in the streets. In the misery of near-isolation, he discovered he had little to go on, that he had no real resources within himself.

When Myra came down with a serious illness, Babbitt suddenly discovered he really loved her, that all the while a profound reality had been lost beneath an overgrowth of the superficial. He broke with Judique, and turned away from her liberal friends, returning to his wife and family. Myra recovered. Babbitt joined the Good Citizens League and became again one of the Booster Club's best boosters. After his brief bit of probing at the edges, he settled back into essentially the same old groove. It was all he knew, and he knew it wasn't enough, but there he was.

His son Ted chose to become a mechanic rather than go to college and married the girl next door. Babbitt had always wanted Ted to have a college degree, and although shocked by this development, he was privately pleased that his son had the courage to chart a course and do his own thing. To Ted he confessed that he had always been afraid of himself and of Zenith, saying pathetically, "I've never done anything I wanted to in my whole life."

Since 1922, when Sinclair Lewis wrote the story of Babbitt, this man's name has represented the preeminence of materialism in mind and spirit.

The name is used to denote strongly peer-conscious people who are covetous of local esteem and who devote themselves wholly to the pursuit of the prestige and power that can be bought with money. Their methods are not necessarily dishonest, but they are not precisely scrupulous either. In the social spectrum, Babbittry is ordinarily an ugly, uncomplimentary word.

Babel   As this old story begins, the whole earth is of one language and few words—which would appear to be a desirable state of affairs. There is a migration of people into a land called Shinar, later known as Babylonia. Having no stones with which to build, but an ample supply of mud, these people learn the art of making bricks and are proud of their new skill. A strong wall made of these would shelter them well from the attack of enemies. Better yet, they could build a whole city in which refuge could be taken.

So the people say, "Let us build ourselves a city, and a tower with its top in the heavens; and let us make a name for ourselves, lest we be scattered abroad in the earth." They start constructing the city, which has at its center a tower.

But God is displeased; these people are too arrogant, too ambitious, and too self-centered. Their power is becoming too god-like, so God sends a mighty confusion into their midst; suddenly they are unable to understand the speech of one another. The mortar-mixers cannot understand the masons, nor the hod-carriers the scaffold-builders; no one can understand anyone else.

Because of this, fights begin, blame is cast, and everyone is suspicious of everyone else. There is a lot of shouting, communication completely breaks down, and the work eventually stops. The people scatter; little groups go their separate ways, doing the very thing they had sought to avoid in the beginning.

What is remembered most from this biblical tale is all the confusion, commotion, and ferment. And in our speaking, we refer to it a lot— a Babel, or a Babel of sounds. It's any confusion of noises, any state where divergent voices clamor for attention, where there is much speaking, but little is said, and even less is heard.

Beau Brummell   Born into English aristocracy, educated at Oxford, inheriting a fortune, he never did anything notable or earthshakingly important in his entire life. But his renown has spread into the far corners of the English-speaking world, and his name is a household word.

His name was George Bryan Brummell (1778–1840), known commonly as Beau Brummell. *Beau* was something of a nickname; a *beau* was a *dandy*—a man obsessed with his appearance, who gave inordinate attention to the clothes he wore.

Brummell was all of that. It is said that he usually spent about eight hours getting dressed for a social occasion, aided by a valet! He moved in the most elevated circles of British society, and his manner of dress was always a matter of considerable interest. Generally considered a model of fashion and elegance, he was also regarded as a wit. Popular at parties, he was himself a topic for much of the party patter.

In his earlier years, Brummell was an intimate friend and companion of the prince of Wales who later ruled England as King George IV. But in 1813 the two men quarreled, and this petty bit of peevishness parted them permanently. By Brummell's account, he was riding with a friend in a London park when they met the prince, who spoke affably to Brummell's companion, but not to him, whereupon Brummell loudly asked his riding buddy, "Who's your fat friend?" He intended for the prince to hear the question, and the prince did.

As a consequence of this rift, Brummell's name thereafter was often absent from many London guest lists. Then, after he squandered his inherited fortune and stacked up gambling debts, he fled to France in 1816. There, twenty-four years later, he died in a hospital for the insane.

But his name survives him. A Beau Brummell is a man obsessed with his own appearance, addicted to fancy dress. The expression can be heard in humorous or good-natured reference to someone who at the moment just happens to be well dressed—and sometimes it's used concerning one who never is, as in, "A Beau Brummell he isn't."

Bird in the Hand   First was Aesop (perhaps a legend only) and later came Theocritus (a very real person actually), two ancient Greeks. Between the two of them we get the saying, "A bird in the hand is worth two in the bush," meaning that it is better to cherish and appreciate what we have than to look longingly upon the things that are beyond our reach; better to hold onto what is sure than surrender it to grab for the uncertain.

Among the stories of Aesop was one concerning a nightingale who happily sat on the branch of an oak. Seeing him there, a hawk swooped down, seized him, and carried him away. High on a towering precipice, the hawk was preparing to eat the nightingale when the victim began to beg for his life, contending that he was much too small a bird to satisfy the hunger of a monstrous hawk.

The nightingale argued that the hawk should go after the bigger birds, that he was wasting his time and energy in pursuit of birds unworthy of his great strength and skill. After listening to the smaller bird's clever plea, the hawk replied, "You seem to think I'm a skillful hunter, which I am. But you must also think I'm stupid, which I'm not. It would indeed be stupid of me to let go the food I already have in my claws to pursue some other bird which as yet I cannot even see." And those were the last words that nightingale ever heard.

In another of his fables, Aesop told of a commercial fisherman who one day, despite all his labor, caught only one small fish. The poor creature began instantly to implore the fisherman's mercy. "Please, sir," he begged, "please put me back into the water. I'm too small to be of any worth to you. If you let me go, I will in time grow up to be a really big fish. Then you can catch me again and can sell me for a great deal of money." Rejecting this entreaty, the fisherman responded, "It would be most foolish of me to give up the small gain I already have for the chance of a greater gain which is by no means certain."

Three centuries after Aesop, Theocritus emerged as a giant on the

Greek cultural scene. A pioneer poet and literary innovator, he developed new poetic styles and dealt extensively with new themes. His poems were largely the pastoral type, cast in rural or natural settings, glorifying common things—telling stories of animals and people, mountains and forests and flowers, lakes and flowing streams.

Since it was from these scenes that Aesop had drawn his fables, it was virtually inevitable that Theocritus would make use of them. Among those that appeared in his poetry were the tales of the hawk and the nightingale and the fisherman and the fish. The point of both being the same, Theocritus summarized the two, giving us the expression "A bird in the hand is worth two in the bush."

Blast from Astolpho's Horn   What was it like, this blast from Astolpho's horn? Well, for one thing, it created a panic. And since that horn's first blast, the event has stood for any force that causes a sudden commotion among people, producing fear or some chaotic uproar. To say that something comes like a blast from Astolpho's horn is to say it is abruptly upsetting, disturbing, or alarming.

The story is from Italian poet Ludovico Ariosto, an episode in his long narrative poem *Orlando Furioso*. Although they have an historical setting, the Orlando tales are largely myth, offering a great deal of fascinating fiction surrounding sorceries, enchantments, and magic of various kinds.

In one such episode, Astolpho was given a magic horn by the Indian enchantress Logistilla. Astolpho, an English knight, had come to France as one of Charlemagne's twelve paladins to assist in the struggle against the Moors and Pagans. In the belief that Astolpho would need some special weapon, the friendly enchantress gave him the horn. A horn a weapon? So it proved to be, and a mighty one too.

With his companions, Astolpho was caught in a violent four-day storm at sea. Driven off course, the ship was thrust into the harbor of a land controlled completely by women, their strange history dating back 2,000 years to the Trojan War. When the Greek patriots then returned after many years of combat, most found that their wives had taken up with other men and that their homes were filled with children not their own (many now grown to maturity). These unfaithful wives were forgiven, but the illegitimate children were forced out.

One of these outcasts was Phalantus, who fitted a ship for piracy and, with a hundred others, took to the high seas. Remaining for a while at a Cretan city, these handsome youths attracted a large number of interested women. Leaving there, they took these women with them, and the women in turn took all the jewels and treasures they were able to scrounge. Landing in an uninhabited area, these fellows enjoyed ten days of connubial frenzy, then left their women, taking all their treasures, and returned to the seas.

Quite understandably, the women vowed everlasting revenge against all men. Becoming known as the killer women, they unceremoniously murdered every man who crossed their paths and sacked every ship that came into near waters.

Realizing at last, though, that without men their race would soon perish, they devised a plan to recruit a few sturdy males for breeding purposes. Any captured man was given a choice between becoming one of the daily sacrifices at the Temple of Vengeance or fighting ten captive knights all at one time. He who killed all ten men must then have sex with ten of the women that night. Any man who thus qualified himself was spared to become a breeder.

To control the male population, women could have only one male baby each; all other male babies were killed. After nearly 2,000 years of this, the strange colony had grown to more than 20,000 women, all trained, vicious warriors. In all this time, no man had ever gotten away from them alive.

Into this weird world came Astolpho with his magic horn. He and his friends, now captives, were able to arrange for a ship, but escaping to the ship—with 10,000 of the women around them in the arena and another 10,000 standing guard at the exits, along the seaside, and around the harbor—was an apparent impossibility.

Small as their chances were, the escape party undertook to fight their way out. From the outset, their attempt was doomed; the arrows and lances were too many, and the women's rage too strong. But then an eerie, unearthly sound was heard through the precinct—it was a blast from Astolpho's horn! There was immediate pandemonium as every person tried to flee, somewhere, anywhere. Some were trampled in the gates, some leaped into the sea and were drowned, and there were even some who ran for ten miles, never stopping.

In the shake-up, Astolpho's party reached their escape vessel and, in their confusion, hastily sailed away without him. Later, with the continued aid of his terrifying horn, he made his escape by another route.

Bluebeard   Any young woman who aspired to be a wife of Bluebeard should have chosen to be his seventh—he murdered the first six. This infamous character was created in 1697 by French poet Charles Perrault and has since been re-created by numerous others. In the beginning, the story was a fairy tale, although there was little of the fanciful about it; mostly, it was cold-blooded villainy.

The man known as Bluebeard did indeed have a blue beard. Not the most popular fellow around, he became something of a mysterious recluse. He did, however, persuade seven women to marry him. Maybe they married for money, for the fiend was filthy rich. Each wedding was quickly followed by the strange, unexplained disappearance of each bride—until the seventh, that is.

The seventh bride had a sister and several brothers with whom she was very close; but leaving all these, she went to live nearby in Bluebeard's fabulous castle. Not long afterward, the groom announced that he must go away on an extended business journey. Before leaving, he gave his new wife keys to all castle doors, urging her to use the place freely and to have friends in as she wished. He took extreme care, however, to point out one of the keys that was never, never to be used; he was also careful to specify which door that key would open: "But don't open it; don't ever, ever open that door," he said.

Just as Bluebeard knew she would, his wife opened that door. Naturally, she simply had to know what was inside the forbidden room. As she stood there, the key in her hand, peering into the darkness of that dank, windowless chamber, her vision slowly adjusting to the dark, what finally took shape before her terror-stricken eyes were the bloody bodies of Bluebeard's six former wives. The key fell from her hand, but she snatched it up quickly, closed and locked the door, and ran away as though all hell were snarling at her heels.

But when she had dropped the key it had gotten blood on it. Lest Bluebeard see that blood and realize what she had done, she tried to wash the blood away. But this was no ordinary key—it was magic. The blood was indelible, and when it was cleaned off of one side, it reappeared on the other.

Very soon, having curtailed his journey, the master of the castle returned. "My keys?" he said, and held out his hand. The trembling girl watched, as one by one he looked carefully at the keys, giving most careful attention to one. He pronounced immediate judgment: "You must die!" and he drew his sword. "No, wait!" the girl cried. "Give me a few minutes to say my prayers." Bluebeard, a generous soul, allowed the terrified girl exactly seven and one-half minutes.

The condemned hastily retreated to an adjoining room, not for praying as Bluebeard believed, but to call out to her visiting sister who was within hearing distance. "Are our brothers coming?" she cried. They were, two of them, both professional fighting men.

Bluebeard tried to run, but the brothers struck him down even before he reached the porch. None of the six former wives lived long enough to have babies, so Bluebeard had no other heirs and his vast estate became the property of his widowed bride—and her devoted family, of course.

The character Bluebeard was so impressive that for three centuries he has reappeared numerous times in literature. And his name has persisted as a figure often used in our speech; a woman slayer is often known as a Bluebeard.

Bowdlerize   If you had stood quietly near the chancel of the Church of the Holy Trinity at Stratford-upon-Avon one day in 1818 and listened carefully, you might have heard a muffled sound coming from beneath the paving stones, which might have been that of William Shakespeare turning over in his grave.

In 1818 Shakespeare had been dead just 202 years. In that interval, his plays and poems had garnered critical esteem and public regard that was, and arguably still is, unparalleled in literature. Thomas Bowdler, however, was unhappy with Shakespeare's work and felt it should be improved.

Bowdler (1754–1825) was an English clergyman, physician, and editor who looked upon Shakespeare's writings as sometimes risqué. Seeing great worth in Shakespeare generally, he nevertheless viewed some of the language and scenes as indecent and suggestive—inappropriate "for gentlemen to read aloud in the presence of ladies."

So Bowdler undertook to "clean up" Shakespeare, and by his standards he did. Editing out all portions he considered offensive, in

1818 he issued the bard of Avon's work in ten volumes entitled *The Family Shakespeare.*

In literary circles, this expurgated edition of the great bard's work was universally damned as a travesty. The reading public, however, reacted differently. Prior to Bowdler's death, *The Family Shakespeare* went through four complete editions, and it went through at least three afterward. Not content with his treatment of Shakespeare, Bowdler also worked over Edward Gibbon's *Decline and Fall of the Roman Empire.*

Even in his own lifetime, Bowdler's name entered the language as an expression in general use, and so it remains today. Any prudish expurgation of a literary work is known as bowdlerism. To bowdlerize is to delete what is deemed inappropriate or in some way morally or aesthetically offensive.

Boycott   In 1880 there came into our language a one-word expression to describe an ancient and complicated economic and social phenomenon. Boycott has a meaning quite clear to us now, but the word would be meaningless apart from an episode of Irish history. That episode took a man's name and made it a household word almost worldwide.

Captain Charles C. Boycott was manager of the immense real estate holdings of Lord Earne. Very severe in his treatment of the tenants who lived on and used the lord's property, Boycott became extremely unpopular with them, even despised. They petitioned Lord Earne to replace Boycott with a man more considerate of them, but Earne did nothing about it. Finally, the tenants and their sympathizers joined in a covenant: They would have nothing whatever to do with Captain Boycott.

They refused to work for him or to permit others to do so. His farm workers and servants deserted him. No one would have any business dealings with him. Anyone attempting to assist him was immediately put under the taboo as well. As a consequence, his former friends and associates turned away from him. He was effectively isolated.

Afterward, the strategum used against Captain Boycott was also used against others. It became a favored technique of the Land Reform Movement in dealing with owners and landlords. Wherever it went, the name of Boycott went with it. Before 1880 ended, published news stories were using Boycott's name quite freely, for example, "Opponents of land reform are yielding to the fear of being Boycotted."

The name stuck. It may be a coercive action against an individual, a group of individuals, a business concern, or a specific product. No doubt Boycott would have preferred fame for some other reason, but this is the niche in which circumstance has placed him.

Braggadocio   "All gan to iest and gibe full merilie." A line from *The Fairie Queen*, it was penned by Edmund Spenser around the year 1596. Written in Old English, many words were not spelled then as they are now, and many didn't have the same meanings. In our present way of speaking this quotation is, "All began to jest and cheer quite merrily."

There is, for instance, the word *brag*. In Spenser's day and earlier, this word was used differently than it is today. A brag was the braying of a trumpet.

The Fairie Queen is a long narrative poem, an allegorical epic, in which the many characters are representative of certain important people or social factors. The Fairie Queen herself is Elizabeth I, ruler of England at that time, who is named Gloriana in the poem. The Red Cross Knight represents righteousness and holiness. A partial roster of others includes Guyon, representing temperance; Arthegall, justice; Britomart, chastity; and Una, religion. And then there is Braggadochio.

The story opens with the queen's annual twelve-day festivity, during which anyone having a problem may appear at court and request a "champion"—a knight who will take the case and make things right. Una, a beautiful young woman, appears to report that her father and mother are held captive by a dragon, and the Red Cross Knight offers to slay the beast. Many adventures follow, with many knights participating, and chief among them is Guyon.

Guyon's horse is stolen by a vain, boastful fellow who pretends to be everything he isn't. Pretending to be a man of highest courage, he is a coward. Pretending to have done many noble and valiant deeds, actually he has done none. All his bravery is in his tongue; it will venture anything, and does—freely, glibly, and almost incessantly.

Spenser names this character Braggadochio. After all, the fellow's behavior is like a trumpet braying—it makes no music, just noise. He speaks at length, and loudly, always in praise of himself. In other words, he toots his own horn. He brays, he brags. And from Spenser's time until ours, *brag* has been a close synonym for *boast*, and *braggadocio* (different spelling from Spenser's character) is *boastfulness*.

Riding away on Guyon's horse, Braggadochio manages to steal armor, weapons, plummage, and even, by enchantment, a woman (a clone of the lovely lady Florimell). He runs away or weasels out of every fight, but always manages to maintain a haughty demeanor and appearance.

At length comes a great gathering of knights, numbering 100 or more, all taking part in various competitive events, all this in honor of Florimell. Arthegall, a noble knight, arrives in company with one whom he does not know, a knight he has chanced to meet along the way. This is none other than the infamous Braggadochio himself, who vainly struts his way into the assembly. When Trompart ushers in Braggadochio's false Florimell, Arthegall challenges the braggart to give some evidence that he has gone to battle before, evidence that is not forthcoming.

Guyon recognizes and reclaims his stolen horse and Sir Marinel recovers his stolen shield. The real Florimell is sent for, and when she stands alongside the imposter, the latter vanishes; her clothing remains in a heap on the floor. In the presence of the whole assembly, Talus shaves off Braggadochio's beard, breaks his sword, and completely humiliates the man. Whereupon, as Braggadochio sneaks away, all begin "to iest and gibe full merilie."

By the Skin of Your Teeth   Behind this phrase is the biblical story of Job, a prominent citizen who lived in a land called Uz. He was rich and powerful, and he was also a good man who was righteous and just.

He had sheep by the thousands and shepherds to tend them; he had thousands of camels and drivers for all of them. He had 500 yoke of oxen and other possessions in proportion. He had one wife, ten children, and all was going well.

Then one day a messenger came running, shouting to Job, "While your servants were plowing with the oxen, the Sebeans came and murdered all the men and took away all the animals." While this messenger was still speaking, another came, saying, "Lightning from the heavens struck with a mighty bolt and burned up all the sheep and the shepherds with them." And before this second messenger had finished speaking, a third came, also with bad news, "The Caldeans have taken all your camels and slain all the drivers." While messenger number three was still speaking, number four arrived with the worst news of all: "A windstorm destroyed the house where your seven sons and three daughters were gathered, and all are dead."

In a second round of calamities, Job was stricken with boils, and his body was one huge sore from the soles of his feet to the top of his head. He sat in an ash heap, scraping dead flesh from his body with broken shards of pottery. He still had his wife, but her presence was probably worse for him than her absence would have been; as she looked at Job's condition with a coldly practical eye, her word to her husband was this one bit of advice: "Curse God, and die!"

In the midst of all this, Job had a long conversation with a committee of visiting friends, who, incidentally, were no more helpful than his wife. After speaking to these counselors, Job reviewed all the losses he had suffered and concluded, "My friends abhor me; those I loved have turned against me; I am skin and bone, and have escaped death by the skin of my teeth."

There isn't much skin on a tooth. And an escape made by the skin of one's teeth is a narrow one, a really close call. Narrow as was the escape, it was one that Job made. Job neither cursed God nor died. He lived for many years remaining faithful to the God he trusted and eventually saw his fortune restored manyfold.

– C –

Cambuscan's Horse, Mirror, Ring, and Sword   All of these objects had magical powers, and there are various times of need when we might wish we had one of them. They appear in *The Canterbury Tales* by Geoffrey Chaucer, written in the late fourteenth century. The tale is told by one of the Canterbury pilgrims, the Squire, a twenty-year-old apprentice knight traveling with his father from London to the shrine of Thomas à Becket.

In the tale, the great Tartar king Cambuscan, who has ruled for twenty years, is now with his lords and ladies at his annual birthday celebration. Into the midst of this festive scene rides a strange knight on a strange horse—the latter is completely made of brass. At his side the stranger carries a sword, in his hand he holds a mirror, and on his thumb he wears a golden ring. He announces that he comes with greetings and bears gifts from the king of Arabia and India. The gifts are:

• The brazen horse—A sort of symbiotic marvel, it takes its rider anywhere in the world in less than twenty-four hours. All the rider needs to do is twist a certain wire in the horse's ear and whisper the desired destination. The horse can fly as well as run, when left standing it cannot be moved, and when running it cannot be stopped except by its master's command.

• The mirror—A gift for Cambuscan's daughter Canace, it identifies one's friends and foes and tells if a love is true or false.

• The golden ring—Also for use by Canace, the ring enables her to understand the language of birds and communicate with them. In addition, it reveals the medicinal qualities of every herb that grows.

• The sword—It cuts through the thickest armor with a single stroke, and the wound inflicted by it will never heal unless the smooth side of the sword is laid upon it.

While walking in the woods soon after the birthday celebration, Canace hears a falcon crying out in baleful lamentations and learns the bird has lost her lover to a kite, a lesser creature of low estate. The princess takes the case in hand to befriend and assist the grieving bird.

Chaucer's storyteller, the Squire, promises to relate the manner in which the falcon wins back her lost love and then to provide exciting revelations of events yet to come. But he doesn't. The story is never finished. In midthought, the narrative is left hanging, and after 600 years, there it still hangs.

We'll never know more about how these remarkable powers were used. These gifts, and the Squire who told of them, lived in the mind of Geoffrey Chaucer, and they died when he did—in 1400. What remains for us is the wish that these magical items were real and that they were ours. Who wouldn't want Cambuscan's horse when stuck in a traffic jam! Unfortunately, though, we'll never know what became of the broken-hearted falcon.

Camel Through the Eye of a Needle   "That's like putting a camel through the eye of that needle!" exclaims an employee to the boss. What is meant by this phrase is that the task is an impossible one.

Picture it: a camel, a large and ungainly creature, trying to squeeze itself through the eye of a sewing needle! It's preposterous to think the animal might ever succeed, and ridiculous he should try. The story is told three times in the Bible, and it is a good one.

Somewhere just east of the Jordan where Jesus was teaching, a handsome, intelligent, rich, yet troubled young man approached the gathered crowd.

Uncertain and apprehensive about death, he asked Jesus, "What must I do to inherit eternal life?" Jesus replied, "You know the commandments," and he began to recite them. When the young man protested that he had always observed all of these, Jesus said, "Then go, sell all you have, give it to the poor, and you will have treasure in heaven, and come, follow me."

Because he had great possessions with which he was unwilling to part, the young man turned and walked sorrowfully away, and Jesus sadly watched him go. Then he spoke to his disciples: "It is easier for a camel to go through the eye of a needle than for a rich man to enter the kingdom of God!" And it's from this biblical lesson that we get this phrase referring to something that is impossible or nearly impossible.

Canard   If in French a canard is a duck, why then in English is it a fraudlent tale that is usually preposterous and malicious? The answer is to be found in a story—and in a fascinating quirk of human nature.

We tend to be afflicted by fits of gullibility. Know about the Brooklyn Bridge? That 1,595-foot span across New York's East River was completed in 1883. Soon afterward, though, certain shady shysters were going around the country selling shares in the Brooklyn Bridge. Hit-and-run characters, they would systematically work one city then jump quickly to the next, staying one step ahead of the law.

This performance gave rise to a new saying. If a person felt conned into a bad deal, he was apt to say, "I think I just bought the Brooklyn

Bridge!" Tricksters who perpetrated hoaxes or promoted scams were spoken of as sellers of that same bridge. And if someone makes an offer that seems too good to be true, one often asks, "Are you trying to sell me the Brooklyn Bridge?"

The French had their way of saying the same thing: *vendre un canard à moitié*, in English, to "half-sell a duck." Of course, a duck is either sold or not sold, never half-sold. Therefore, if some pettifogger had pulled a fast one, that person could say, "I just half-sold a duck."

So much half-selling of ducks was going on that somebody decided to test the public's level of gullibility. He wrote and published a yarn about twenty canards (ducks) he said he had owned. Feigning utter seriousness, he reported that he killed and cut up one of the ducks and fed it to the other nineteen. Then he cut up another, which in turn was consumed by the remaining eighteen. In the same manner, number eighteen was eaten by the other seventeen. Thus, one by one, all the ducks were fed to their surviving buddies until at last only one duck was left, which meant this one duck had eaten all nineteen of his companions.

The preposterous tale was published again and again—and believed to be true—throughout France. And from that time, there and elsewhere, any groundless and preposterously false story has been called a canard, especially when it is repeated over and over. The parade of canards can be long and monotonous, and many are particularly malicious, so watch out!

Carry a Message to Garcia   To be faithful, to have integrity, and to be courageous against overwhelming danger—these are the marks of one who has what it takes to carry a message to Garcia. This dramatic catchphrase first appeared in 1899 and quickly became an inspirational rallying cry often heard on school campuses and wherever attention was given to deeper commitments and higher ideals.

The phrase is not as common as it once was. But it does retain a place in our speech, and perhaps we are the poorer for not using it more and understanding it better.

The story begins with the advent of the Spanish-American War in April 1898. U.S. President William McKinley urgently needed to have a message delivered to the insurgent General Garcia, who was fighting the Spanish somewhere in the Cuban wilderness. But could General Garcia be located and could anyone get through to him?

Andrew S. Rowan—native of the Appalachian hills, graduate of the military academy at West Point, a forty-one-year-old lieutenant in the army—was summoned to the White House in Washington. The president gave him a sealed envelope, saying, "Take this to General Garcia; he's somewhere in Cuba." Rowan offered no hesitation, nor did he ask any questions. The lieutenant simply thanked his commander-in-chief, saluted, and walked away. He sealed that envelope in a waterproof pouch and strapped it to his body directly over the heart. Four nights later, he stepped from an open boat into the darkness of Cuba's north shore. Less than three weeks afterward, having located Garcia and delivered the message, he emerged from the jungles on the island's south side.

This is one story of resourcefulness, courage, and heroism of which there are many. This one, though, became especially popular in 1899 as the theme of a remarkable essay by Elbert Hubbard. Under the title *A Message to Garcia*, Hubbard used the Andrew Rowan episode to create an inspiring bit of English prose that quickly found its way into virtually every nook and cranny of America. And so today, those who are fit to carry a message to Garcia are those who can accept a difficult task and assume the personal responsibility needed to see it through.

Casanova   Giovanni Giacomo was Casanova (1725–1798) a clergyman, ecclesiastical secretary, soldier, writer, alchemist, lottery director, violinist, gambler, spy, diplomat, librarian, and through it all a thoroughgoing libertine.

Today a Casanova is a promiscuous, adventurous, roguish sort of man, who is generally likable and usually irresistible among women. The original—and the prototype of all Casanovas—was a student in the seminary at St. Cyprian who was expelled for immorality and scandalous conduct in general. He was sixteen then. Immediately, he launched himself on a devil-may-care career that took him all over Europe and involved him in one outrageous escapade after another.

An engaging fellow and something of a wit, he smoothly wormed his way into the upper strata of society wherever he went. While good at making first impressions, apparently his friendships and liaisons were of short duration, for he migrated often from the court of one king to that of another, from country to country, city to city, notably Paris, Dresden, Prague, and Vienna. Returning to Italy, he was arrested in Venice and sentenced to five years' imprisonment for impiety and general chicanery.

Making a spectacular escape from prison, he fled to Paris, where he represented himself as a financial genius, got himself accepted by the French aristocracy, and contrived to institute a lottery and manage it for a while. Within three years, though, he owed so many people money that he fled Paris to escape his creditors.

Changing his name to Chevalier de Seingalt, he circulated among the elite circles of Europe, but never remained long in a place (perhaps because his welcome quickly wore out). His next round of predatory meanderings included Germany, Switzerland, England, and such cultural and power centers as St. Petersburg, Warsaw, Riga, London, and Rome. And everywhere—there were women, women, and more women; not by the dozens or even the scores, but by the hundreds! As ancient kings had a passion for conquering territories, it was this fellow's passion to make conquest of females.

A persistent cuss, although his passion got him into trouble from time to time, he never gave it up. On one occasion, he was expelled from the French Riviera. On another, when one of his escapades created a scandal and a duel followed, he fled for his life, seeking refuge in Spain. Permitted at last to return to Venice, he served the Venetian inquisitors as a spy and then finished his life in Bohemia as a librarian at the Château of Dux.

Throughout his career, Casanova did some writing, although little of it was well done. His most important work was the story he wrote of his own life, *Memoires de J. Casanova de Seingalt*. Mostly the boastings of a vain man, his *Memoires* were, nevertheless, an illuminating critique of social life in eighteenth-century Europe.

Although written in his old age, he terminated the story with age forty-nine; after some of the early fire had burned out, he relived those years by writing of them. Apparently in his bizarre career as the world's most notorious adulterer and seducer, he never felt that anything might be amiss in his manner of living. He believed to the end that he had been a godsend to the women of Europe. Some of them probably agreed. Others felt differently.

Cassandra   A Cassandra is a prophet or prophetess of doom whose warnings are always unheeded. The story of the original Cassandra, however, is somewhat more complicated. This young woman was a daughter of Troy's King Priam and Queen Hecuba. Apollo was the Greek god who presided over the human skills of music, medicine, poetry, and prophecy. Being strongly attracted to Cassandra, he presented to her a very special gift—an unlimited power to foresee the future.

It would seem this power would be quite useful and make its possessor a person of much distinction, but in the case of Cassandra this is not the way things worked out. Having given her this remarkable gift, Apollo apparently believed she would then agree to anything he wanted. But she felt otherwise, and when she steadfastly resisted his amorous advances, he turned hostile.

Apollo did not have power to take away the gift he had given, but he could fix things so the gift would always be a burden for her, and he did. He decreed that whenever Cassandra prophesied the future nobody would believe her. For the rest of her troubled life, the poor woman suffered the torture of knowing what was about to happen and being totally unable to convince anyone of it. She was seen as the victim of a mental disorder, and until the very day of her death, she bore this misery alone.

Through the ten years of the Trojan War, she tried again and again to warn her people of various impending calamities, but her efforts were always in vain. When the Greeks left that huge wooden horse outside the city gates, Cassandra begged the Trojans not to take it into the city, but nobody would listen. When Troy fell, the Greek commander Agamemnon seized her as his captive and took her away with him to his home in Mycenae. There, upon arrival, Agamemnon was murdered by his own wife, and that same day she killed Cassandra as well.

Cassandra was a pathetic figure. Today she is a symbol of a powerless insight and an ineffectual knowledge. In addition to being a doomsayer, a Cassandra may be one who knows a great deal, but is unable to use that knowledge to make a difference.

Cast the First Stone   We are throwing stones when we severely criticize, accuse, or condemn someone. When it is said, "He gets his exercise by throwing stones," it means that he is always finding fault with other people. Or when someone comes under suspicion, a person may say, "I don't want to be the first to cast a stone," meaning that person is unwilling to participate in the speculation or condemn the accused.

Stone-throwing expressions were all given birth one day in Jerusalem almost 2,000 years ago. On that day, Jesus was conversing with the crowd when a group of men strode forward, dragging a frightened and disheveled woman. Thrusting the woman forward, one of them said, "Teacher, this woman has been caught in the act of adultery. Now in the law, Moses commanded us to stone such. What do you say about her?"

Expected to render judgment on the woman, Jesus didn't. He said, "Let him who is without sin among you be the first to throw a stone at her." After only moments of silence, during which furtive glances ricocheted from face to face, somewhere in the company a hand opened, a stone fell to the ground, and one of the older men turned and walked away. He was followed by others—until all had left.

Jesus said to the woman, "Where are they? Has no one condemned you?" She replied, "No one, sir." Then Jesus said, "Neither do I condemn you; go, and do not sin again."

An instructional story worth remembering, it reminds us to look at our own faults before hurling the first rock.

Casting Pearls Before Swine   Jesus of Nazareth was born into a world where life was hard. During the three years of his public work, Jesus devoted much attention to life's significance and meaning, seeking to put it in its proper perspective of worth and beauty. Nowhere does there exist a better guide to personal fulfillment, self-realization, and interpersonal relationships than in his "Sermon on the Mount."

This sermon was delivered to the Jewish people, among whom eating pork was strictly taboo; hogs were "unclean" and looked upon with total disdain. In the Jewish scale of things to be scorned, hogs were followed closely by dogs, and these creatures were common symbols of anything held in contempt.

Thus Jesus' statement was packed with power: "Do not give what is holy to the dogs, and do not throw your pearls before swine, lest they trample them under their feet, and turn and tear you to pieces."

Jesus was speaking of life. He was saying don't throw it away; don't give it to the dogs, as they will have no appreciation of it. The "dogs" of which he spoke are the life-destructive forces, whatever they are. Life is a precious jewel, he was saying, so don't toss the pearl that is you into anybody's pigpen. If you throw your pearls before swine, they will trample them, never knowing their value nor caring what they are.

Any figure as powerful as this must inevitably live on in language, and this one does. A picture of the worthy being given over to the unworthy, it has broad use in modern speech, sometimes seriously, sometimes humorously, and sometimes cynically.

Catch-22   In the final year of the Second World War, Captain John Yossarian was fed up with the U.S. Air Force and wanted out so desperately that he pretended to be crazy. Medical officer Daneeka explained that he could release anyone who was crazy, but that, "Anyone who wants to get out of combat duty isn't really crazy." Yossarian's wish to get out was sufficient proof of his good sense.

This frustrating scenario—a classic catch-22 situation—is found in the 1961 novel by Joseph Heller, *Catch-22*.

Heller's novel seems to represent World War II as one enormous catch-22, a no-win situation, an exercise in futility. The war is presented as a sort of mass madness, and everyone involved can cope with it only by being at least somewhat mad.

Yossarian's friend Orr also fell victim of the same catch. Orr was crazy, confirmed by Doctor Daneeka, but the doctor couldn't ground Orr until Orr asked for this change of status. Since Orr was too crazy to do this—and if he ever did, it would prove he was sane—he was therefore ineligible for grounding.

Absurd? Yes, one of the absurdities that sometimes occurs in human affairs. Heller's novel gave a name to this type of phenomenon—a problem situation that denies its only possible solution. He called it catch-22, and we continue to use this phrase today.

Cat's Paw   Traditionally, monkeys have been famous for two characteristics: their intelligence and their tendency to imitate or "ape" whatever they see humans do. There's an ancient tale concerning a monkey who once used both of these characteristics quite skillfully. This particular yarn dates from early in the sixteenth century, and may be considerably older. Some trace it to Julius II, supreme Roman pontiff from 1503 to 1513, and believe this event actually occurred in his household. Whatever the source, the story is somewhat as follows.

A pet monkey had the freedom to run at will about his master's large house. One day, a weary, hungry soldier stood outside gazing longingly into the kitchen. When the cook disappeared into an adjoining room, the man entered, attracted by the fragrance of chestnuts roasting on the hearth. Thinking that a few of these might assuage his hunger a little, he plucked some from among the coals.

This action was keenly observed by the monkey, who decided that raking chestnuts from the fire was a really splendid idea and something he definitely ought to be doing. So, as the soldier went away, the monkey moved in to do his monkey thing. But those coals were hot, very hot, and the chestnuts burned him.

At one end of the hearth lay the family cat, half asleep and at peace with the world. But not for long. The monkey intruded with the suggestion that the two of them play a little game. "Here, give me your paw," he said to the cat, and she did. Then he said, "Now let's pretend that you are me and that this forepaw is mine, and I'll show you what I'm going to do with it."

With that, the monkey made a wide swipe with the cat's paw among the coals. Out came a few chestnuts, and from the cat came shrill cries of pain. The story represents the monkey as compelling the cat to let him use her paw time after time to rake out more chestnuts. For anyone who knows cats, though, this is a doubtful scenario. It's more likely that after that first swipe, there was an instant and blinding flurry of flying fur, a lightning flash of bared teeth, a frenzied flailing of four sharp-clawed feet, and all this with blood-chilling sound effects, as that cat squalled and yowled and spat, and the monkey ran for his life.

Anyway, from the story we have a vivid way of saying an important thing. So if someone wants you to do something he ought to do for himself or something that will get him out of difficulty, relieve him of a responsibility, make a favorable impression of him with somebody, or clear him of blame, you can respond, "No, I won't. I refuse to be a cat's paw for you. If you want to get those chestnuts out of the fire, pull them out yourself."

Charon's Boat   This Charon—who was he? On occasion one hears his name mentioned, usually in connection with his boat or the toll he charges. Well, it all goes back to about 3,000 years ago when this character figured largely in the mythology of the ancient Greeks. Almost every person needed to deal with Charon sooner or later.

When a person died, that person, or that person's soul or spirit or "shade," went into the Underworld. There was a department in the Underworld called the Elysium or the Elysian Fields, which was a place of happiness for people of virtue, and most people aspired to go there. To get there, though, one had to cross the River Styx, a slow stream of black, murky water that flowed through a dark, ghostly valley.

Charon was the ferryman who took the dead people across. He kept his boat tied up at the shore, and as the shades of recently departed folks arrived, this austere old man would take them aboard and row them to the other side.

But he didn't exactly run a charity operation. He made a charge of one small coin, and sometimes two or three. Those who prepared a body for burial anticipated this and normally placed a coin or two in the mouth of the dead body or perhaps in the hand.

Charon also had another requirement: The deceased must have had a proper funeral. Without the benefit of a funeral, the departed one was condemned to wander for 100 years up and down the riverbank. (After that time, the old ferryman's hard heart would soften a little, and he would take the wandering spirit across.)

But, like all the Greek mythological figures, Charon was not infallible; sometimes he broke his own rules. For example, when Eurydice, the beloved wife of Orpheus, had been taken into the Underworld, Orpheus went on a rescue mission. Reaching the ferry landing at the river's edge, he played upon his lyre and sang so enchantingly that old Charon was charmed into forgetting all about the toll he usually collected.

Likewise, Hercules managed to cross without payment. On his venture into the Underworld to steal Pluto's three-headed dog, he made such dire threats and manifested such terrific strength that Charon had the very living daylights scared out of him.

But Orpheus and Hercules were the exceptions. Folks of the run-of-the-mill variety had to play the game by Charon's rules. He ran the ferry concession, and nobody could cross the River Styx any other way. The old man had his price and his way of doing things, and that was that.

And he is still with us, in language at least. To die is to take Charon's boat. To pay Charon's toll is to go through the mysterious process of dying. Like "kicked the bucket" and "bought the farm," Charon's boat is one of several crass circumlocutions taken to avoid speaking directly of an unpleasant subject—death.

Chauvinism   For a dozen years at the beginning of the nineteenth century, France (and for a time much of the rest of Europe) was under the control of one enigmatic little man, Napoleon Bonaparte. Sweeping into power on the crest of the French Revolution, Napoleon set out, to consolidate by force all European countries into one mighty empire with himself as emperor. He would have succeeded if it had not been for his disastrous invasion of Russia in 1812 and his encounter with the British duke of Wellington at Waterloo in 1815.

Whatever else may be said of Napoleon, for or against him, he was an incredibly gifted leader. Many of his followers were intensely loyal. One of these was a fellow named Nicolas Chauvin of Rochefort. Chauvin fought in most of Napoleon's wars and was often wounded, some say seventeen times. But his devotion to the "little corporal" was so total as to be fanatical.

In Chauvin's view, Napoleon could do no wrong. Not only did he follow his commander in everything but he always assailed every listening ear with the highest praise of the man. To him, humanity's highest good was the glory of France, and that glory was best exemplified in the life of Napoleon Bonaparte.

Even after Napoleon's dream of empire collapsed, even after Russia and Waterloo, Chauvin continued everywhere singing the praises of Napoleon and his wild vision of conquest. In clubs and bars, in government circles and on the streets, he extolled Napoleon to the point of becoming ridiculous. Ultimately, the man was looked upon as a laughingstock and a bore.

Probably the matter would have ended here, had not this obsessed war veteran been written into some of the popular literature of the time. But he was, and this gave him a kind of self-perpetuating notoriety. For example, there was *La Cocarde Tricolore* by the Cogniard brothers in 1831. In this very successful comedy, Chauvin was caricatured as an unreasoning and bellicose patriot who carried his patriotism to the extreme.

His name became a byword for an exaggerated patriotism that exalts its own country to such heights that all others are considered of no importance. Now, as then, chauvinism is a militant, unreasoning, and boastful devotion to country, an ultranationalism that can see no value or virtue in anything else. The expression is often broadened to include a pugnacious and offensive attitude of superiority—over other people, other places, or other ideas. In modern times, the expression has made a place for itself in speaking of relations between the sexes. A male chauvinist is a man who takes a superior and intolerant or patronizing attitude toward women.

Chicken Little A small chicken, immature and inexperienced, is under a tree when an apple falls on her head. "Getting more out of the experience than there is in it" (thanks for this phrase to Mark Twain), she stupidly concludes the sky is falling. Running wildly about to spread the alarm, and encountering Henny Penny, she cries out, "The sky is falling! The sky is falling!" How does she know?, asks Henny Penny. "By experience," Chicken Little replies. "I saw it with my eyes, I heard it with my ears, a piece of it fell on my head!" Seeing, hearing, feeling—empirical evidence, all of it, and rather convincing.

So Henny Penny is swept into the panic. "We must go and tell the king," she exclaims; and the two of them, in headlong flight, soon come upon Cocky Locky. He too is swept into the gathering current, and now the three of them go racing away to see the king. On the way they see Ducky Lucky swimming in a pond, and her calm is quickly shattered by the frightful news: "The sky is falling! Oh how terrible!" And she wobbles away with the others.

The next encounter is with Turkey Lurkey, who when she hears the news, says, "Follow me, and I will take you to the king." By now, there are five in the party; and as their numbers increase, so does their hysteria. Carried away by the excitement, nobody has yet bothered to question the truth of Chicken Little's report, much less doubt it.

The group never reaches the king; instead, they come upon Hooty, the wise old owl, dozing on a low tree limb. Disturbed by the ruckus, he opens an eye, and inquires, "What's all this noise about?" In a clamor of screeching voices, the fowls all speak at once: "The sky is falling! Falling! A piece of it fell on Chicken Little's head!"

Sagely unperturbed by all the uproar, Hooty says to Chicken Little, "Can you show me a piece of the sky that fell?" All atwitter with apprehension, the group leads Hooty to that portentous point underneath the tree; and there, taking one calm look at the object that had created the commotion, the owl quietly declares, "That's not a piece of the sky; that's an apple."

Thank goodness for some good sense at last. Thank goodness for somebody who understands that the whole sky is not coming down because one apple falls.

Well, a chicken little is an alarmist, one who doesn't see the whole picture. A chicken little may lift a solitary disturbing fact out of context, move it over to a position of centrality, build a whole system around it, and then, not content to worry about it alone, must also worry everybody else. Usually quite sincere, but sincerely mistaken, this family of alarmists usually predicts some spectacular doom for us, something like being flattened beneath the weight of a fallen sky.

Cinderella Story A Cinderella is a person of unrecognized worth or beauty, usually a woman. It's a Cinderella story when such a person suddenly achieves recognition or success, rising rapidly from some lowly place to a position of eminence—or when a team goes from last place to first. (And, somewhat incidentally, a Cinderella dance or party is one that must conclude before midnight.)

The story of Cinderella is one of the oldest fairy tales, appearing initially among the French. Over several centuries, it has been told in many forms. Sometimes the young lady has been aided by a fairy godmother and other times by friendly white doves and sundry other birds. Sometimes a pumpkin has been changed into a fine coach and sometimes there has been no reference at all to a pumpkin in the story. The famous slipper has been at times made of gold or fur or glass. But the general direction of the story has always been the same: To the amazement of everyone, a poor little noone is abruptly made into somebody of much importance.

In its briefest form the story might go something like this: A young girl's mother dies, her father remarries, and the new stepmother has two mean, ill-tempered daughters who make the young girl's life as difficult as possible. Forced to sleep among the cinders on the hearth, the girl is first called Cinderwench, a name which, because of her sunny disposition, is later changed to Cinderella.

The king holds a marvelous festival, inviting all the realm's young women so that his son, the prince, may choose a bride from among them. Cinderella's two unsavory stepsisters dress in their very finest and set out for the festival ball. Cinderella would like to go, but of course cannot—not until her fairy godmother appears and changes a garden pumpkin into a plush coach, six mice into white horses, six lizards into footmen, and a rat into a coachman. Transforming Cinderella's ragged garments into elegant apparel of silver and gold, the fairy sends the girl off to the ball, with the instruction, "Don't stay beyond midnight, for at midnight that coach will again become a pumpkin."

At the ball, the prince is utterly smitten by the elegant grace and beauty of this "princess." Just before midnight, though, she abruptly leaves, climbs into her coach, and quickly disappears into the night. At home, the two ugly stepsisters tell her of the stranger at the ball, a beautiful princess of unknown identity.

On the following evening, the three of them again go to the ball, separately of course, and again the prince gives his whole attention to Cinderella. In the excitement, Cinderella forgets about her midnight curfew. When she finally runs away, she goes in such haste that she loses one of her slippers, the left one, a slipper made of glass. Her coach has changed into a fat, hollow pumpkin and the six white horses into mice; but, swift as the wind, she runs home to her place beside the hearth.

Finding the slipper where Cinderella has lost it, the prince knows it to be hers, and announces that he will take as his bride the girl whose foot fits that shoe. The palace attendants go everywhere trying that shoe on the left feet of young women throughout the kingdom. But it fits none of them. In due time, though, the king's attendants come to the house of Cinderella's father, and here the slipper proves too small for either of his overeager stepdaughters.

"Let's see if the shoe will fit me," says Cinderella. Her stepsisters laugh, as does their mother. But the shoe is tried, and it does fit, perfectly. Just then appears the fairy godmother, working miracles with her magic wand, and instantly Cinderella is a princess again. Of course, she and the prince are soon married. The stepsisters are properly penitent, or pretend to be; and in the palace Cinderella makes a home for them for as long as they may live. . . . Aren't fairy tales wonderful?

Clay in the Potter's Hand   One of Israel's major prophets, Jeremiah, lived and labored in a time of national crisis. Israel was in danger from three world powers—Assyria, Babylonia, and Egypt. There was also a fourth danger, a peril from within. Israel was in a state of moral decay, in jeopardy from its own poverty of spirit and loss of vision.

It was this inward condition that troubled Jeremiah most. His message was plain: The people of Israel must repent and return to righteousness and faith; Jehovah was requiring this of them. Failing to do this, they would be overcome by the enemies around them.

One day in a pottery shop, Jeremiah observed a potter working at his wheel, "and the vessel he was making of clay was spoiled in the potter's hand, and he reworked it into another vessel, as it seemed good to the potter to do."

Leaving the pottery, the prophet went forth to the people, saying to them, "This is the word of the Lord Jehovah: 'O Israel, can I not do with you as this potter has done? Like clay in the potter's hand, so are you in my hand.' " Jeremiah went on to give them an ominous explanation of what this meant: Oh Israel, if you don't shape up into what the Lord wants you to be, then you need to know that the Lord is devising an alternate plan. Putting it another way, if you don't shape up, you'll be broken and remade.

At length, the breaking came, and Jeremiah lived to see it. For more than forty years, he had loved and labored and wept, but his efforts were all in vain. When the Babylonians came in 598 B.C., and again in 587 B.C., a degenerate nation had no strength to withstand them, and broken pieces of the spoiled vessel were scattered across the Mideastern world.

Clay in the potter's hand is used today to describe a person who is weak and subject to the will of another.

Clean the Augean Stables   The expression to clean the Augean stables has been in use for centuries to indicate the huge task of purging away pollution or corruption of one sort or another—or, for that matter, the huge task of doing anything that is extremely difficult or seemingly impossible. It comes from the saga of the Greek strong-man Heracles (Latin: Hercules) and from the story of the sixth of his twelve labors.

In this particular assignment, the task of Heracles was to clean out the stables of Augeas, a rich king who must have been inexcusably neglectful of his possessions. These stables of his housed 300 oxen and had not been cleaned for thirty years! No doubt they needed cleaning by now, and cleaning them would be an arduous task, especially for one man—and Heracles was required to do it in just one day.

Well, of course, being Heracles, Heracles did it. While not a civil engineer, he did it by an innovative feat of civil engineering. The stables stood alongside a river, and the clever Heracles dammed the water's flow, diverted the stream, and forced it through the stables, washing them clean.

Cobbler, Stick to Your Last   The most celebrated painter of antiquity was a Greek who flourished in the fourth century B.C. Court painter to both Philip II of Macedon and to his son Alexander the Great, Apelles saw his work praised by contemporaries as the finest of all time. Pliny proclaimed as a masterpiece his painting of Macedonian general Cyclops on horseback. His most widely acclaimed work was a picture of the goddess Aphrodite rising from the sea. And there was his powerful painting of Alexander in the Temple of Diana at Ephesus wielding the blazing thunderbolts of Zeus. From others we know much about the man and his work; but of all he did, not a single scrap remains.

But something concerning Apelles does survive—an anecdote having a pithy and pointed insight. The story behind it involves a cobbler who visited the painter's studio one day. To understand this story, it is necessary to know that a cobbler is a shoemaker and that the frame on which shoes are made is called a last.

As the cobbler observed the work of Apelles, he found fault with the shoes the painter had put on the feet of one of his figures. The great painter agreeably accepted the cobbler's criticism and immediately made the suggested correction. This apparently gave the cobbler a surge of self-confidence, for he began to speak critically of the figure's legs.

This was too much. Apelles turned upon his visitor, crying, "Cobbler, stick to your last!" In other words: Cobbler, you may know shoes, and I respect that; but I know the human form, and you're in no position to tell me how to paint it.

That day, the Greek artist, of whose art we have none, gave us an expression of speech that has endured more than two millennia, overleaping cultural boundaries, spanning philosophical chasms, and translated from language to language. Cobbler, stick to your last is a way of saying: You take care of your business and stay out of mine.

Cooking a Goose   To say that one's goose is cooked is to say that he or she is finished. "I will cook your goose" means I will ruin you, foil your plans, or stop you.

But why say goose? Why not chicken or duck or some other bird or other animal that's cookable? The answer is to be found in a story now centuries old, an episode in the career of the flamboyant Eric IV of Sweden.

With a small contingent of soldiers, Eric rode into an enemy town. In comparison with his ridiculously small army, the forces of the enemy were mighty and well armed. They could scarcely believe that this erratic character, historically known as "the mad king," had actually come to fight them. After all, they thought, for so small a force to engage in battle would be unthinkable.

To express their disdain, they decided to taunt Eric in a most demeaning sort of way. To provide a target equal to his abilities, they hung up a solitary, live goose for him to shoot at.

Ignoring the goose, and with the intent of drawing his enemies out for a fight, Eric set about burning and demolishing things throughout the area. As his enemies saw that their province was being destroyed, they sent messengers demanding to know his intentions. His reply was short and to the point: "My intentions? I intend to cook your goose!" And apparently he did, sacking and subduing the area.

Count Chickens Before They're Hatched   Many hundreds of years ago in an eastern land, a farmer had some cows, or goats maybe. He also had a daughter, young and beautiful, but perhaps not quite as beautiful as she imagined. Neighborhood boys had begun to look at her admiringly, but probably not to the extent she fancied.

One bright day in springtime, as the girl went about her morning chores, she took the milk pail and went out to do the milking. As the pail gradually filled, the idea came to her that the pailful of milk was worth a lot of money. She thought: "I will take it to the market and sell it. With the money, I can buy at least four dozen eggs, which I will put in four nests, and set hens on them. In three weeks I will have forty-eight young chicks; these I will feed table scraps that would be otherwise wasted. When the chicks are grown I will sell them for a great deal of money."

By this time, the girl had the filled pail atop her head, as was then the customary manner of carrying things, and was going from the barnyard back to her house. Her thoughts continued: "With the money I get for the chickens, I will buy a beautiful blue dress with frilly white lace, and silk stockings, and fine silver shoes, and fresh red roses for my hair; these I will wear at the autumn festival, and one after another all the boys will come and timidly ask me to dance with them, and I will be coy, and make them beg, and I will toss my head and say—"

Just then, reflexively acting out her thoughts, the girl gave her head a saucy toss, and off came the pail and out poured the milk—all of it—onto the ground. In that moment, all the girl's silly dreaming screeched to a sudden stop.

According to Aesop, who was first to tell the story of the milkmaid and her pail, the girl sat down beside the path, saying, "I should never have counted my chickens before they were hatched."

As she expressed herself then, so have we ever since. By saying, "Don't count your chickens before they are hatched," we warn against a premature and unfounded optimism, and advise caution about the accomplishment of some desired end.

Cricket on the Hearth   The cricket had first chirped the night John Perrybingle brought his bride into the modest cottage he had long called home. She was younger than he, much younger. Her name was Mary, but he always called her Dot, for she was so small. He, a carrier who drove a one-horse wagon delivering parcels for folks, was a big, slow, honest, gentle, kind-hearted man. John and Dot were poor people, but there was much love between them. And now after a year, there was the baby, and the cricket had chirped through it all.

Not far away lived Caleb Plummer and his blind daughter Bertha, their circumstance one of extreme poverty. "You may have knocked down Caleb Plummer's dwelling with a hammer or two, and carried off the pieces in a cart." But, lovingly, he gave to his sightless child a priceless gift, the impression that she was surrounded by beauty on every side, that the squalid house was cheerful and bright.

Caleb was a toymaker. He worked for Tackleton, the toy merchant who hated children—a bachelor and a hard man whose heart pumped ice water in place of blood and who never showed any feelings. He always killed his crickets. "I hate their noise," he said; "scrunch 'em," he once said to John as he ground his heel heavily into the floor. There were no crickets on his hearth, and he was resolved there never would be.

And there was May Fielding, Dot's good friend from childhood days, who Tackleton had persuaded to marry him. She had loved, and still loved, Bertha's older brother Edward who had gone away to sea and was now believed dead. She had candidly confessed to Tackleton that she had no love for him, but with this man her lack of love was of no importance. The wedding was soon to take place.

But before it did, an old stranger came seeking lodging for a short time at Perrybingle's house. Dot soon discovered that the old man was not old at all, but he was really Edward Plummer. Having returned from the sea and learning of May's engagement to Tackleton, he wished secretly to determine if her forthcoming marriage was one she really wanted. Keeping Edward's secret, Dot didn't tell anyone who he was, not even John.

Then one day, John saw Edward (disguise removed) in an animated conversation with Dot and concluded that this handsome young man was a former friend or lover who Dot could not forget. His big heart broken, all that night John sat alone at the hearth, and all that night the cricket chirped.

By morning, John had figured it all out: He had been grossly inconsiderate and unfair to ask his beloved Dot to give up her youth to marry him; therefore, he would "release her from the daily pain of an unequal marriage." Learning of John's plan and the reason for it, Dot understood anew how big of heart he really was. For her, there were no other loves and there never had been.

Now Edward reappeared with his bride. Bride? Yes—May Fielding.

And what of Tackleton? Was he angry? No. For anger is a feeling, and Tackleton didn't have feelings, or never had any until now.

But now he experienced something new. He had caught it from those around him. To express it, he contributed his unused wedding cake for the celebration at Perrybingle's house. Arriving at the reception, he said, "My house is lonely tonight. I have not so much as a cricket on my hearth. I have scared them all away. Be gracious to me; let me join this happy party!" And join it he did, and one supposes he never scrunched another cricket.

Nor should anyone. The cricket on our hearth is the feeling that reminds us that life has its brighter side, that there's always something to be hopeful for. The cricket's chirp is a call to assert our better self.

This story is by Charles Dickens (1845), a tale told not in chapters but in "chirps"—Chirp the First, Chirp the Second, and Chirp the Third.

Cross to Bear   "I have a heavy cross to bear" and "A cross has been laid upon me" are frequently heard expressions. When we feel burdened with some unwelcome or unpleasant load, we may say that we are bearing a cross.

None of us, though, however awful our burden of suffering, will ever carry a cross in the same way a cross was carried in the story from which these expressions originate. The cross-bearer was Jesus of Nazareth. The cross was an instrument of death, upon which a human body could be impaled. It got its name because it was nothing more than two heavy timbers crossed and fastened together at right angles.

Condemned to die, Jesus had been stripped of his clothing and lashed with whips; his foes had spat on him and, in mockery, pressed down on his brow a painful wreath made of thorns. And then Jesus was further humiliated by being forced to carry his own cross, while strong soldiers with whips and prodding spears followed.

Out from the judgment hall of Pontius Pilate, along the streets of Jerusalem, beyond the city's outer wall, and up the slope of Mount Calvary to Golgotha, the place of execution—Jesus carried this burden along the *via dolorosa*, the way of sorrows. Weakened by many abuses, at some point along the way Jesus faltered beneath the burden, and the cross was laid upon the back of another. The cross was delivered to the hilltop, the body of Jesus was secured to it, and on it Jesus died about midafternoon that day.

That's the story behind this expression—a story that, by comparison, may help make our burdens seem lighter!

Cry Wolf   To cry wolf is to spread a false alarm or a warning of danger when no danger is present. The story comes from the seventh century B.C. or earlier and is one of the many attributed to Aesop. It is the story of an irresponsible shepherd boy who found out the hard way that to be trusted one must prove trustworthy.

In his community, wolves were a perpetual problem for the shepherds who grazed their flocks on the hillsides above the village. Men took turns keeping watch during the long winter nights, calling for help if the wolves attacked. On one occasion, a man who was unable to take his turn at watch sent his young son instead.

Alone with the sheep and the stars, the lad felt the excitement of high adventure and, as is characteristic of adolescent boys, wanted to make the most of it. Shortly after midnight, he shouted, "Wolf! Wolf!" again and again as loudly as he could. From the village the men came running, bearing sticks and staffs for fighting off the wolves. But there were none, only a mischievous boy making sport of the whole affair, and he thought it was great fun.

Annoyed, but in a forgiving mood, the shepherds returned to their homes; gloating over the trick he had perpetrated, the boy settled in for the night's vigil. As the darkness deepened, however, his mood quickly changed. Shadows assumed strange forms and the nighttime sounds suggested weird shapes moving in the dark.

Soon, feeling a desperate loneliness and seized with fear, the boy imagined wolves everywhere. Again, in their village homes, the shepherds heard the cry, "Wolf! Wolf! Wolf!" This time there was real panic in his voice; and again, armed for combat, the men came running; but they found no wolves, only a frightened boy. Again they went back to their homes, and this scenario was repeated two or three times during the next few hours, until finally the men resolved to pay no attention to any further calls from the boy.

Then it happened: In the wee hours of the morning, the wolves swooped in on the flock. The terrified lad, running about in utter panic, screamed, "Wolf! Wolf! Wolf!" But nobody came. Snug in their beds, and exhausted from all the false alarms, the men assumed that, because they had been deceived several times already, they were being deceived again.

That night the wolf pack killed and devoured many of the sheep; and, according to one version of the story, they also killed the boy. He had cried wolf so many times when it meant nothing that when the danger was real his cry went unheeded. Not much attention is paid to the watchman who is forever crying wolf.

Cupid's Arrows Everyone knows of Mr. Cupid. He's that mischievous cherub who goes around shooting arrows into hearts, causing folks to fall in love. We hear expressions such as, "He's been shot by Cupid's arrow," or "Cupid is in pursuit of her." (Occasionally, the word *Dan* appears before the name, making it Dan Cupid. *Dan* is a title of honor such as the Spanish *Don* or the English *Sir*.)

Now this Cupid character has always had some trouble deciding just who he is. He is mythological, of course. He started out being a Greek, but after a few centuries he became a Roman, as did many of his mythological compatriots. As a Greek, his name was Eros, son of Hermes and Aphrodite, the love goddess. It was as a Roman that he became Cupid, the son of Mercury and Venus, and it is as a Roman that we know him best.

One thing about him, though, which many do not know, is that he had arrows of two kinds, gold and lead. If he shot someone with one of his golden arrows, the result was genuine love for the very first person of the other sex who happened by. His leaden arrows, however, had a different effect. Whoever was shot by one of these became an immediate menace to everyone in the neighborhood, for this arrow produced sensual passion.

When Cupid was a child, his mother was playing with him when her bosom was accidentally penetrated by one of his golden arrows. Before the wound healed, her eyes fell upon Adonis, and becoming utterly captivated by him, she lost interest in everything else. She even left heaven, Adonis being more attractive to her than heaven itself. So we know that this Cupid chap carries a powerful weapon!

— D —

Damon and Pythias Syracuse was a Greek city on the island of Sicily, across the Ionian Sea, about 400 miles from Greece. In the mid-fourth century B.C., Syracuse was ruled by Dionysius I, a complex personality in whom were combined some fine qualities and a great many of the other kind. He was an absolute ruler, having power of life and death over everyone in the city and the whole surrounding area. Quick to anger, he was often mad at somebody about something, and the punishment was usually a death sentence.

For some frivolous reason, one who incurred the wrath of, and subsequent death sentence by, Dionysius was a fine young man named Pythias. The young man begged for a little time and permission to go to Athens and care for certain matters, promising to return for his execution. At this, Dionysius laughed scornfully, being absolutely sure that if Pythias ever got out of sight, he would never come back.

It was then the old tyrant received the strangest proposal that he had ever heard. Pythias said, "I have a friend who will stand surety for me; he will remain until I return, and if I fail to return by the specified time, my friend will die in my place." In immediate confirmation of this, a stalwart young Greek named Damon stepped forward, saying, "This is true. I will stand for my friend."

Having never before seen evidence of such devotion, Dionysius was impressed, so impressed, in fact, that he agreed to the proposal. The execution date was then set, and Pythias hurried away on his mission to Athens.

As the weeks went by, Damon manifested no anxiety, professing full confidence that Pythias would return. The deadline drew near, and still there was no word from Pythias. The people of Syracuse did not know that the ship carrying him was delayed by a terrible storm.

The execution day arrived. Saying he was sure Pythias had been somehow unavoidably detained, Damon stood by as preparations were made for his death. As this was being done, the storm-battered ship from Athens limped into Syracuse harbor. Leaping from the deck at the first possible moment, Pythias ran to the execution site, breathlessly arriving within minutes of the appointed time. Embracing Damon, Pythias stepped forward to face the executioner.

Dionysius was so affected that he issued a pardon for Pythias. These young men were Pythagoreans, followers of the most advanced and idealistic philosophy of their time. Dionysius was so deeply moved by their courage, high purpose, and faithfulness in friendship that he summoned them to his private chambers seeking information as to how he himself might become a Pythagorean. (He quickly lost interest, however, upon discovering the required level of discipline and commitment—the cost was more than he was willing to pay.)

This classic drama of personal devotion has enriched our language in various ways. A Damon and Pythias is proverbial for inseparably devoted friends. To be a Damon for another is to be ready for any sacrifice; to be a Pythias is to be utterly faithful, even to the point of death.

David in Saul's Armor   Saul stood head and shoulders above the other Israelites, over whom he ruled as king. He was a strange, brooding, enigmatic character, displaying at times broad streaks of nobility and at other times appalling brutality. Subject to fits of deep depression, he could sink into dark moods that seemed to hold him like a prisoner in their power.

People close to the king were desperate for some way of dealing with this problem. In due time, someone came up with the suggestion that music might help, a suggestion that Saul himself accepted gratefully. Someone knew of a citizen at Bethlehem, a sheep farmer named Jesse, who had a son named David, who was an exceptionally skilled harpist. So this young man was brought to the king's palace, and when the dark moods were upon Saul, he was often soothed and restored by the playing of this stripling shepherd from Bethlehem.

For a while, David was a sort of commuter between the king's palace and his father's house. Then one day, his father sent him with provisions for his three older brothers who were on the western frontier with Israel's army fighting the Philistines. Here David saw the nine-foot-tall Philistine giant, Goliath, and here he heard the giant's blood-chilling challenge, daring any Israelite to come forth and fight him. All were afraid to do so, but David decided that he would.

It looked a lot like suicide; how possibly could this shepherd lad hope to survive a battle with the hulking giant? David told the king what he intended to do, and it must have been an emotional moment.

David had no battle armor, neither breastplate nor shield. With what rationale one can merely guess, Saul dressed David in his own suit of armor, many sizes too large. Unable to even more, and knowing the armor was too heavy for him, David said, "I cannot go with this," and he removed it.

Then, walking to a nearby brook, he carefully selected five small stones, worn round and smooth by the washing of the water. These he placed in his shepherd's bag, and with his shepherd's sling in hand, he went forth to meet Goliath.

And David won. One stone, expertly flung from that sling, struck the giant squarely in the forehead, bringing him down, unconscious. David then ran to him, pulled Goliath's sword from its sheath, and cut off his head. David didn't need Saul's armor; the stone and the sling, though not much, were enough.

From this story we have not one but two expressions that sometimes appear in our speech. The first, "a David in Saul's armor," is someone unable to perform up to potential due to the well-intentioned restrictions imposed by others.

The other expression has to do with David's sling, which is any meager equipment, physical or personal, used to undertake a great task. Like facing a charging bull with a pea-shooter, we sometimes must fight the giants with dwarf-size weapons, for sometimes this is all we have. (See also GOLIATH.)

Delilah   A Delilah is an enchanting but terribly treacherous woman, fascinating but deceitful. The original was a woman of Sorek, a Philistine. The story concerns her relationship with a very strong man who was too weak to resist her feminine wiles. That man was Samson, an Israelite.

Following their return from Egypt and before the establishment of their kingdom, the people of Israel were ruled by a series of indigenous leaders called judges. One of these was Samson. He really wasn't very smart and didn't have much leadership ability, but he did have enormous strength.

In Samson's time, the area immediately east of the Mediterranean Sea was occupied by both Israelites and Philistines. Between these two peoples there was communication, but also fierce rivalry and a substantial amount of hostility. Samson had a giant-size grudge against

Philistines in general and often used his phenomenal strength to wreak havoc among whole armies of them—on one occasion doing in 1,000 of them with a weapon no more deadly than the jawbone of an ass.

Among the Philistines, Samson was a man with a price on his head. This state of affairs, however, was no deterrent when Samson met Delilah, Philistine though she was. As soon as the Philistines learned of this liaison, they went to Delilah with a proposition: "Entice this man, and find out wherein his great strength lies, and how he may be bound, that we may subdue him." For her services, they promised 1,100 pieces of silver.

So Delilah cozied up to Samson, sweetly beseeching him to reveal the secret. He teasingly said, "If they bind me with seven fresh bowstrings, I'll not be able to break them." Later, while Samson slept, and a small army of armed men waited in an adjoining room, Delilah bound Samson tightly with the bowstrings. Then she shouted, "The Philistines are upon you!" Instantly Samson awoke, and instantly snapped his bonds. The Philistines hid quietly in the other room.

Delilah poutingly pretended personal offense that Samson had deceived her and begged him to tell her the truth. This time, he declared that new ropes would do the trick; and while he slept, she thus bound him, but with no more success than before. Then in a third inning of this little game, while Samson slept, Delilah plaited his long hair, but to no avail.

By this time, Delilah was beginning to see all that silver slipping between her fingers, as the Philistines were growing impatient. So she turned up her charms to their full power, and Samson's willpower wilted. He confessed to being a Nazarite. This meant that never in his life had his long hair been cut, and that it must never be.

Knowing now that at last she had the desired information, Delilah called the Philistine authorities, and they came. By the time they arrived, Samson was asleep. One of the men gave Samson his first haircut. Awaking Samson found that his hair and his strength were gone. The Philistines then gouged out his eyes, and put him to slave labor grinding grain at their mill in Gaza.

Delilah got her silver. And since then her name has been used to denote a deceitful person, especially a woman.

Devil and the Deep Blue Sea   Somewhere around the Peloponnesian peninsula there was a narrow strip of water between towering stone cliffs. Among all the dreaded segments of that rugged coastline, none were more hazardous or terrifying than this strait, through which ancient Greek mariners had to sail.

Sailors had more than massive stone mountains to worry about. On one side was a powerful whirlpool capable of swallowing the strongest of ships and men. This dark vortex was called Charybdis. On the other side was a huge cave in which lived the hideous monster Scylla. She had six heads, each at the end of a long, serpentine neck. She also had a voracious appetite, as each head was equipped for eating.

On his journey home from the Trojan War, Odysseus (in Latin, Ulysses) undertook the perilous passage between Scylla and Charybdis. Trying to steer clear of the whirlpool, he let his ship get too close to the cave, and Scylla stretched out her six long necks and snatched up six of his men, devouring them instantly. According to one version of the story, Odysseus got his ship safely through; in another, his ship went down in the whirlpool and he saved his own life by seizing the branches of an overhanging fig tree.

Anyway, to steer between Scylla and Charybdis required consummate seamanship of all who ventured to pass that way. The names of these hazards have become fixed in our language to denote any two perilous alternatives between which we must carefully make our way.

Apparently, "between the devil and the deep blue sea" also originated with this story—possibly because folks who wished to make use of the imagery were unable to pronounce *Scylla* and *Charybdis*!

Die for Want of Lobster Sauce   Louis XIV was the king of France, and had been for many years (1643–1715). During his reign, French royalty had reached a new summit of prestige, and French culture had risen to new levels. Cultural amenities were in vogue; fashion, manners, and protocol were observed with a devotion that approached the religious. Economically, the nation may have been near bankruptcy, international relations may have been in utter disarray, internal strife may have brought the country to the brink of ruin, but if France were to go down, it was certain to go down in style—no question about that.

In France there was an eminent citizen known as The Great Condé or Louis II de Bourbon, Prince de Condé. A distinguished soldier, the

Great Condé was now retired. At his estate in Chantilly, he gave a state dinner in honor of the king, served by Vatel, a chef of impeccable repute.

Here the drama begins—and ends. Vatel was informed at the last moment that one ingredient needed for the menu had not arrived: the lobsters from which the sauce was to be made for the turbot. The news was devastating. No lobster sauce for the king and this company! What was to be done?

Of course, any one of a number of things might have been done—substitutions could have been made, or apologies. But no, a disaster of this importance called for drastic measures. Vatel could never face that elite company with a dinner less than perfect. So he promptly withdrew to a nearby room and ran himself through with a sword! End of drama. Vatel died for want of lobster sauce!

As word of the man's death went the rounds of eighteenth-century Europe, a new expression came into general use. Although not used much anymore, it's a warning that is still with us. Don't die for want of lobster sauce is a warning against over-reaction.

Die Is Cast   Julius Caesar, although born into an aristocratic Roman family, identified himself with the common people and their causes. He soon achieved a position of national prominence, and after a quarter-century in the chaotic world of Roman politics, he was made ruler of Gaul (France), presiding over portions conquered by Rome and commanding an army of four legions.

In the nine years of his service there, his achievements were heralded as phenomenal. A military genius of highest rank, he was preeminently successful in the Gallic Wars and adored by his men. He shared all their hardships, and it was commonly believed he knew every soldier by name.

It was apparent to most that Caesar loved Rome and served her well. But in the capital city, there were some jealous people who felt otherwise. One of these was Pompey, who had been married to Caesar's daughter Julia until her death in 54 B.C. Pompey then turned violently hostile, and the Roman senate gave him its support to elect him sole head of state in 52 B.C., a position to which Caesar himself aspired. Because of Caesar's military successes and his extreme popularity with the people, the senate feared him desperately.

As the tension increased, in 50 B.C., Caesar offered to give up his army if Pompey would also surrender his. The senate rejected this offer, declared Caesar an enemy of the people, and demanded that he immediately and unconditionally disband his legions. In response, Caesar assembled his army in Gaul and asked if his men would support him against the Roman senate. The answer was a decisive yes, and then with the assistance of Marc Antony and others, Caesar marched south toward the Italian border.

A small river called the Rubicon marked the border between Gaul and Italy. Reaching this river, Caesar hesitated; to cross it meant a bloody civil war. Crossing that river would also mean a committment from which there could be no retreat.

As the commander hesitated, so legend says, a stranger of immense size appeared, seized a trumpet from the hand of a trumpeter, blew loudly a few stirring blasts, and plunged into the water and crossed the river. Observing this, and saying decisively, "The die is cast," Caesar ordered his army to advance. Crossing the river on January 19, 49 B.C., Caesar's legions began an almost uninterrupted march that brought them at last to the city of Rome and to a victory of major historical importance.

The die is cast means the decision is made, the final word has been said. After all the ambivalence, circumstance has spoken, and no longer is there any question about it.

Dog and Dart of Procris   Procris was a beautiful young woman, a favorite of the goddess Diana. Being the goddess of the woodlands and the hunt, Diana gave Procris two quite useful gifts. One was a dog that always caught its prey and the other was a dart that never missed its mark. To possess a dog so unfailing and a dart so unerring would seem to prove a great advantage to the owner.

When we are struggling against heavy odds or trying to perform difficult tasks, we may say we need the dog or dart of Procris or both. We mean that we need a fail-safe way to get something done. In the story of Procris, however, these possessions became instruments of tragedy.

Procris's husband, Cephalus, was a fine young man, and the two were deeply devoted to each other. Cephalus loved the woodlands and the hunt. Procris gave Cephalus her dog and her dart.

It wasn't long, however, until that dog, put to chasing a fox, was instantly turned into stone. Why? Because the gods could not approve either the dog or the fox outdoing the other. The fox was so strong and wise and the dog so swift and cunning that each deserved better than to be conquered by the other. So the gods stopped the contest, thus ending the dog part of the story.

The dart part of it, though, goes on, sadly and tragically. Cephalus was out hunting with Procris's dart, almost daily in the forest. Often warm and weary, he would lay aside his clothes, lean back against a tree or moss-covered stone, and talk aloud to the natural world around him. "Come, sweet breeze," he would say, "come and fan my breast, come and quench this heat that burns me."

Once Cephalus was seen and heard by a neighborhood busybody who assumed he was talking with some unseen woman nearby. The busybody went directly to Procris with the unsettling report. Needing to know the truth, she went into the forest the next day, concealed herself, and listened as Cephalus carried on his fanciful conversation with the cooling breeze. It sounded to her as though "breeze" were the name of a woman as well.

Shocked and startled, Procris let out a small gasp of astonishment. Cephalus heard this, and believing it was the sound of a wild animal, he sent that unerring dart flying in the direction from which the sound had come. The dart, which never missed its target, again found its mark.

Parting the undergrowth, Cephalus found the beautiful, young Procris striving to pull the dart from her body. She lived barely long enough to understand that "breeze" was indeed just a light wind, nothing more. And there in the arms of her grieving husband she died, victim of her own dart.

Dog in the Manger   A dog and a pair of oxen lived on the same farm. The oxen were a big, gentle, plodding couple who wore their yoke well, and faithfully did their work, plowing fields and pulling heavy loads. The dog was a feisty little rascal who usually went about as though he owned the place.

The oxen took their meals at a manger that the farmer kept generously filled with hay. The dog, of course, never ate hay, his menu consisting mostly of meat and bread.

One day, however, the dog found a good use for the oxen's hay; in it he curled up for a late afternoon nap. Soon the oxen came in from their day's work, arranged themselves alongside the manger, and began nibbling the hay.

By this disturbance, the sleeping pooch was awakened. He shouldn't have been startled or frightened by the oxen, for these animals were his friends and neighbors; he knew them well. Nevertheless, upon awakening, he began to bark vigorously. Running back and forth from end to end of the manger, he saw to it that neither animal could possibly have access to any of the hay. If they tried to reach it, he ran snarling to them, barking, growling, and nipping at noses as though he were a dog many times his size. Here were those huge, docile creatures, tired from their day's work and hungry, and this pesky pooch wouldn't allow them to enjoy their evening meal.

Finally, the oxen gave up and backed away into their stalls. Frustrated and much perplexed, one said to the other, "I don't understand this dog. I just don't understand him at all. He can't eat that hay himself and will not permit it to be eaten by those who can."

Of course, everybody knows that oxen can't talk; but this is a fable, one of Aesop's, and in fables animals can talk, and usually do. A dog-in-the-manger attitude is a selfish and offensive one. It says, "If I can't have something, I'm not going to let anyone else have it either."

Don Juan   A survivor of more than three centuries in the literature of the Western world is the legendary character named Don Juan Tenorio.

For his first hundred years or so, he lived as an oral legend among the people of Spain. Then in 1630, he appeared in a drama by Tirso de Molina, *The Seducer of Seville.* Here, he was notorious for having seduced the daughter of a prominent citizen and then killing her father in a duel.

By 1665, he had migrated to France and served as the main character in a drama by Molière. In this representation he was an out-and-out philanderer who seduced women, never paid his debts, dishonored his friends, violated all laws, and hurt people in almost every way with absolutely no qualms at all. After flippantly scorning a ghost's warning that he faced a horrible punishment, he was seared by an invisible flame, and amid thunderous sounds and lightning flashes, the earth opened up and swallowed him.

He reappeared again and again, however, notably in 1787 as the featured rogue in Mozart's opera *Don Giovanni*. In this story, he and his servant Leporello were involved in one villainous adventure after another. The servant bragged that the Don had many mistresses in most lands—700 in Italy, 800 in Germany, 91 in France and Turkey, and 1,003 in Spain—so it's no surprise to learn that Don Giovanni ended up somewhere in the infernal regions of the damned.

From 1819 to 1824, he moved suavely through the long meanderings of Byron's *Don Juan*. Here, he was a first-class charmer, a clever, popular chap who women found irresistible. He was not so much a seducer of them as they of him, but it should be noted that he never offered much resistance.

Back in Spain by 1844, he was picked up by José Zorrilla y Moral and made the main character in a drama bearing his name. A wild and reckless gallant, he wagered a friend that in a year's time he could perform more evil deeds than the other. Naturally, Don Juan won the wager, but in doing so, left in his wake a tortured and bloody trail of suffering. In spite of all this, a female admirer pulled him back to safety just as he was about to be dragged away to hell.

He was still very much a survivor in 1903 when George Bernard Shaw had him figure largely in *Man and Superman*. Here, Don Juan was in hell, and he was weary of the place. In a long, philosophic discourse with the devil and others, he reasoned that the highest good of man is the cultivation of intellect; that all which hinders such cultivation is to be avoided; and that because woman, in the nature of the circumstance, cannot be avoided, woman is man's undoing!

According to Shaw, the rake was so fed up with hell that he decided to try for a different place. His final words were, "I can find my own way to heaven." One might wonder about that, and, as well, about his acceptance should he ever get there.

No great wonder, though, that this infamous character's name should have become a descriptive cognomen for any man of similar mien. However, his record being what it is, think at least twice before calling any man a Don Juan. Libel suits have been filed for less!

Doubting Castle   *See* SLOUGH OF DESPOND.

Doubting Thomas   Perhaps the most singular event ever reported in all history was the resurrection of Jesus Christ. The first person ever to wrestle with the resurrection mystery was one of the disciples of Jesus, an apostle named Thomas. It was on a Friday that the enemies of Jesus crucified him, and at about midafternoon that day he died. His body was taken down and, just before sunset, laid in a garden tomb.

Soon after sunrise on Sunday, however, it was discovered that the body was not there; a group of women said they saw Jesus alive on a garden walk and that he spoke with them. Afterward, during a period of forty days, he was seen by numerous people.

On one of these occasions, when eleven of the twelve apostles were assembled in one place, Jesus appeared in their midst, saying, "Why are you troubled, and why do questionings arise in your hearts? See my hands and my feet, that it is I myself."

The absent apostle was Thomas. The others later reported to him that they had seen their Master, risen and alive. Now, Thomas was a good, honest man, and the very idea that Jesus could be alive again was one his practical mind just could not accept. So he said, "Unless I see in his hands the print of the nails and place my finger in their mark, and unless I place my hand in his side, I will not believe."

Eight days later, all of the apostles were together again in a room. Suddenly, Jesus stood in their midst, saying to them words he had said so often to them before: "Peace be with you!" Then, turning immediately to Thomas and holding out his hands, Jesus said, "Here, Thomas, put forth your finger and touch my hands," and then, probably pulling his robe aside, he added, "And put your hand into my side." Thomas did neither. Instead, standing awestruck and forever convinced, he murmured, "My Lord and my God!"

This Thomas has long been known as "Doubting Thomas," although it is probably a grave injustice to call him that. Anyone who requires absolute proof before accepting an idea or proposition may be known as a Doubting Thomas.

Draw the Bow of Ulysses   As the spoken or written expression of an idea, to draw or to string a bow of Ulysses is to do something nobody else can do. The story comes from Greek mythology and is dramatically told by Homer near the conclusion of *The Odyssey*.

Ulysses (actually the Greek Odysseus), the king of Ithaca, had completed ten years at the siege of Troy and then had spent another ten years making his way home. Traveling incognito as a lone wanderer, and arriving in his realm, by a combination of chance and design he encountered his son Telemachus, who had been only a small child at the time he had gone away to war. He was able to convince Telemachus that he was indeed the long-absent Ulysses, and the old bond between father and son was strongly renewed.

Telemachus reported to his father concerning affairs in the kingdom. The lead story had to do with Penelope, the courageous and devoted wife of Ulysses who had faithfully awaited her husband's return for twenty years. But hanging around the palace was a passel of male bums living off the king's wealth and trying to convince Penelope that Ulysses must surely be dead by now and that she should marry one of them.

Accompanied by his son, and still disguised as a tramp, Ulysses went to the palace. Arriving, he learned that Penelope had arranged a contest for the men, promising to marry the winner. Actually, she knew this to be a contest none of them could ever win; the contest was actually a tactic of delay, and learning of it, Ulysses understood this. A series of twelve rings were arranged in line with each other, and the man who could best shoot through these, striking a mark beyond, would win—using the bow Ulysses had left at home twenty years before.

The bow of Ulysses was a powerful weapon made especially for him and for his use only. As it turned out, and as Penelope had anticipated, not one of those men had the strength even to string or draw that bow. When all had failed, Ulysses, still posing as a stranger and sitting at one end of the courtyard, begged permission to try it. He was given the bow and he examined it carefully, pretending to be unfamiliar with such things. Then in the flash of an instant, he fixed the arrow, pulled back the bowstring, bent the mighty bow, aimed, and fired—straight through all the rings and into the mark beyond.

Nor was this the last arrow Ulysses fired that day. Ordering the palace gates shut so none of the men could escape, with the aid of his son and two old friends, he slaughtered the whole cowering mob. He then compelled twelve of the servant women who had notoriously consorted with these characters to clear away all the blood and gore. This done, he killed them as well.

Shortly afterward, Ulysses was able to prove his identity to Penelope, and following their joyous reunion, we assume they lived happily ever after!

Drink at Angelica's Fountain   *Orlando Furioso* is a long narrative poem, written by Italian Ludovico Ariosto and completed in 1532, that combined a little history and a lot of myth. Set in early ninth-century Europe, Charlemagne was the king in France, and around him were his twelve paladins who were knightly assistants in the management of public affairs. Among these were Orlando and Rinaldo, nephews of the king, and a cousin of theirs, Astolpho, an English prince who had come to aid in the struggle against Moors and Pagans.

The king of Cathay had a bewitchingly beautiful daughter, the princess Angelica. He sent her to France to stir up dissention and cause confusion in the court of Charlemagne. With skillful use of her charms, she did her work well; she quickly had the knights fawning over her and fighting among themselves.

Orlando was one who, overcome by her charms, fell madly in love with the woman—so madly that when he lost her, he did in fact go mad. Astolpho, however, restored Orlando's lost wits. Getting a lift on Elijah's chariot and with the guidance of Saint John, he made a journey to the moon. There he found Orlando's wits stored in a vial and brought them back to him.

At one point, Angelica fell passionately in love with Rinaldo, although he utterly detested her. Up in the Ardennes were twin springs that ran so close the same water flowed from both. It happened that Rinaldo drank from one of these and she from the other. Instantly, her love turned to loathing and Rinaldo's loathing to love. Apparently the water of these fountains always had a reversing effect on people who drank it—always turning loathing into love and love into loathing.

To our present day, if one has a sudden change of heart, such as moving abruptly from love or to it, the question is likely asked, "Have you been drinking at Angelica's fountain?" Sometimes it may seem so, for sometimes no better explanation is discernible!

Back to the story: In the end, Angelica married neither Orlando nor

Rinaldo. Instead, having saved the life of Modoro, a Saracean knight, she married him and went home to Cathay. With her leavetaking, things in France simmered down considerably.

Drink the Cup   On one occasion, the brothers James and John, disciples of Jesus, asked him to grant them an enormous favor. They wanted places of special privilege in his kingdom. His reply to these impulsive young men was, "You don't know what you are asking." Then he added, "Are you able to drink the cup that I am to drink?"

Much later, these two disciples, together with another named Peter, stood by when Jesus wrestled in agonizing prayer. The time was the night before his crucifixion, and the place was a garden known as Gethsemane. As he was praying there, the disciples heard him say, "Father, if you will, remove this cup from me." Then, as Jesus continued in prayer, "If this cup cannot pass away, except I drink it, your will be done." Jesus called it a cup—the demeaning mockeries, the cruel taunts, the lash of whips, the crown of thorns, and the crucifixion on the cross—and the cup did not pass.

When we seek to describe the worst of suffering, we may speak of it as a cup to be drunk. To drink a cup is to experience grief or pain. The cup is trouble we hope won't come, but often does.

Drive Like Jehu   To drive like Jehu is to drive wildly, which some people seem inclined to do. A Jezebel or a painted Jezebel is a woman of high spirit and low morals, the very epitome of wickedness. A Naboth's vineyard is anything so passionately desired that it is sought or gotten in any deceitful or underhanded way. These three expressions all come from a single story, told mainly in Jewish and Christian scriptures and confirmed somewhat in the historic monuments of ancient Assyria.

For nineteen years in the ninth century B.C., a self-indulgent despot named Ahab was the king of Israel. Traditionally, his people were worshipers of Jehovah, but Ahab was no stickler on this point. Neighboring peoples of other cultures worshiped various other gods called Baals, usually in wild and sensual carousings, and Ahab saw no harm in embracing their pagan practices. He also embraced one of the most rabid of the Baal worshipers, a woman named Jezebel, who he married and moved into his palace at Samaria. Jezebel was a daughter of the king of Sidon, who was himself also a priest of the goddess Astarte.

Jezebel was a scheming, violent, totally unscrupulous woman. On one occasion, she found her husband in a gloomy mood and, inquiring about it, learned that he wanted a vineyard that he was unable to get. The vineyard was owned by Naboth, who refused either to sell or trade it. Jezebel took things into her own hands at once, arranging a fine feast in honor of Naboth. But she also arranged for two liars to sit opposite Naboth and, at the very height of the festivities, to accuse him of cursing God and the king. This being done, and the people believing the lie, Naboth was stoned to death, and Ahab took possession of the coveted vineyard.

When Ahab was killed in battle, two of his sons, in turn, took control of the realm, acting as puppets, while Queen Mother Jezebel pulled all the strings. One of these fellows was Ahaziah and the other Jehoram.

Another main character in this drama was Elisha, a prophet; Elisha had grown weary of the way things were going. Knowing of a fiery, dynamic young man named Jehu, Elisha arranged to have him anointed king of Israel, as an alternate to Jehoram.

Jehu was never a man to spend much time thinking about things; he was a man of action. And he acted now, quickly. Knowing that Ahaziah, Jehoram, and their mother were together at their summer palace at Jezreel, Jehu mounted his chariot, gathered his men around him, and stormed away in a cloud of dust.

Not long afterward, a watchman at the wall of Jezreel saw that dust cloud appear on the horizon. Jehoram sent out a messenger to ask, "Do you come in peace or for war?" But that messenger never returned, and when a second one was sent, neither did he. By this time Jehu was drawing near the city, and seeing more clearly now, the watchman shouted an alarm: "The messenger has reached them, but is not coming back; and the driving is like the driving of Jehu, the son of Nimshi; for he drives furiously."

Both Ahaziah and Jehoram, in their separate chariots, then raced forth to meet Jehu. Reaching him, Jehoram called out, "Is it peace, Jehu?" The shot of an arrow could not have been sharper than Jehu's answer, "What peace can there be as long as the harlotries and sorceries of your mother Jezebel are so many?"

Shouting to his brother, "It's treachery!" Jehoram swung his chariot about; but before he could gain speed for flight, an arrow from Jehu's bow struck him dead. They were just then passing the field for which Jezebel had murdered Naboth, and Jehu shouted to his men, "Dump his body here," and they did.

In Jezreel, Jezebel heard that Jehu was coming. She painted her face, adorned herself, and waited by an upstairs window. As Jehu approached, she hurled taunts and epithets toward him. From his chariot, Jehu glanced up, and seeing the woman there, called out, "Who is on my side?" When two or three faces appeared at the window, Jehu commanded, "Throw her down." And throw her down they did, and her body was crushed to pulp beneath the grinding wheels of chariots and the pounding hooves of horses.

A little later, now in command of the city, Jehu said to his men, "Go now and see about this cursed woman, and bury her; for after all, she is a king's daughter." The men went. But, as it is written, "They found no more of her than the skull and the feet and the palms of her hands."

Drive the Horses of the Sun   When someone of extreme ambition deals with power he or she may be unable to control, it is sometimes said the person is trying to drive the horses of the sun. The expression comes from the story of Phaethon, an episode of Greek mythology.

Phaethon was a very young man, probably about sixteen. Among his circle of boyhood buddies, he was known as the swiftest and strongest, but they taunted and teased him about one thing. He claimed that his father was Helius, the sun god, and his friends did not believe him.

Eager to prove himself to his crowd, he wanted to do something spectacular that would demonstrate his relationship with the mighty Helius. So he went on a long journey to the east, seeking the palace of the sun god. Arriving before daybreak one morning, he told Helius he sought some way of identifying himself as his father's son. This pleased Helius very much, for Phaethon was indeed his son. The proud father then, in a moment of fatherly foolishness, promised to give Phaethon anything he asked.

Just at that time the grooms were bringing out the four great white horses and preparing the chariot for the day's run pulling the sun across the sky. Although surrounded by servants, Helius always drove that chariot himself. It struck the adolescent mind of Phaethon that the most spectacular thing he could do would be to drive those four horses that day and so he asked for his father's permission.

Helius hesitated, but he had promised anything his son asked and felt, despite the danger, that he should keep his promise. So that day Phaethon mounted the chariot and took into his hands the reins of those powerful horses. At precisely the right moment, the mighty animals leaped forward, running at a speed Phaethon had never dreamed possible and rising to heights he never knew existed.

Up and away across the sky the animals ran as though made of blazing fire. As it always is with horses, they quickly sensed the absence of the master's hand on the reins. Then they went wild, swerving far from the appointed path. Phaethon was unable to control them; the great chariot careened wildly across the sky, swerving erratically right and left, up and down. As the chariot came closer to earth, mountaintops caught fire and smoked like volcanoes. In some areas, the heat was so intense that all the people there became dark of color. Some rivers dried up, and many areas of forest land were burned, leaving only sandy deserts.

Phaethon was powerless, and he knew it. He was terrified; even his hair was on fire. Watching from the highest heavens, Zeus, majestic overlord of all gods, found it necessary to send one of his thunderbolts to destroy Phaethon to save the earth, and this he did.

One who would drive the horses of the sun must hold the reins in strong and steady hands. It is hazardous business to covet management of a power one cannot control.

− E −

Eat Crow   When someone says "I had to eat crow" it means that the person was compelled to admit to a mistake, to apologize for some misdeed or blunder, or to do some unpleasant or disagreeable thing due to that person's fault.

Crow is an extremely unpalatable bird, and to eat it would be a rather distasteful experience. This experience, though, was suffered through by two men many years ago, during one of our American wars. There are several versions of the story, and at least two settings for it—the Civil War and the War of 1812. The Civil War version goes as follows.

A Northern regiment was encamped near the estate of a wealthy plantation owner somewhere in the South. One of the privates went hunting on the plantation grounds. Encountering nothing of note to shoot at, the soldier finally fired away at a crow and killed it. Approaching the dead bird, and laying his gun on the ground, he picked up the carcass.

At that moment, the planter emerged from the woods, seized the soldier's rifle, and pointed it straight at him. He cursed, "That crow, fellow, was our family pet; and now that you've killed it, you've got to eat it. Eat it, now! Eat it, or I shoot!"

The soldier had no choice. Stripping away a handful of feathers, he took a couple of bites of raw drumstick and, with excruciating effort, swallowed it. "More," said the planter; and more it was, for several agonizing minutes. The planter then asked, "Well, how do you like my crow?" The soldier stammered, "I . . . I can eat it . . . , but I don't exactly hanker after it."

Pleased with himself for having put the soldier through this ordeal, the man said, "Now get off my land, and don't ever come back—you hear me? Here, take your blasted weapon, and be gone!" But the rich landlord was in for the surprise of his life: With gun now firmly in hand, the soldier took dead aim at him, commanding, "It's your turn now, sir. Part of this crow is yours, sir. Eat it. Do it now, right now." And the man did; he had no choice.

Next day, the irate planter appeared at the Union camp to complain about the fracas. The soldier, called in to give an account of himself, was asked by the presiding officer, "Have you seen this man before?" With one brief glance toward the planter, the young man replied, "Yes, sir; we . . . we dined together yesterday!"

Eaten by Your Own Dogs Actaeon was the grandson of a powerful king; he was a young man of much vigor, the adventurous sort. Having a pack of hunting dogs, he had trained them to viciously attack any forest animals they might encounter. And with his hunting pack, he often went into the woodlands seeking prey.

On one occasion, he led his dogs into a sector of the deep woods he had never been in before—the province of the goddess Diana and her nymphs. The area was off-limits to all forest creatures and to all humans; even the strongest and most courageous dared not enter, as it was known to all that the goddess could cast a spell causing their wits to leave them. Actaeon knew he was trespassing upon the territory of the gods, but he kept going anyway. You see, he wanted to find the beautiful goddess and her playful nymphs and hopefully spy on them without their knowing he was watching.

Suddenly he came upon them, bathing in a sparkling pool at the entrance of a cave. He meant to remain concealed, observing them in their naked beauty, but they saw him and were startled. A quick splash of water forced him to blink, and upon opening his eyes everything appeared strange. He tried to speak and found that he could not. In confusion he turned away, and putting his hand to his forehead, he discovered that antlers were growing there. Attempting to walk, he realized that hands and feet were now the hooves of an animal. Looking at his reflection in a pool, what he saw was a huge woodland beast; he had been changed into a stag.

He began to run in panic, but he could not outrun his dogs. Snarling savagely, they were at his heels. Well trained as they were for killing stags, when his antlers caught in the brush, the dogs were instantly upon him, tearing him apart. And so Actaeon died, devoured by his own dogs. He had created a ruthless hunting pack and now they destroyed him.

The picture is a vivid one: A person sets up a powerful device to work his will in the world, and then, when circumstances change, this device causes the person's downfall or destruction. If you become the victim of your own scheme, it can be said that you were eaten by your own dogs.

Eldorado   The search for Eldorado began in 1530 and it continued in earnest for nearly 400 years—and some say it hasn't ended yet. Only 38 years after the first voyage of Columbus, Spanish adventurer Francisco Pizarro and 180 men were in South America plundering for riches.

They captured the Inca emperor Atahualpa, who offered gold in exchange for his release. The offer accepted, Inca porters delivered enough gold to fill a room twenty-two feet long and seventeen feet wide to the level of the emperor's upraised hand. Unfortunately, it didn't help Atahualpa; Pizarro killed him anyway. But where had so much gold come from? And was there more?

Five years later, Sebastian de Belalcázar, in the same area for the same reasons, heard from Indians a tale of great riches. In this fantastic land of golden spires and domes was, reputedly, a sacred lake where the people made ceremonial sacrifices of their most precious possessions by throwing them into the water, and where the king once a year covered his body completely with gold and washed it away by bathing there.

Belalcázar called this mysterious king El Dorado, The Golden Man. In time, the realm over which this king reigned was known as Eldorado, and the legends of that land and the search for it constitute a fascinating tale of adventure, intrigue, and mayhem.

Expedition after expedition set out, criss-crossing South and Central America, warring with natives, sometimes fighting among themselves, struggling against wilderness and disease, all searching for the Eldorado they never found. Their greed was fed by tales of enormous wealth that was just beyond the next mountain or far away in some mysterious land, so they passionately persisted in the quest even though the journeys often resulted in suffering and the loss of human life. There was, for example, the 1568 expedition of Gonzalo do Quesada, which set out from Bogotá with 2,800 men, to return after three harrowing years with just 68.

During an earlier attempt, Quesada had located a lake named Guatavita, where, by some rumors, El Dorado had held his annual cleansing ritual, but very little gold was ever found. In 1595, British adventurer Sir Walter Raleigh met the Spanish at Trinidad, obtained what information a few heavy-drinking bouts could provide, and launched his own expedition. Raleigh afterward reported the existence of an immense lake named Parima. Although no one else had ever actually seen it, for many years maps had located and identified the lake; it remained for Prussian explorer Alexander von Humboldt early in the nineteenth century to prove that no lake existed in that place.

Lake Guatavita, however, continued to fascinate many adventure-seekers, and over the years attempts were made to search its murky floor, some even in modern times. A few golden articles were found, but nothing that approximated the reputed wealth of Eldorado.

The trail to this fabled land and its fabulous lake is strewn with the blood and bones of thousands and with much frustration and heartbreak, but as yet the city's golden spires are nowhere to be seen. We do, though, have this poetic word, created in 1535 by Belalcázar, and while not as priceless as all that gold might have been, it is useful nevertheless. It is often said, "He spent his whole life looking for Eldorado."

Eldorado? It's a state of ease and plenty, of opportunity and privilege without limit. In short, it's something that doesn't exist.

Eleventh Hour   The eleventh hour is often used to indicate lateness, the last possible moment, something that happens just in the nick of time, or the instant of final opportunity.

The expression comes from one of the parables told by Jesus. It concerns the business dealings of a well-to-do farmer who had much land, with many crops growing in his fields, among these a vineyard. Needing laborers for work in his vineyard, the farmer went out one day early in the morning looking for workers. Finding several men, he offered them one denarius each if they would work for him that day. Accepting the offer, the men went to work.

At about the third hour (that is, 9 A.M.), the landholder found several other fellows who weren't doing anything, and he put them to work, saying, "You go into the vineyard also, and whatever is right I will give you." The same thing happened at the sixth hour (noon), at the ninth hour (3 P.M.), and at the eleventh hour (5 P.M.). This last group of men had only a short time to work, since the workday was almost over.

At quitting time, the men were paid, and all received one denarius each, regardless of how long they had worked. Men who had worked all day objected that this was unfair and that they deserved more. The farmer replied, "Have I not given you what I agreed to give, one denarius? Have I not kept my promise? If I choose, then, to give others as much as I have given you, is not this my right to do? Am I not allowed, if I choose, to give away what belongs to me?"

Thus, as things turned out, the men who came to work at the

eleventh hour got there just in time to receive the full benefits of the day. For them, this was that day's final opportunity, their last chance.

Eureka! At the moment of a sudden discovery, this exclamation is often heard. It usually comes with the finding of something long sought and much desired, whether a coveted treasure, a lost article, or the answer to a perplexing question. It's a Greek word, with a dramatic story.

Archimedes, Greek mathematician and physicist (287–212 B.C.), lived most of his life in Syracuse, a Greek city on the island of Sicily. During a portion of Archimedes' lifetime, the tyrant of Syracuse was Hiero II. Archimedes, an ancient to whom modern science owes much, was a relative of Hiero and a close friend.

On one occasion, the tyrant had commissioned a new golden crown, but he suspected the finished product was an alloy of gold mixed with silver. He asked Archimedes to resolve the question for him. No such test was known, and for many days the great scientist puzzled over the matter.

Then one day at a public bath, Archimedes stepped into a nearly filled tub. As he did so, the water overflowed. His attention instantly captured, he stepped out and then in again, carefully observing the result. Realizing that when immersed, a body displaces an amount of water equal to its own volume, and knowing that a given weight of silver has greater volume than an equal weight of gold, Archimedes knew how to test the purity of Hiero's crown! With great excitement, he leaped from the tub crying, "Heureka! Heureka!" The word is the Greek verb for "having found," and *eureka* is literally "I have found it."

This episode in the life of Archimedes is historically well founded and it marked the beginning of his original work in hydrology—a work that has given us accurate and useful principles. Tradition adds an interesting postscript: Eager to test his discovery and too excited to remember his clothes, Archimedes ran naked all the way home.

Every Cloud Has a Silver Lining The story behind this phrase is *Comus*, a long narrative poem by John Milton, written in 1634. Circe, mistress of a mysterious island, has developed a powerful potion that when drunk turns a person into a pig. The infamous Bacchus, his ship driven by a storm, is cast upon Circe's island. He freely fraternizes with the sorceress and fathers a child whom she names Comus.

Inheriting his mother's powers of sorcery, Comus later inhabits and controls a dense forest where unwary travelers, conned into drinking his concoctions, become hogs or goats or other lowly creatures. The Attendant Spirit, usually in some disguise, also inhabits the woodland to protect travelers against the deceptions of Comus.

Into this forest come a virtuous young woman and her two brothers. Separated from them, she wanders lost and bewildered. In the darkness of a clouded night she sees suddenly a sign of hope, and says,

> ... There does a sable cloud
> Turn forth her silver lining to the night.

(From here come all our phrases having to do with clouds and silver linings.)

As the girl's wanderings continue, Comus appears in shepherd's garb and offers to take her to a cottage. She accepts, but is taken as a prisoner to his castle.

Elsewhere in the forest, the two brothers, also lost, are concerned for the safety of their sister, and between them there is long discussion as to whether her virtue will protect her. The Attendant Spirit appears to the brothers and reports that their sister has been led away by Comus and is in great danger. Led by The Attendant Spirit, the brothers strike out immediately for Comus's hidden palace.

In the palace, the young woman refuses to drink from the glass Comus offers. It is a battle between his perfidy and her virtue. In the midst of it, the brothers burst in with swords drawn and snatch the drinking glass from Comus's hand and rescue their sister.

Comus and his gang vanish; but as the story ends, he is somewhere near, his evil-evoking wand still in his hand.

Eyes of Argus   Io was a princess, the daughter of King Inachus, and Zeus was the high god who ruled the heavens and much else. Zeus fell in love with Io, but his wife, Hera, did not look approvingly upon this development. She changed Io into a white heifer, assuming that Zeus would not be as attracted to a young cow as he had been to the beautiful young Io. An effective way of eliminating competition, one would think, but Hera wasn't satisfied, so she hired a watchman to keep an eye on Io.

His name was Argus, and he was well qualified for his assignment; he had 100 eyes, located all over his body, so that he was capable of seeing in all directions at once. No matter how many of these eyes were asleep or closed at any time, at least two were always open and watching. This watchman's full name was actually Argus Panoptes, meaning "Argus the All-Seeing." The Io heifer was surely well guarded; not much hanky-panky would be possible under those 100 watchful eyes!

Zeus, however, didn't give up his interest in Io. He summoned one of the lesser gods, Hermes, a sort of divine messenger and general trouble-shooter, whose shoes had wings on them. Zeus sent Hermes on a mission of liquidation—to do in Argus. And Hermes did it, and by an innovative method.

Approaching Argus, Hermes began to sing and tell stories, repeating them over and over again. One by one, the eyes of Argus began to close in sleep, until he was sound asleep in every one of his 100 eyes. Having thus immobilized Argus, Hermes cut off his head.

This, of course, was the finish for Argus, but his fame and name continue to linger with us. To be Argus-eyed is to be jealously watchful. To need the eyes of Argus is to need a more complete and penetrating view of complicated matters. To say that we lack the eyes of Argus is usually to admit that we do not comprehend the meaning of something.

Eyes of Argus in the Peacock's Tail   To put the eyes of Argus in the peacock's tail is to do a very difficult thing. And to continue the story from the previous entry . . .

Hera desired to honor her late guardsman, Argus, in some way. Her favorite bird was the peacock, and when its tail was spread in a proud strut, it provided a lot of usable space. So Hera took those 100 eyes from the body of Argus and, with great difficulty, set every one of them like jewels in the tail of the peacock. And to this day, whenever a peacock spreads his fanlike tail, the eyes of Argus can be seen.

— F —

Fabian   For about 400 years, the Fabius family was a powerful factor in Roman public affairs and politics. Our story has to do with one Quintus Fabius Maximus and the singular role he played in the Second Punic War, 218–201 B.C. The conflict was between Rome and Carthage; Carthage was the center of a sprawling empire across the Mediterranean on the coast of Africa. The Carthagean leader was Hannibal, the most formidable enemy Rome ever faced.

From his position at Cartagena on the Spanish coast, Hannibal marched his armies 800 miles in five months, northward across the Pyrenees, eastward across Gaul, and then southward across the Alps into Italy (his crossing of the Alps stands as one of the most remarkable military events in all history). With severe losses to gorilla fighters, weather, and avalanches, Hannibal survived the march with 20,000 infantry, 6,000 cavalry, and only a few of the elephants with which he started.

Roman general Scipio was waiting for him with well-disciplined and rested troops. But they were no match for Hannibal; during the next months, Hannibal won every encounter with the Romans. After the 218 B.C. defeat of the combined Roman legions at the River Trebia, Fabius was made commander of the Roman forces. Realizing that his army could never win in a head-on battle with Hannibal's, he developed a strategy of evasive harassment. Engaging in a kind of guerilla warfare, he broke up his army into small units, raiding the invaders' supply lines and preying upon their foraging parties, but always avoiding contact with the main Carthagean force.

In this way, Fabius was gradually wearing Hannibal down. But the proud Roman traditionalists felt humiliated that Fabius would never stand and fight, and they fired him. Then in 216 B.C., under other leadership, the Roman armies met Hannibal's main force at Cannae. The Romans suffered disastrous and decisive defeat. Fabius, recalled then to his former command, resumed his tactic of harassment. After thirteen years, without fighting another major battle, the mighty Hannibal was forced to leave Italy.

Now reformers who want to bring about change gradually and peacefully think of theirs as a Fabian philosophy. To promote this type of socialist reform, an organization known as the Fabian Society was founded in England in the 1880s (among its first members were George Bernard Shaw and Sidney Webb). And thus the origins of our current Fabian expressions.

Face That Launched a Thousand Ships   A face that can launch a thousand ships is one that is incredibly beautiful. The expression comes from two stories.

The first is the story of the Trojan War as told by Homer in 800 B.C. Menelaus, king of Sparta, was married to a beautiful woman named Helen. Paris, a handsome young prince and the son of Priam, king of the Trojans, absconded with fair Helen and took her away to his father's palace across the Aegean Sea in Troy.

This shenanigan on the part of Paris displeased Menelaus immensely, and he persuaded the kings from a good number of the Grecian states to join him in an effort to rescue his wife. The result was the ten-year Trojan War. The Grecian kings raised huge armies, combined their forces, and launched a fleet of 1,000 ships to sail against Troy.

The second story begins in the sixteenth century A.D. with Englishman Christopher Marlowe. Born the same year as Shakespeare, he too became a dramatist. About 1588, he wrote a play entitled *Doctor Faustus*, which was the story of a man who literally sold his soul to Satan in exchange for certain favors. The contract provided that Faustus be granted his every wish for a period of twenty-four years, after which his soul would belong exclusively and entirely to the devil.

Faustus understood that Helen of Troy had been one of the world's most beautiful women, so one of his wishes was that she be conjured up for him. When she appeared—her "shadow," that is—Faustus burst forth in praise of her beauty. His speech is perhaps one of the finest passages in English literature. It begins, "Was this the face that launched a thousand ships?" Apparently, Helen's was a face that men fought over and sold their souls to get!

Falstaffian   Sir John Falstaff: a witty, self-indulgent braggart, winsomely insincere, a lovable lech, and one of the most complex characters in literature. He was the prodigious creation of William Shakespeare, who marched him by devious routes through three of his plays: *Henry IV*, *Henry V*, and *The Merry Wives of Windsor*. Fat and lazy, a hard drinker and glutton, he was a schemer and rascal, yet a fascinating fellow who was welcome in most circles and generally popular. To call anyone Falstaffian is to pronounce him jovial but deceitful, agreeable company but insufferably vain.

Typically Falstaffian was this fellow's behavior at the battle of Shrewsbury when Prince Hal managed to kill Hotspur, the enemy leader. During the battle, to protect himself from injury, Falstaff pretended to be dead on the field. The battle over, he boasted of all sorts of heroic fighting that he had done, including the killing of Hotspur. The prince soon put the record straight on that one—but being caught in such shenanigans never fazed Falstaff since he was a master of the face-saving art.

He was also a master con artist. On one occasion, Mrs. Quickly, the hostess at the Boar's Head Inn, ordered Falstaff arrested for debt as he had failed to pay for sundry libations consumed at her establishment. In the end, the rascal successfully wheedled a sizable loan from her and an invitation to dinner besides.

In his earlier years, as Shakespeare presents him, Falstaff was a beer-hall buddy of Hal, the prince of Wales. When Hal became king (Henry V), Falstaff and his cronies hastened to London, anticipating favored positions and easy lives in the lap of royal luxury. They were rejected by the newly crowned monarch, who, along with his crown, had acquired also a new sense of duty.

When Falstaff died, as eventually he did, Mrs. Quickly (by now the wife of Falstaff's pal Pistol) was present to witness the event. She reported, "He cried out, 'God, God, God' three or four times. Now I, to comfort him, bid him he should not think of God; I hoped there was no need to trouble himself with any such thoughts yet." Certainly, up until that time, he had never been much bothered by thoughts of God or of anything else of great importance.

Fates   We commonly hear it said, "The fates are against me," or "The fates have smiled upon him," or, "It's in the hands of fate." The term *fate* is from the mythology of ancient Greece, where people believed a large number of divine or semidivine beings watched over and managed mortal affairs. There were, for example, the Three Graces who presided over the areas of beauty and charm. There were the three (later, nine) Muses who were in charge of music and poetry.

But the consortium whose activity was most decisive for humans was a third threesome, the Three Fates. The fortunes of all people were, literally, in their hands. These three industrious females worked upon the thread of human life. Clotho spun the thread, Lachesis drew it out and measured its length, and Atropos cut it off with her great, gleaming scissors. Thus, in their assembly-line operation, the Three Fates took the raw fibers, formed them into a continuous strand, gave it smoothness and strength, and at length brought it to an end.

If the thread of life was cut off early or became tangled or tied into knots, well, this was blamed on the Fates. It was assumed, though, that the Fates knew what they were doing, and they were trusted as experts at their work.

These ancient people sought some way of explaining the mysteries of life, the answers to why things happened as they did. Sometimes we speak of the thread of destiny, and in doing so, we hark back to the busy careers of Clotho, Lachesis, and Atropos.

Faustian Bargain   *The History of the Damnable Life and Deserved Death of Doctor John Faustus* was the title of a strange tale that in 1587 made its way from Germany into England. There it was picked up by Christopher Marlowe, by whom it was immediately rewritten as a drama for the British stage.

Doctor Faustus, a respected scholar at the University of Wittenberg, becomes engrossed with the occult, giving himself over to a consuming passion for the shadowy world of necromancy and magic. In an ever-deepening involvement, he yearns for the power that some liaison with spirits might bring. Soon Mephostophilis appears. This demonic personage is a primary lieutenant of Lucifer, the chief of devils.

With Mephostophilis, Faustus works out a deal by which for twenty-four years he will be granted everything he wishes, and Mephostophilis will be his constant, unseen companion and servant. At the end of this period, however, the soul of Faustus will belong wholly to Lucifer. The agreement is sealed and signed in blood.

The contract time soon passes, though, and Faustus hasn't done much with his powers but pull off a few pranks and conjure up a few folks who have been long dead. As the day of reckoning approaches, Faustus realizes for the first time what he has done. He wants out of his contract, but that is not possible.

The doctor says to his Wittenberg associates, "O, would I had never seen Wittenberg, never read a book!" But now, for twenty-four years of service rendered, Lucifer must be paid. The cost is high; for the little he has gotten, Faustus must now give his immortal soul.

It is nearing midnight of his last day, and in a room at Wittenberg he bids his fellow scholars a last goodbye: "Gentlemen, farewell! If I live till morning, I'll visit you; if not, Faustus is gone to hell." He sends them away to await the morning in an adjoining room, saying, "Whatever noise you hear, don't come."

During the night there are horrible shrieks and screams; and when morning comes, the scholars find only the man's mangled arms and legs. Faustus has paid the first installment only, as other payments will come little by little in tortures that will last forever.

Here ends the story of Dr. Faustus as told by Marlowe. But the strange career of John Faustus has been the subject of many literary works. Most notable of all was the masterful *Faust*, a dramatic poem by Johann Wolfgang von Goethe. In Goethe's poem, Faust does find salvation at last. Yet the obsessed doctor's deal with the devil is such a bad one that to speak of the very worst of all possible deals is to call it a Faustian bargain.

Feet of Clay One night Nebuchadrezzar had a disturbingly vivid dream, and it troubled him. He desperately wanted to know the meaning of it, for in those days all dreams were believed to have meanings, and those meanings were important. Being the king of Babylon, and having access to the best brains in the world, Nebuchadrezzar called in all his wise men and said to them, "Tell me what I dreamed."

They replied, "Nobody can do that; but if you will only tell us the dream, we will then tell you what it means." The king did not like that suggestion and he ordered the men put to death.

Now in Babylon at that time was a Hebrew named Daniel, who Nebuchadrezzar had brought as a captive to Babylon when Jerusalem was overthrown in 586 B.C. By the power of his personality, intelligence, and integrity, Daniel had risen to a position of respect and leadership. Learning now of the king's condemnation of the wise men, he went to the king, saying, "Do not destroy the wise men of Babylon; I will give you the interpretation of your dream."

But first he had to tell the king what it was he had dreamt. He said, "O king, in your dream you saw the great image of a man, with head of fine gold, breast and arms of silver, belly and thighs of brass, legs of iron, and feet that were partly iron and partly clay. And in your dream you saw a huge stone come crashing down from a mountain, striking those feet and smashing them, and bringing down the whole image, so that all parts of it were broken into pieces so small that the wind blew them all away. Then you saw that stone grow into a mountain that filled the whole earth."

Daniel was right, but what was the meaning of the dream? Daniel went on to say, "You, sir, are the head of gold; but after you will come another king and another kingdom, and others following this, each inferior to the former, until at last the worst and weakest will utterly fall, and a new kingdom will fill the whole earth, and this will be the kingdom of God."

Having feet of clay refers to having a fatal imperfection. It denotes a hidden flaw, an unapparent and incongruous point of vulnerability.

Fiddle While Rome Burns   To do nothing in a time of impending calamity or to stand by idly when circumstance calls for action is to fiddle while Rome burns. The phrase is often used to suggest a neglect of duty or a shirking of responsibility. It comes from a story that is historically based, but probably not historical; it is probably not an account of events as they happened, but as many wished they might have been.

It was July A.D. 64. A fire started not far from the imperial palace where Emperor Nero had, for ten bloody years, managed and manipulated the affairs of the Roman Empire. This despicable bigot was the fifth and final emperor to come from the family of Julius Caesar and the worst of the lot.

He came to the throne through the scheming of his unscrupulous mother, Agrippina, who was also his mistress for a period of time. Later, he had her murdered. Indeed, it was hazardous to the health of any woman to be involved with Nero. He murdered his wife, Octavia, so he might marry another, and after a short time also killed that one.

In that rather freewheeling time, the Roman citizenry were accustomed to a lot of perfidy on the part of their rulers, but Nero's blatant immorality, insufferable vanity, and inhuman brutality were too much for them. They detested the man.

So, when the great fire broke out in Rome, there were many who believed that Nero started it. Early historians uniformly treated the episode in this way; and the report that the man fiddled while the city burned was rumored from the beginning. Later versions of the story had Nero fifty miles away at the time, speeding to the city the moment he heard the news and behaving quite responsibly. Who knows?

We do know, though, that if Nero did some fiddling in A.D. 64, it wasn't with a violin; that instrument wasn't invented until several centuries afterward. As a matter of fact, the earliest reports never called the instrument a violin, but a lyre. Whatever the instrument, and the tale's validity, the story was widely believed from the start and has persisted through the ages.

So who really started the fire? Claiming that he didn't, Nero blamed the Christians. They were a new religious order in the world then, and it was commonly believed that Nero deliberately perpetrated a catastrophe so that he might blame the Christians for it, thus providing the justification for launching a campaign against them that took the lives of thousands.

As for Nero, his career following the fire was brief. By his outrageous behavior, he had alienated virtually everybody. At last, after fourteen years in power, and finding himself deserted by even his closest companions and cronies, he took his life. That was in the year 68. He was thirty-one.

Fifth Column   For many years, Spain was torn by internal strife. In the era of the monarchy, when rival segments of the ruling family fought with one another, and later during attempts at democratic government, civil war was an almost normal state of affairs. In 1931, King Alfonso XIII was deposed and a republic was established. From the beginning, however, the new government was torn by dissention, and by 1936 the country was embroiled in nationwide civil war.

The Loyalists held the capital city, Madrid, as well as other segments of the country here and there. General Francisco Franco, having led a revolt of Spain's Army of Africa in Morocco, brought the army across to the Spanish mainland, obtaining there widespread military support for the revolution. In northern Spain, General Emilio Mola led other revolutionary forces in some very successful ventures.

In autumn of 1936, with the support of Franco, General Mola launched an all-out attack against the Loyalist forces in Madrid. Four separate columns of the well-trained and well-equipped rebels were poised to march against the city. Mola was confident of a quick victory. In a radio broadcast addressed to the city's defenders, one of his generals declared, "We have four columns on the battlefield against you and a fifth column inside your ranks."

This fifth column referred to the rebel sympathizers secretly located throughout the city who would join the fighting from within, while the four approaching columns made their attack from without. From that day on, a fifth column has been an enemy within or a secret force on the inside that is waiting for the right opportunity to make its move.

The Spanish revolutionaries, however, failed to take Madrid at this time. They succeeded nearly three years later. In March 1939 the capital city was finally conquered, and this rebel victory made General Francisco Franco the dictator of Spain for the rest of his life. During this bloody struggle, Ernest Hemingway picked up this thread of current history and published a play entitled *The Fifth Column* (1938). The survivability of the expression was thus assured.

Finger in the Dike   *See* LEAK IN THE DIKE.

Fleshpots   Due to an acute food shortage in their homeland, the Hebrew people fled from Canaan to Egypt. There, at the mercy of the Egyptians and considered the underclass, these refugees quickly became a race of servants and slaves who were assigned menial and laborious tasks. They were, however, provided living space on the fertile delta of the Nile, with family units maintained. Although they were a people in bondage, they were well housed and well fed.

After four centuries of this treatment, a remarkable leader named Moses arose from among the people, and his purpose was to lead them back to their homeland in Canaan. Following a long and difficult struggle, Moses at last managed to get all of the Hebrew people out of Egypt, across the Red Sea, and into the barren wastelands of the Sinai peninsula. The long trek to Canaan—which took forty years— was plagued with difficulties. Again and again, the people became restive and rebellious.

Less than three months after leaving Egypt, the people feared starvation because the barren wasteland provided very little food. They turned against Moses with a burning fury, saying, "It would have been better to have died in the land of Egypt, when we sat by the fleshpots and ate our fill of bread; for you have brought us out into this wilderness to kill this whole assembly with hunger."

At that moment, the people were remembering the cooking vessels of Goshen and could almost smell the savory meats they once had eaten in abundance. Right now, it didn't matter to them that then they had been slaves; right now, they put the fleshpots ahead of freedom.

The feeling of those people was so tragically typical of our humanity that their story adds an expressive word to our vocabulary, *fleshpots*. To lust after the fleshpots is to have a passionate longing for luxuries and material possessions. The concept is so compelling that the word has many specific uses in our time; for example, prostitutes are sometimes coarsely called fleshpots.

Fly in the Ointment   Solomon, as portrayed in the Bible and elsewhere in history, was an intelligent and astute man. For about forty years he was the king of Israel, the third in succession after Saul and David. A son of David and Bathsheba, he inherited the throne in fulfillment of a dying wish of his father, who left for him a well-established, rich, and powerful kingdom. Upon assuming the throne, the new king quickly established himself as the unquestioned sovereign of the land; his first order of business was the cleverly engineered elimination of all opponents.

Solomon was an accomplished diplomat. While his father's reign had brought almost forty years of constant war, under Solomon's rule the country enjoyed its longest period of peace. He brought Israel to a position of high respectability among nations. He was also a builder of wide renown. Under his leadership, a magnificent temple of worship was built in Jerusalem, and all through the realm great structures took shape—palaces, roads, bridges, fortresses, stables, waterworks, and entire cities.

Solomon had one notable weakness: women. He squandered much of his nation's wealth on women, and because of his obsession with them, his principles were compromised. Solomon actually married 700 wives. One would think that this would be enough for any man, but not for this fellow. In addition to his 700 wives, he also had 300 mistresses. In that day polygamy was common, but not to that extent! His flagrant excesses triggered a reform movement which, after his death, outlawed polygamy in Israel.

How does a man like Solomon feel about such behavior? We may have a clue in the biblical book of *Ecclesiastes*, which was long believed to be the work of Solomon (although many now doubt this).

Whatever the authorship, however, there is in this book one sentence that Solomon may logically have written: "Dead flies make the perfumer's ointment to give off a stinking odor; so does a little folly outweigh wisdom and honor." Dead flies are small things, but in ointment, they make it smell bad, and the bad smell overcomes the good. Likewise in a man's life, a little folly outweighs a lot of wisdom and honor. Solomon ought to know. He had great wisdom and was internationally honored, but he was afflicted by a folly that proved to be enormously burdensome and expensive.

"The fly in the ointment," as used in common speech, is whatever messes up something. It is the thing, usually small, that fouls what otherwise would be appealing or desirable; it is the troublesome intruder who spoils the scene.

Frankensteinian Monster   It has been often said that in splitting the atom we unleashed a power we may be unable to control. Victor Frankenstein also created a thing mightier than he, and it destroyed him. Since it had no name, it has been called after its creator "the Frankenstein monster." And now anything capable of overpowering its maker is commonly called a Frankensteinian monster, and one who makes such a monster may be known as a Frankenstein.

The story of Frankenstein and his creation is told by Mary Shelley in 1818. It's an ugly tale with frightening implications. The son of affluent and high-minded Swiss parents, young Frankenstein is a student at Ingolstadt. His mother is dead, but at home in Geneva are his father, his youngest brother, William, and Elizabeth, a bright and delightful young woman who his parents adopted when she was a small child.

At the university, Frankenstein becomes obsessed with the notion that he can create a human being, and secretly sets out to do so. Over a period of two years, gathering body parts from graveyards, laboratories, and dissecting rooms, he assembles an eight-foot male body and, by electrical impulse, brings it to life. It is only in this instant that he realizes, in panic, what he has done. Seized by an utter revulsion, he flees the scene and for many months suffers a "nervous fever."

Frankenstein knows nothing of the monster's whereabouts or activities until word comes that in Geneva his beloved brother William has been murdered. He is horribly distressed and secretly knows that the monster has done this, and he is horrified when an innocent neighborhood girl is hanged for the murder.

Retreating into the icy summits of the Alps, he is confronted by the monster who has now mastered the art of speech and a great deal more. In prolonged conversation, this grotesque, soulless creature reveals his superior intelligence. He is a being of enormous physical strength and diabolical cunning. He complains that his own creator abandoned him and that he stands ready to wreak vengeance upon men, especially the one who has brought him into his miserable existence. What he wants is a female companion, like himself, and demands that Frankenstein make one for him. Frankenstein finally agrees to do it, at least to try. The monster warns that he will be somewhere nearby monitoring the entire process.

After some delay, Frankenstein goes away to an island off the coast of Scotland, sets up his laboratory, and begins his work. His misgivings multiply until at last, in a fit of utter disgust, he destroys all his work. The monster appears, vowing he will destroy everything precious to Frankenstein. And eventually he does.

Almost immediately, the monster kills Frankenstein's best friend, Henry Clerval. Somewhat later, when Frankenstein marries Elizabeth, the monster strangles her on their wedding night. Giving up everything else, Frankenstein starts out in pursuit of this murderer. The monster taunts him by deliberately giving clues to follow, but always arranging to be somewhere beyond reach. This desperate pursuit covers much of the world, until eventually the monster goes into the frozen wastelands of the far north.

Here, his dogsled crushed by moving mountains of ice, Frankenstein is taken aboard a ship, where sometime later he dies. The night following his death, unearthly screams are heard coming from the room where his body lies. Rushing to investigate, the ship's master finds the monster, torn by a terrible grief, standing above the body. After expressing profound regret for his deeds, the creature leaps onto an ice flow and disappears into the Arctic night. He swore to the ship's master that the world will never hear from him again. As far as we know, it hasn't.

– G –

Galahad   The epitome of pure manhood is Galahad. Having all the virtues and none of the vices, Sir Galahad has stood since Arthurian times as a symbol of the best of gentlemanly character. Some say he is too good to be true, but whether he actually lived or not, Galahad shines like a light amid the oft-shadowed goings-on of King Arthur's Court.

At Arthur's Camelot there was the Round Table with seating for one hundred and fifty knights; it was round so no man could feel himself either higher or lower than any other. The idea was noble; but in practice the knights weren't always as noble as they were expected to be.

At the table one vacant place was always left, reserved for the Holy Grail, the chalice from which wine was drunk at the Last Supper. It was the understanding that the grail had been brought to Glastonbury and hidden, so Arthur's table had a place waiting for it, should it ever be found. Finding the grail was a major objective of every man.

Here, then, was the stage on which the ongoing drama of Arthur and his knights was played. The players were a varied lot, Sir Lancelot a chief among them.

In many ways a noble knight, Lancelot had one major weakness, Guinevere the queen, and wife of Arthur. Whenever the king's back was turned, these two consorted freely together. Then, too, there was Elaine, a young princess, who was utterly possessed by her own passion for Guinevere's surreptitious lover. By trickery, Elaine got Lancelot into bed with her, making him believe she was Guinevere. The result: Arriving about nine months later was a baby named Galahad.

The child grew up to become a strong, handsome, generous young man. When eventually presented at the Round Table, the king said to him, "God make thee as good as thou art beautiful." As events developed, it seemed that God or someone did precisely this. Occupying the Round Table chair that Merlin had lost his life by sitting in, Sir Galahad said, "If I lose myself, I save myself." Whereupon, the coveted grail came gliding through the room on a beam of light. As Tennyson tells it, the young knight later said,

> I saw the Holy Grail and heard a cry—
> Galahad, O Galahad, follow me.

Galahad followed. And in following he demonstrated that almost all temptations can be overcome. In following, he aided, encouraged, and uplifted many people. In following, pursuing the cup of Christ, he found it at last somewhere in the distant East, reposing there in a sacred chamber. Many others, having sought the grail and failing in their search, had returned to Arthur's court, all of them with the word, "This quest was not for me."

But Galahad traced the holy thing to its chamber, and only he was able to enter the room where it stood. And only he was allowed communion from that holy chalice.

Some say that Galahad never found the grail at all and that his life was used up in futile search. Others say that, never finding the grail, his search was not a futile one. They say that in all his seeking, he found legions of people who needed him; that in seeking and serving, he drew nearer to Christ than he would have had he ever drunk from the grail; and that in seeking the grail of Christ, he found not the grail but the Christ.

Gargantuan   The story of Gargantua is unabashadly grotesque and intentionally unreal. François Rabelais, the author, meant it to be so utterly outlandish as to be comical, and it is. It is also a barbed and biting satire on the institutions and customs of sixteenth-century France.

At eleven months pregnant, Gargantua's mother ate too many tripes, and later that day Gargantua was born from her left ear; instead of crying, as newborns are expected to, this one called for a drink. He got his drink, and later a very good education that he never used much.

Gargantua was a giant; even in comparison with other giants, he was huge. As an infant, the milk of 17,913 cows was required to feed him. Later, 2,502 yards of cloth were needed to make his shirt and breeches, and 1,100 cowhides were used for the soles of his shoes. He rode a mare as large as six elephants, and once he stole the bells from the tower of Notre Dame to use as jingles around the mare's neck. Once when stung by wasps, the mare switched her tail and wiped out the Forest of Orleans. The comb Gargantua used on his hair was 900 feet long, and sometimes, when he combed, cannonballs fell out.

At the age of 400 years, Gargantua fathered a son, Pantagruel, who was also a giant. When just a baby, one day he got an arm free of his swaddling clothes and ate the cow that was nursing him. Perhaps the son's appetite was inherited from the father, for the appetite of Gargantua was enormous. On one occasion, Gargantua made a salad of lettuces as large as walnut trees and inadvertently ate up six pilgrims who had taken refuge among them.

In everyday speech, we sometimes speak of a gargantuan feast or a gargantuan appetite, or of anything big described as gargantuan. There is, though, more than mere bigness to be noted in the story of Gargantua. The giant is basically a gentle, peace-loving fellow, but he is often embroiled in conflict. His career as a fighting man begins in his community when the bakers refuse to sell cookies to the shepherds, and war breaks out.

From then on, it's a matter of his prodigious power pitted against piddling problems that are but trifles in comparison with his might. On this framework Rabelais constructs his scathing satire of French royalty and the establishment in general who waste enormous resources on miscellaneous, little ends.

Pantagruel has also made a place for himself in our language, albeit not an enviable one. As a giant, he was even bigger than his enormous dad. Born thirsty in the midst of a three-year drought, he always drank a lot, and not just water. Indicative of the confusion that usually attended him, at the time of his birth there were three Thursdays in one week. Something of a lamebrain, he spent most of his life in the constant company of his crony Panurge, who was totally dull. An oafish and rowdy fellow, Pantagruel's name has become metaphoric for coarse and boisterous buffoonery.

Gerrymandering   Gerrymandering is the dividing of voting districts in a region to unfairly concentrate the voting power of one political party or group over the others. The expression has been a part of our language since the early nineteenth-century tenure of Elbridge Gerry as governor of Massachusetts.

A Democrat presiding over a Democratic government, Gerry arranged or approved an arrangement by which redistricting confined Federalist strength to one or two districts. The result was many convoluted boundaries, as divisions were made without regard to geographic location.

One district was of such ungainly shape that Benjamin Russell, a newspaper editor in Boston, had a map of it hung on his office wall. Upon seeing this map, Gilbert Stuart, the renowned painter, said that it had the shape of some monstrous animal. Then, adding a few quick lines with a pencil, he said, "There, that will do for a salamander." "Salamander?" said Russell, who was an ardent Federalist, "Let's call it a gerrymander." In that instant a new word was born into our language. Today, gerrymander can be used generically for any division that is made to give someone or some group an unfair advantage.

Gilderoy's Kite   After a particularly heinous crime has been committed, an irate citizen may declare, "When they catch the brute who did this, they ought to hang him higher than Gilderoy's kite!" This person is calling for maximum punishment of the criminal, but where does the expression originate? For the answer, we must go back to the seventeenth century and a Scottish chap named Patrick MacGregor.

A bright, energetic, red-haired youth who could have been successful in any one of many good endeavors, MacGregor turned to crime instead. Becoming a cattle thief in the Highlands and then a sort of general-purpose highwayman, he was soon the leader of an outlaw band that terrorized the countryside, taking from anybody whatever they wanted. No Robin Hood stealing from the rich to help the poor, this fellow was apparently without redeeming qualities.

In February 1636, seven of his gang were captured, tried, condemned, and hanged at Edinburgh. A large reward was offered for MacGregor's capture, and the prospect of easy money was a temptation too strong for Peg Cunningham, his mistress. She turned him in, and when the authorities came to arrest him, he killed eight of them and stabbed Peg. But they got him.

And in July of that year, at the town of Gallowlee near Edinburgh, they hanged him, along with five others of his band. The gallows on which they hanged MacGregor, however, was much taller than the others—thirty feet high, they said. They gave him special treatment; an ordinary hanging wouldn't do, not for this rogue who had preyed so much on women and the poor. So they put him up very high, perhaps for all to see, perhaps to give him a long way to fall. And fall he did.

But what of this bit about Gilderoy's kite? Well, you see, MacGregor was Gilderoy, or so he was called. In the Gaelic tongue *roy* was the word for "red" and *gillie* was "laddie" or "young man." Thus, because of his youth and red hair, MacGregor was called "Gillie-roy," or Gilderoy," a name change for which all law-abiding MacGregors in the region were undoubtedly grateful.

And *kite* was Gaelic for "belly" or "stomach," a man's bulging middle. By extension, the word was often used in reference to the whole body. So here we have it: Patrick MacGregor's body hanging high on a gallows. And how high is this? Well, precisely as high as Gilderoy's kite!

Go the Second Mile   In the time of Jesus, Palestine was a land occupied by the Romans. The Jews were a proud people, their national identity of paramount importance to them, and so it had been a devastating blow to their patriotic spirit when, in 63 B.C, the Romans had moved in and taken control.

A Roman governor was now in Jerusalem, and units of the Roman army were garrisoned at strategic locations throughout the country. A Roman soldier had authority to impress any citizen into his service at any time and in virtually any way. To the average Jewish citizen, this was an odious and demeaning practice.

Into this scene came Jesus, teaching forgiveness and nonviolence, advocating an attitude of extreme self-giving in the interest of others. He was saying that however others may treat us, we should treat them well. For a people whose philosophy of interpersonal relationships was "an eye for an eye and a tooth for a tooth," this nonviolent posture was an alien idea. For the Jewish victims of this Roman occupation, this teaching was a hard one to accept, but Jesus insisted. He even used the Roman oppressors to illustrate his point. He said, "If one of those soldiers accosts you on the road, lays his pack on your back, and compels you to go with him a mile, then go with him two miles."

And why go this second mile? Probably because there is a difference between doing what one must and going on to do what one can, an immense difference between a compulsory service and a voluntary one, and the difference is the effect on the people involved—both the one who serves and the one who is served.

From this story, we have the expression to "go the second (or extra) mile." After nearly 2,000 years, it is very much with us, usually meaning to do more than would normally be done to please or placate another, to go beyond normal expectations of what is required of helpfulness or accommodation.

Goliath   Saul was king in Israel, and Jesse had a sheep farm somewhere near Bethlehem. Saul had a problem: the Philistines, who were forever harassing the western frontier of his kingdom. These Philistines were an ornery lot, terrorists really, who came in waves to invade, striking like lightning and then disappearing. But they would always come again, killing, looting, burning, and each time leaving a trail of destruction. To make matters worse for Israel, these Philistines were a race of near-giants, and at least one of them was actually a giant. His hometown was Gath, his name was Goliath, and he stood nine feet tall.

For forty days, this monstrous hulk of a man would approach the armies of Israel twice daily, bellowing a challenge to any man who would dare to come out and fight him. Hurling insults and taunts and cursing Israel's God, he put terror into the heart of every man, and no man dared stand up against him.

Here is where the son of Jesse, David, comes into the story. He had eight older brothers, and three of them were in Israel's army, struggling against those Philistines on the western border. In those days, troops in the field were not well supplied, requiring frequent assistance from home.

This being the situation with Israel's army, Jesse sent David with foodstuffs to locate his three brothers, give them food, and find out how they were doing. David found them, but he also found something else—that irksome giant. He heard those defiant bellows and observed the cowering fear of Israel's soldiers.

Assured that great riches and many advantages would be given to the murderer of Goliath, David set out to liquidate the big fellow. From a brook he selected five round, water-polished stones, and put these in his shepherd's bag. Then he took them and his sling and went out to confront the giant. Goliath laughed at him. But David soon brought that laughter to an end: He flung a single stone, which struck Goliath in mid-forehead, knocking him to the ground, unconscious. David then ran to him, pulled the giant's sword from its scabbard, and cut off his head.

That was the end of Goliath. But his name remains as a synonym for something that is large. Whatever is called Goliath-size or as big as Goliath is large. (See also DAVID IN SAUL'S ARMOR.)

Good Samaritan   A good Samaritan is any person who helps another, often a stranger, and usually at some personal sacrifice. The expression is from a story told by Jesus.

In his day the land of Palestine was divided into three major parts: Galilee in the north, Judea in the south, and Samaria in the middle. Due to a long history of conflict, Judeans looked down on Galileans as a sort of under-class, and both groups despised the Samaritans as a class even lower. Both Judeans and Galileans, traveling from one end of the country to the other, normally avoided passing through Samaria by crossing the Jordan River and detouring eastward.

Against this hostile background, Jesus told the story of a man traveling in Judea, who was on his way from Jerusalem down to Jericho. Thieves robbed him of all he had, beat him brutally, and left him naked and half-dead at the roadside.

Sometime later, a priest who was also a Judean, came by on his journey toward Jericho. But the priest did not stop and help the poor, wounded man; he just moved over to the opposite side of the road and went on. Not long afterward, a Levite, one of the elite, also came along, and he too crossed to the other side and passed by.

Then came the Samaritan, a stranger in Judea, who was not well thought of by Judeans and was a long way from home. Would this wounded man appreciate his help? Apparently, he didn't even think of asking this question. Were those thieves still lurking somewhere near, waiting to pounce on him also? Apparently, he never even considered the risk. And what about his liability: Would he be sued if something went wrong? Fortunately, he didn't even have to worry about this. A man needed help, and he gave it.

Placing the injured man on his own donkey, he walked beside to steady him there, and guided the little beast to the nearest hotel. He gave the inkeeper money in advance to care for the man, saying, "If the bill is more than this, I will pay you when I return."

Jesus, telling the story, did not use the term *good Samaritan*. But we do—often.

Goody Two Shoes   This small book was issued in 1765 by John Newberry of London, the first publisher to specialize in children's literature. The full title: *The History of Little Goody Two Shoes*. The title page dedication, written by the publisher, was addressed to the children of London: "To all young gentlemen and ladies who are good, or intend to be good, this book is inscribed by their old friend in St. Paul's church-yard." Its authorship has always been in doubt, but evidence points strongly to Oliver Goldsmith.

The story begins with a girl named Margery Meanwell; she and her brother Tommy were alone in the world as their mother and father were deceased. So poorly clothed were they that Margery had only one shoe. Taken into the home of a kind clergyman and his wife, Mr. and Mrs. Smith, they were well cared for for a brief time.

Then came a deep sadness when Tommy was taken away to be trained as a sailor. Margery's grief was somewhat relieved, though, when a caring gentleman provided her with a new pair of shoes. So thrilled was she that wherever she went she always said to everyone, "Look, two shoes; I have two shoes." It was in this way that she became known as Little Two Shoes and later, as a grown-up, Margery Two Shoes.

Evil men forced the Smiths to put Little Two Shoes out of their home. Homeless now, she was compelled to make her own way. Concluding that an ability to read would be the key to everything, she borrowed books from the children who went to school. Learning the alphabet, she made wooden blocks with letters on them, and these she could arrange and rearrange into words.

Showing other children how this was done, she made a game of the learning process. Soon she had many children gathering around for the excitement that was to be found in spelling and reading. Growing into her teen years, she was given a position as teacher in a school where she continued to make learning an adventure. Always cheerful, always helpful, and always kind, she was loved by everyone. She believed in everyone, was always hopeful, and had a way of making things turn out well for herself and everyone around her.

The time came when a fine gentleman asked her to marry him and she accepted. As the ceremony was about to commence, a finely dressed young man burst into the room—her brother Tommy, having made a fortune from his seagoing ventures. The rest of her life was spent doing nice things for folks on all sides, especially helping the poor. The story ends with the writer's comment that "her life was the greatest blessing and her death the greatest calamity" the people around her had ever known.

So we have the expression "goody two shoes," which takes its place alongside *Little Lord Fauntleroy* and *Pollyanna*, names of three children of exceptionally fine and refined qualities. It is most often used, unfortunately, by people who look upon the quality of goodness as being soft and weak. It is commonly a put-down by which one person castigates another as being naively out-of-touch with "the real world."

Goose That Laid the Golden Eggs   A poor peasant and his wife were worried about having enough food to see them through the winter. One late autumn day, as their anxiety was approaching panic, a stranger appeared at their cottage carrying a large, white goose. He said, "If you will care for this goose, the goose will care for you." And then, without a further word, the stranger was gone.

The two impoverished people wondered about this peculiar happening, but they began immediately to provide for the new arrival. They prepared for her a nest and gave her all the food scraps they could find, hoping that by the next day she would lay an egg. Sure enough, she did—an egg unlike any ever seen in all the history of goosedom, an egg of pure gold!

With great excitement they took the golden egg to the marketplace and sold it for a great deal of money, with which they bought many of the things they needed. The next morning, another golden egg was laid, and the day after that, yet another! And so it went, day after day, until their larder was well stocked with the finest food, their cottage fitted with new furniture, and the couple was seeing visions of a gilded mansion with servants to attend to them.

Soon, they could scarcely wait from one day to the next, so eager were they to supplement their accumulated treasure. They did little else but watch that goose and wait for the next egg. Day by day, they seized each new egg with a greed that grew proportionately with their ever-increasing store of gold; the more they had, the more they wanted.

As the weeks went by, the couple thought more and more about the source of all that gold. Inside that goose, so they thought, there must be a huge reservoir of the precious yellow stuff. One day, the wife said to her husband, "Why do we have to wait day after day to get all that gold? Why not kill the goose and get all of it now?"

No less greedy than his wife, the husband considered this a good idea. Eagerly, he took ax in hand, seized the goose, laid her neck across the chopping block, and cut off her head. Then, in nervous anticipation, he did surgery on the lifeless body. And you know what he found inside? Nothing more than anyone has ever found inside a goose.

This ancient story of Aesop enjoys almost daily use in many languages. To kill the goose that lays the golden eggs is to selfishly and wantonly shut off at its source the flow of that which is desired. Often heard in affairs of government, "A confiscatory tax will kill the goose that lays the egg."

Gordian Knot   One day, about 2,400 years ago, a farmer drove his team and wagon into the west Asian city of Phrygia. As he approached the temple of Jupiter, the unsuspecting countryman was suddenly surrounded by an excited multitude, giving him adoration as though he were someone great.

To them, he was someone very great. Their prophet, or oracle, had told them to seize the first man who approached the temple with a wagon and make him their king. This man happened to be Gordius, the farmer.

Well, since a king doesn't much need a farm wagon, Gordius left his right there at the temple. In fact, he made an offering of it! Lest someone later abscond with his offering, Gordius tied it to a temple beam with a rope and a knot so intricately looped, twisted, intertwined, and woven that nobody would ever be able to untie it.

Over the following years many people tried to loosen the knot, but no one succeeded. Gordius's ingenious knot became famous, and the curious came from all over to see it and to try to untie it. The legend grew that whoever could untie the knot would rule over the entire Eastern world.

That knot was still there when Alexander the Great invaded the land about 334 B.C. Alexander, son of Philip II of Macedon, was only about twenty-two years old at the time, but he was already a phenomenally successful ruler and military commander. Highly educated, cultured, and sophisticated, he was not inclined to put up with a lot of nonsense.

While in Jupiter's temple at Phrygia, Alexander was shown the knot, and told that it could not be undone. "No?" said Alexander. "Really? Well, then, here's how to do it!" And drawing his sword, he slashed the knot in two with one stroke.

So ended Gordius's famous knot, and did Alexander rule the world? For a very brief time he ruled almost all of the known world. But Alexander is gone, Jupiter's temple is gone, and even Phrygia is gone, but in one sense that knot of Gordius is still with us, as a figure of speech. The Gordian knot may be any intricate, complicated, difficult problem. To cut the Gordian knot is proverbial for any bold, decisive action that terminates a stalemate or overpowers paralyzing complexities to get things moving again.

Gotham Pose   An intelligent person who plays dumb to achieve some purpose may be called a gothamizer. To assume the Gotham pose is to pretend stupidity to avoid some responsibility. But sometimes it may be wise to appear foolish, as the Gothamites did many years ago.

In England during the early thirteenth century, King John was seeking a parcel of land for major development. He wanted to build a palace, roads to serve it, quarters for his soldiers and horses, and all the other facilities needed for the royal court. In lovely Nottinghamshire there was the village of Gotham; the king looked upon this as the perfect location for his project. The people of Gotham felt otherwise, however, not wishing to upset the pastoral tranquility and not wanting to be responsible for maintaining all that royalty.

When John sent his emissaries to make a survey of the situation, they were amazed at what they found. While the countryside was beautiful, the forests lush, the grass green, and the waters fresh and clear, the people were strange. None among them appeared normal. Here, a group of citizens was attempting to rake the moon's reflection from a pool. There, another bunch stood in a circle with joined hands around a bush to keep a cuckoo imprisoned among the branches. Yet another party was earnestly attempting to drown an eel, expressing amazement at the creature's ability to survive underwater.

What king would want to establish his court among a people who were as crazy as loons? Not John. After all, what would the French ambassador think? Or, for that matter, what would anyone who visited think? And who would grow the grain for bread or the beef for steaks? These people were clearly too nuts to be responsible for any of this. King John, therefore, vetoed Gotham and looked elsewhere, seeking a locale where the population, while perhaps not intellectual giants, at least had normal, good sense.

When the king's men had completed their investigation and ridden away, the people of Gotham exulted, "More fools pass through Gotham than are in it!" They had entered into a clever conspiracy to deceive the king, and their act had served them well. They had defended themselves by the pretense of being crazy. In this way they accomplished quite effectively what neither argument nor force of arms could ever have done.

Greeks Bearing Gifts   *See* TROJAN HORSE.

Green-Eyed Monster   Shakespeare's play *Othello* is the tragic story of one man's sinister scheme to destroy the lives of three good people. The schemer is Iago; the intended victim is Othello; and the two other, incidental victims are Othello's wife, Desdemona, and Othello's friend and associate, Cassio.

Othello is commander of the naval fleet at Venice, in Italy. He has promoted Cassio to serve as his first lieutenant. Iago, another officer, resents this appointment as he had wanted the position for himself, so he embarks upon a campaign of deception aimed at the undoing of his superior.

Always pretending total loyalty and love, Iago develops and carries out an elaborate plot that gets Cassio fired from his new position. Not satisfied with this, he goes after Othello with a maliciousness that is totally without scruples.

Professing always to be Othello's devoted friend, he insinuates to Othello that Desdemona and Cassio are having an affair. He pretends to know things that his "honor" will not permit him to reveal. When Othello had courted Desdemona, Cassio had served as a go-between on his behalf; now, Iago implies that there had been a lot of hanky-panky going on between these two and that it continues.

Othello and his wife are deeply in love and a faithful pair, so Othello is in agony to hear of his wife's infidelity. Iago also suggests that Othello shouldn't be surprised by any philandering on the part of Desdemona, for she is a beautiful woman who is enormously desirable to any man.

In pretext of giving friendly advice, Iago then warns Othello against being jealous of his popular wife. He says, "O beware, my lord, of jealousy! It is the green-eyed monster which doth mock the meat it feeds on," referring to felines—cats, lions, leopards—that torment their prey before eating it.

Driven to desperation, Othello murders his wife. Too late he learns from Iago's wife of the awful plot perpetrated by her evil husband. Realizing the horrible wrong he has committed, Othello does what he can to make amends to Cassio, and then takes his own life. Discovered for what he is, Iago is condemned by the authorities to a lifetime of torture.

Because of this tragic tale, we often refer to jealousy as the green-eyed monster.

Gung Ho   Loosely translated, the Chinese *gung ho* means "work to-gether." In English, to say that someone is gung ho is to say that he or she is enthusiastic about something. The story of how that Chinese word became this English expression is a rather interesting piece of modern history.

In the 1930s, gung ho became the slogan of Chinese leftists. Bent on reforming or overthrowing their regime, gung ho became a rallying cry heard throughout the land.

Then came World War II and, during the 1940s, a prolonged struggle against the Japanese. American forces were stationed in China to assist in this struggle. Notable among these were units of the Marine Corps; from among these masters of derring-do there was organized a kind of commando batallion that operated stealthily behind the Japanese lines.

The commander of this batallion, Lieutenant Colonel Evans Carlson, arranged a series of strategy meetings with groups of his men. Because commando warfare required precise coordination and unfaltering teamwork, Colonel Carlson called these sessions gung-ho meetings, using the word that best expressed the idea of working together.

But these U.S. Marines soon gave that word a new meaning. An audacious lot, these men were an intrepid band of doers who went about their hazardous missions with a danger-defying gusto. Calling themselves the gung-ho battalion, their character quickly gave new color to the name and forever changed the meaning of the word for the Western world. From their time until ours (among English-speaking people), to be gung ho is to be fervently in support of something.

~ H ~

Halcyon Days   Juno was goddess of good women, who always rejoiced in women's happiness and stood ready to help them in their troubles. At her throne sat the beautiful Iris, granddaughter of the Ancient Ocean and sister of the Dark Clouds. Iris was always ready to assist Juno, and her bridge to Earth was the arching rainbow.

On Earth, one deeply devoted to Juno was the youthful Halcyone, daughter of the wind-god Aeolus and wife of the good King Ceyx of Thessaly. A time came when her husband had to go away on a long voyage across the sea. Knowing well the awesome power of her brothers, the Wild Winds, Halcyone feared for the safety of the man she loved so much.

Her fears were well founded, for the Wild Winds did indeed stir the Ancient Ocean into an awful fury, and the ship of King Ceyx was torn apart by the ferocious waves. In her heaven, Juno saw it all happen, and knowing the torment her beloved's loss would bring to Halcyone, she quickly devised a plan to help.

Summoning Iris, Juno dispatched her with urgent speed to the cave of Somnus, the god of sleep and dreams. Alighting from her rainbow and following the River Lethe upstream to its source, she found Somnus sleeping soundly on an enormous bed of black feathers, with great heaps of dreams piled high around him awaiting distribution. Awakened by the bright light Iris brought into his cave, he received Juno's message.

Obedient to the wish of the high goddess, the god of sleep immediately sent a dream to Halcyone. In it, she saw a rugged shoreline littered with the broken timbers of a devastated ship. Awakening, and running quickly to the place she had seen in her dream, she looked with horror upon the scene. In the water, near the shore, she saw the body of her husband floating amid the ship's broken timbers.

Driven by a terrible grief, she plunged into the water, desperate to reach the body of the one she loved or to die there with him. But instead of feeling the dark water pulling at her feet, she felt herself lifted as with the buoyancy of a bird in flight.

Just then, the golden crown on the head of King Ceyx changed into a crest of colorful feathers and his dead body was transformed into that of a living bird. Arising from the water, he joined Halcyone in the air, for she too had been so changed.

Juno had made a way for the lovers to be together, as two kingfishers that were often seen flying wing to wing along the shore. And each year in December, when it was time for them to build their nest, they made it boat shaped to float on the water. Here Halcyone laid her eggs, and after fourteen days, the young were born of them. And always during her nesting time, the Wild Winds lay still in their hidden places and the Ancient Ocean lay smooth like glass beneath the sun.

Seafaring men began to notice that each year at this time there were fourteen pleasant days when the weather was good and peaceful; knowing of Halcyone and her love for Ceyx, they called these the Halcyon days in memory of her. Soon, any period of calm weather was known as a Halcyon time, and eventually the meaning broadened to include any period of favorable circumstance. And to this day, days of good fortune and days of smooth sailing are known as halcyon days.

Handwriting on the Wall   In 586 B.C., the Babylonian king Nebuchadrezzar overthrew the city of Jerusalem, destroying the temple of the Jews, carrying away most of its sacred vessels, and taking as captives many of its educated and gifted people. Among these was Daniel, who quickly gained the respect of his Babylonian captors and rose to a position of prominence among them.

Following Nebuchadrezzar, the throne was assumed by Belshazzar, a much weaker and more vacillating ruler, a son or perhaps a grandson of Nebuchadrezzar. The powerful Nebuchadrezzar had had his problems and made his mistakes, and apparently Belshazzar inherited all of his weaknesses and none of his strengths.

There came a night when Belshazzar gave an elaborate feast in his magnificent banquet hall. The place echoed with the boisterous revelries of the lords and ladies of the kingdom. Remembering the sacred vessels from Jerusalem's temple, the king ordered these brought in, and from them the party drank.

In the midst of all this, however, the scene was dramatically sobered by a strange event: high on a wall, the fingers of a giant hand appeared, slowly but unmistakably tracing letters there. The words formed were clear: *Mene, Mene, Tekel, Upharsin.* But what was the meaning of these words?

Actually, the words simply indicated a series of weights, in round numbers: a pound, a third of an ounce, and two half-pounds. Perplexed as to the source of the writing and more so by the meaning of it, the king and all the company stood in utter astonishment and fear.

The king demanded that his wise men tell him the meaning of the message, but none could. His wife then remembered Daniel and his remarkable powers of insight, once telling the meaning of a dream for Nebuchadrezzar. At her suggestion, Belshazzar commanded that Daniel be brought into the hall.

Viewing the perplexing writing, Daniel saw more than a roster of common weights; he saw a capsule of history-in-the making. This, in essence, is what Daniel said to the king: Nebuchadrezzar was a heavyweight; you, sir, are a lightweight; and your kingdom is about to be divided between two mediumweights (meaning the Medes and the Persians).

And it was so. That very night, apparently, the enemy came. They threw a temporary dam across the Euphrates River upstream from where it flowed under the city wall, and in the dried-up channel the soldiers marched into Babylon.

The handwriting is on the wall usually implies that, although we may wish things otherwise, they will be as they will be.

Hanged on Your Own Gallows   The Persian king Ahasuerus ruled at Susa and his queen was the beautiful Vashti. It was the seventh day of a lavish stag party where the king was entertaining the noblemen and chieftains of his realm. After six days of open bar, everyone was quite under the influence, including the king. He commanded that Queen Vashti be brought out for display in all her beauty and royal splendor, but she refused, unwilling to be made a showpiece to please the drunken king.

His authority ignored and his monumental pride offended, the king went into a fit of rage. He and his wise men were convinced the queen had set a bad example for all women: They just might follow her in the disobedience of their husbands, an assertion of independence that was not to be tolerated!

It was therefore decided that Ahasuerus would divorce his wife, which he promptly did. Then, to find a replacement queen, a world-class beauty contest was held. It happened that in Susa there was a man named Mordecai, a Jewish man of importance, earlier brought as a captive from Jerusalem, or more probably a descendant of one. Mordecai had with him his cousin, an orphan who he had adopted as his own child, named Esther. When all the young women were rounded up for the king's inspection, Esther was among them, and from among all the others, not knowing she was a Jewess, it was she he chose.

Now, the king's right-hand man was Haman, a very important man in the kingdom, so important that all citizens were required to do obeisances to him. Mordecai, however, refused to bow in his presence, and by this unforgivable irreverence Haman was gravely annoyed. It was Haman's wife, having an interest in preserving her husband's elevated status, who suggested a gallows be built at their own house (a gallows 75 feet high) on which to hang Mordecai.

Considering this one of the best ideas his wife ever had, Haman built the gallows. But he was afraid to lay hands on Mordecai, to single him out from all others for execution, because Mordecai had a lot of powerful friends. So he offered a huge bribe to the king's treasurer, and issued a decree that on the thirteenth day of the twelfth month every Jewish person in Persia was to be put to death.

Of course, among the Jewish population there arose an immediate lamentation. Behind his palace walls, King Ahasuerus knew nothing of all the commotion; but Esther heard what was going on. Not knowing the consequences of such an act, she informed the king that all Jews were under a sentence of death. His first question was, "Who did this?" Esther pointed to Haman, and announced, "This wicked Haman; he did it!"

As the king was looking for a suitable punishment for Haman, someone said, "At Haman's house there stands a gallows 75 feet high." With no hesitation at all, the king ordered, "Hang him on that." And they did—they hanged Haman on the very gallows he had prepared for the hanging of Mordecai.

By this bit of drama from the biblical book of Esther, our language has been enriched. When one devises a way to ruin another he may be creating the machinery for his own destruction—he may be building a "Haman gallows." One is hanged on his own gallows when he sets a trap for another and then he is caught in it.

Hanging by a Hair   *See* SWORD OF DAMOCLES.

Hare and the Tortoise   Aesop's fable of *The Hare and the Tortoise* is known as well as any of the fables and, one way or another, appears in speech more than most. The hare is the flashy fellow who skyrockets to success only to falter later; the tortoise is the plodder, deliberate and conservative, who wins in the end. The hare looks good for a while, but he doesn't last long. The tortoise may not be spectacular, but he is reliable and can be counted on to the very last.

The simple tale is of a rabbit and a turtle who once ran in a race against each other. It came about because of the rabbit's vanity. Proud of his agility and speed, he had the obnoxious habit of applauding himself by putting others down. One day, hopping jauntily along a path, he came upon the docile turtle half-dozing beneath her shell. As was his wont, he stopped to taunt and tease and boast for a while.

Having heard all this before, the turtle had grown weary of it, and so she did an unturtle-like thing. She stood up as tall as possible on her four strong legs, stuck out her neck as far as it would go, and quite uncharacteristically said, "Rabbit, sir, I'll race you anytime!" Maybe, in the heat of the moment, she didn't realize the apparent hopelessness of the proposition offered, or maybe, in the sober judgment of a quiet and reflective lifestyle, she knew the rabbit better than he knew himself.

Whichever, the cocky bunny laughed derisively. The very idea! What a ridiculous thing to do! A fellow of his prowess in competition with a turtle, a mere turtle! Why, he could run circles around her all the way to the finish line and still get there first! "I mean it," insisted the turtle, "Mr. Fox, sitting on yonder log—we'll have him mark out the course and be the judge."

Rabbit stopped laughing long enough to say, "Okay, you clumsy slowpoke, if you want it, you've got it." He hesitated a little on that part about the fox, for he well knew that foxes love to eat rabbits, and he really didn't trust the fox at all. He surely would never willingly accept the fox's invitation to dinner some summer evening, and he wasn't altogether certain the fox should be involved in this. So self-confident was he, though, that he was quite willing to take the risk. So the fox laid out the course and set himself to judge the running.

At the starting signal, the two competitors were off. It wasn't exactly an exciting start, although the rabbit made a big show of it, displaying his running skills with all the authority of an expert. The turtle simply stretched out her long neck, fixed her eyes on the terrain just ahead, extended her four sturdy legs to their limit, inhaled one deep breath, and started plodding away.

The rabbit was soon out of sight somewhere along the trail, but the turtle gave no thought to that; she kept scrambling along, simply doing as well as she could. As for the rabbit, he had been sure of winning before he ever started, and now he was so far ahead, he thought he had plenty of time to dawdle.

The big show-off had so exerted himself at the beginning that he now felt a bit tired. And there wasn't any challenge in racing against a turtle anyway, not much glory to be derived from it. So, somewhat bored by the whole thing, a little before sunset, he detoured into a clump of bushes for a spot of rest.

And while he slept, the turtle passed him. She gave no thought to it, nor even turned aside to look. She intently kept her neck stretched to the limit and her eyes fixed on the trail ahead. At last awakening, the rabbit saw by the sun that morning had come; he had slept all night. Now, in a panic, he leaped onto the trail and ran as he had never run before.

So he ran the harder, leaping farther than any rabbit ever should, until, breathless and drenched in perspiration, he raced up to the finish line. He could scarcely believe what he saw. There, resting quietly, was that persistent turtle, and beside her the fox, sitting smugly on his haunches, waiting.

Helmet of Perseus In a moment of extreme embarrassment, we may say, "Oh, I wish I could go through the floor!" In other words, I wish I could disappear. Another such wish at such a time might be for the helmet of Perseus. Why? Because this helmet makes the wearer invisible.

Perseus is a part of classical mythology; his story is one of the many loved by the ancient Greeks. A son of Zeus and an ancestor of Heracles (or Hercules), he was a sort of demigod. Incurring the wrath of Polydectes, king of Seriphos, that king devised a plan to have him killed.

The king required Perseus to fight the Gorgons and bring back the head of Medusa, the youngest of them. These creatures were utterly hideous and an ill-tempered and bloodthirsty lot. Medusa was especially dangerous, because anyone who looked upon her face was instantly turned into stone. Polydectes could imagine no way by which Perseus could possibly sever Medusa's head and get away with it.

On his way to the den of the Gorgons, however, Perseus got some good help from some newfound friends. The god Hermes and the goddess Athena saw to it that he received a highly polished shield and a helmet that made him invisible.

Wearing this helmet, he approached the Gorgons, who were unable to see him. Using his polished shield as a mirror, he was able to locate Medusa without looking directly at her and chop off her head.

With his helmet still on his head, and with the head of Medusa securely stashed in a leather pouch, he safely made off with it. Afterward, whenever he wanted to turn someone into stone, all he had to do was open that pouch, look the other way, pull out Medusa's head, hold it up before his victim, and say, "Look! See what I've got here!" Using this technique, he even turned the mighty Atlas into stone. Using that severed head, Perseus produced more statues of lifelike quality than Michelangelo and Thorvaldsen combined!

Hiawatha's Moccasins and Mittens Hiawatha had magic moccasins that enabled him to move with incredible speed; with one step he could advance a mile. He could run more swiftly than the fiercest wind, walk dry-shod above the waters of the widest rivers, and valleys and mountains were but small impediments for him. (Bogged down as we sometimes are in quagmires of modern life, we might wish for Hiawatha's moccasins to cut us loose and get us going. Pressed to keep pace with the hectic hurry of things, we might sometimes say, "I wish I had Hiawatha's moccasins.")

Hiawatha also had magic mittens which, when worn, gave him enormous power. Wearing these, he could crush great boulders in his hands, and no enemy could defeat him. (When one is expected or required to do a very difficult thing, this response may be heard: "You know, I don't wear Hiawatha's mittens.")

With his awesome speed and strength, it was within Hiawatha's power to do almost anything he wanted. He chose to help people.

The Song of Hiawatha, a narrative poem written by Longfellow in 1855, is much more than an adventure story. Anticipating his work on it, Longfellow wrote of "a plan for a poem on the American Indians. . . . It is to weave together their beautiful traditions into a whole." He succeeded superbly, drawing together in the one symbolic character of Hiawatha much of the Indians' philosophy, many of their legends, their comprehensions of spirit, and their perceptions of the natural order.

Hiawatha was an Ojibway, son of Wenonah and the West Wind. Deserted by her fickle and faithless lover, Wenonah soon died, and the child was left to his prudent and prophetic grandmother, Nokomis. Coming of age, the angry youth went in search of the philandering West Wind, wearing his moccasins and mittens. Upon finding the West Wind, an awful battle ensued. But that conflict was resolved, and Hiawatha took his journey eastward, stopping only once—in the land of the Dacotahs, at the Falls of Minnehaha—to buy arrows from

The Ancient Arrowsmith. Here he saw a woman he would never forget, the arrowsmith's beautiful, dark-eyed daughter, Minnehaha, Laughing Water.

Home among the Ojibways, Hiawatha continued his pursuit of helpfulness to his people by fishing for the Great Sturgeon and conquering the Pearl-feather. Then he went west again, to the Falls of Minnehaha, to bring home his bride, the lovely Laughing Water.

Other ventures followed. Then sadness fell hard upon Hiawatha when Chibiabos, the fine musician and good friend, was drowned one winter day when evil spirits broke the ice on which he walked and he fell through. Sadness came again when his good friend Kwasind was murdered by the Little People who pummeled his head with pine cones.

But the deepest sadness was yet to come. It came in the form of Famine and Fever, two sinister enemies, who entered Hiawatha's house without knocking. During the cold of winter, while he frantically hunted in vain for food in the forest, beautiful, beloved Laughing Water died of starvation in the failing but faithful arms of Nokomis.

Then there was the news of strangers coming across the great Big-sea Water on canoes with wings, and the seamen had faces painted all white. At length they came, and Hiawatha welcomed them. Then he said goodbye to Nokomis and to all his people, and at the seaside stepped at sunset into his waiting canoe. He whispered to it, "Westward! Westward! And with speed it darted forward." The people said, "Farewell," as the forests and waves also did, "and the heron, the shuh-shuh-gah, from her haunts among the fen-lands."

Hobson's Choice   During the first third of the seventeenth century, a certain prominent businessman was widely known and highly respected in the city of Cambridge, England. Prosperous and with a solid reputation as a man of integrity, he was a useful citizen and community benefactor. An innkeeper and "carrier," he ran a stage and mail service between Cambridge and London and served as its driver.

During the Great Plague of 1630, the authorities suspended his carrier service. Compelled because of the contagion to remain idle in Cambridge, he fell victim to the disease and died. The poet John Milton, who never wrote an epitaph for any other man, wrote two of them for this one. Two lines from one read:

Rest, that gives men life, gave him his death,
And too much breathing put him out of breath.

This Cambridge citizen's name was Thomas Hobson. Among his several business enterprises he operated a livery stable, which is a place where horses could be rented, much as we rent automobiles now. He kept a fine stable of the animals and cared for them well. He followed, however, a unique sort of rental policy: When a horse was returned after being used, that animal was placed at the end of the line, the others were all moved forward, and when a customer came requesting the rental of one, he was required to take the horse standing nearest to the stable door.

In this rotation plan, no horse was overworked, and all were equally subject to any abuse renters might inflict upon them. Also, no customer could select a particular animal; he took the one Mr. Hobson offered or he did not get a horse.

Among Hobson's most frequent patrons were students from the nearby campus of Cambridge University. These young men were among the most abusive of Hobson's horses, often riding fast and furiously. Although they wanted fast horses, the horses nearest the stable door were the ones they got. One critter might be as slow as molasses in January, but if he stood nearest the door, it was this animal or it was none, and that was that.

Among the students, this situation quickly translated into a metaphor: Confronting a circumstance in which there was really no alternative, one was said to be facing Hobson's choice. The expression soon overspilled from the halls of academia, making a place for itself in our common speech, where it has remained.

— I —

If the Mountain Won't Come to Mohammed   "If the mountain won't come to Mohammed, then Mohammed will go to the mountain." This expression is said when we cannot get what we want for some reason, but we are determined to get whatever we can, and make the most of a situation.

Mohammed, founder of Islam, lived from A.D. 570 to 632. Sir Francis Bacon (1561–1626) wrote a classic series of essays on topics related to manners and motives in human attitudes and behaviors. In one of these, his *Essay on Boldness*, he told a story concerning Mohammed. His source for the story remains a mystery because it has not been found in any literature prior to Bacon's telling of it.

The story has Mohammed announcing that at a specified time and place he would call a distant hill to come to him. A huge crowd assembled; but when the prophet called the hill, it ignored his call, defiantly remaining where it had always been. Bacon wrote that "never a whit abashed," Mohammed calmly declared, "if the hill will not come to Mahomet [Mohammed], then Mahomet will go to the hill." And he did.

As is common, things tend to get bigger with the telling, and somewhere along the way, Bacon's hill became a mountain.

In the Same Boat   First told by Aesop, this tale is about two men in the same boat. They were inveterate enemies, these two, and it wasn't their intention to be passengers in the same vessel; when each booked passage he was unaware the other would be aboard. One of the men found a place at the ship's foremost end, and the other as far to the rear as he could go. From these positions, the two glared at one another, shooting back and forth their invisible darts of hatred.

A severe storm arose, and it was soon apparent to all that the ship would sink. The man at the stern shouted to the captain, "Which end will go down first?" The captain replied, "The bow, sir, the bow." The sternman then said, "That's good; this is what I hoped, for this way I can have the satisfaction of seeing my enemy drown." This man's satisfaction, though, was of short duration, for an instant after the bow went down, so did the stern.

Most of us eventually learn that in many of life's circumstances we are in a boat with many others, some of whom may be very different from us, and that, survive or perish, we must ride out the storms together. Aesop's pithy point was this: Don't rejoice in another's misfortune while you are riding with him in the same boat.

Iron Curtain   This coupling of two, formerly unrelated words may be one of the best-known and most-used expressions of the twentieth century. A curtain is always a barrier to some degree. To say a curtain is an iron one suggests it is formidable, forbidding, and unyielding. Initially having to do with relationship between nations, the expression has a fascinating history and an uncertain future.

As the Second World War was burning itself out in 1945, there was considerable concern about the outcoming political configuration of Europe. At the Yalta Conference in February of that year, the Allied nations called for a division of power and control between the Soviet Union on the one hand and Britain and the United States on the other.

Although they had been allies during much of the war, there was a serious lack of trust between East and West. It was feared in the West that the Union of Soviet Socialist Republics would swallow up the areas placed under its control, making them vassal states in a growing empire.

The war in Europe ended in April 1945, and it was soon apparent that some hard lines were being drawn across the continent. Earlier, even before the war's end, this development had been foreseen by Joseph Goebbels, propaganda minister of Adolf Hitler's Third Reich. A month after the Yalta Conference, Goebbels wrote: "If the German people should lay down their arms, the agreement between Roosevelt, Churchill, and Stalin would allow the Soviets to occupy all Eastern and Southeastern Europe, together with the major part of the Reich. An iron curtain would at once descend on this territory." Goebbels' vivid description of this barrier as an iron curtain was echoed about eight months later in the title of an article in *Sunday Empire News* of London, "An Iron Curtain Across Europe."

The use of the expression that gave it lasting significance, however, was by Winston Churchill in an address on March 5, 1946, at Westminster College in Fulton, Missouri. He said, "From Settin in the Baltic to Trieste in the Adriatic, an iron curtain has descended across the continent. Behind that line lie all the capitals of Central and Eastern Europe."

Was Churchill aware of Goebbels' terminology, or did he think himself the phrase's originator? Whichever, the towering eminence of the man and the dramatic power of his oratory gave the words an importance that would assure them a lasting place in language.

Between 1946 and 1989, these words aptly described the Cold War that existed between the West and communist East. Then rents began to appear, and almost suddenly the curtain was not as formidable as it once had been. Some began to call it a "gauze curtain," and then it virtually faded from the map. But the expression remains as a part of history.

It's Greek to Me   To say, "It's Greek to me," or, "It's all Greek to me," is a way of saying we do not understand. The expression owes its existence to William Shakespeare's character, Casca, in *Julius Caesar*. In the play's opening act, a group of Roman aristocrats are discussing a recent public appearance of their nation's ruler. Caesar has seemed sad and melancholy, and the men are wondering why.

It turns out that Caesar has collapsed and fallen not merely once but twice; perhaps the problem is epilepsy. Cicero had witnessed these episodes, but is not present now. As the men size up the situation concerning Caesar and his seizures, Cassius asks, "Did Cicero say anything?" Casca answers, "Yes; he spoke Greek." Persisting in the matter, Cassius asks, "To what effect?" Casca replies, "Those that understood him smiled and shook their heads; for my part, it was Greek to me."

What Cicero thinks of Caesar is important to Cassius, for Cicero is an influential leader in Rome, and Cassius is the instigator of a plot to kill Caesar. Four years earlier, both Cassius and Cicero, together with Marcus Brutus, had waged a bloody civil war against Caesar. The victorious Caesar, who pardoned all three men, had given Cassius a high position in the national government. But Cassius had continued as a secret enemy of Caesar, and from his privileged post had organized another plot against him.

All elements of the plot are now in place; and on March 14, A.D. 44, by the hand of Brutus, Caesar is stabbed to death on the Senate floor. At the funeral, Mark Antony delivers an oration so powerful that public outrage forces the conspirators to flee. Later they raise an army, but are defeated; and both Cassius and Brutus take their lives. It would appear that in Rome there was a great deal in addition to Cicero's Greek that these men did not understand.

– J –

Jabberwocky   In England, Charles L. Dodgson (1832–1898) taught mathematics at Oxford University for forty-seven years. Never married and always shy and ill-at-ease with adults, he loved children and felt comfortable in their company. Although a noted scholar and respected author, Dodgson had a whimsical and mischievous flair for the fanciful.

The dean of Oxford's Christ Church College was Henry George Liddell; and the Liddells had three children, all girls, one named Alice. Friend and frequent visitor in the Liddell home, Dodgson spent many happy hours reading with the children or telling unusual tales of his own invention.

Since he responded to suggestions that he put some of these stories into written form, we have *Alice in Wonderland* and *Through the Looking Glass*. We know these as the work of Lewis Carroll, Dodgson's pseudonym.

These lively, imaginative tales introduced a variety of characters whose names we often see in print or hear in conversation—the Mad Hatter, the March Hare, the Cheshire Cat, the White Queen, the Red Queen, and the White Rabbit. The word *jabberwocky*, from *Through the Looking Glass*, has assumed metaphoric status in our language.

A bright, chatty, spirited child, Alice was in the family living room playing with a black kitten called Kitty. In due course, her attention turned to the large mirror above the fireplace mantel. Seeing there reflections of things in the room, she wondered if they were actually beyond the mirror, as they indeed appeared to be. She thought of what was beyond the mirror as "the looking-glass house." As she wondered what it would be like over there, she climbed up to the mirror, and it sort of faded away and let her pass through.

Beyond the mirror, Alice discovered that the chessmen, with which she was familiar on this side, were on that side actually little living creatures. She found, too, that the garden flowers had real faces and voices and could smile and wave. And then there was the Jabberwock.

Her discovery of this creature came by way of a book she found, a book that at first appeared to be in some foreign language. Not so, though, for it proved to be a "looking-glass book"; everything in it was printed backward, so when it was held up to a mirror its reflection was quite readable.

What Alice read was a poem entitled "Jabberwocky." It began, "Twas brillig, and the slithy toves," and ended with, "And the mome raths outgrabe," and between these lines twenty-six others of equal nonsensicality, except that somehow the message came through that the Jabberwock was some sort of creature and that somebody probably killed it. We know it "gimbled" and "wiffled" and "burbled," but all this gives no clue as to what it was like.

Alice said of this poem, "It's rather hard to understand. . . . It seems to fill my head with ideas, but I don't exactly know what they are!" The whole poem is a bit of meaningless verbiage, nice-sounding, well-metered, but saying nothing, or if anything at all, not much. So, talk that sounds nice but says nothing is called jabberwocky.

After Alice's encounter with the Jabberwock, she became lost in the woods. At a fork in the trail there were two signposts, one reading "To Tweedledum's House," and the other "To the House of Tweedledee." Both signs pointed down the same path, so Alice followed it and soon came upon two fat, little men, who looked exactly alike. The only way of telling them apart was by the labels they wore, the one "dum" and the other "dee."

When Alice asked for directions from these fellows, she got a long poem about a walrus and a carpenter and a whole passel of oysters. These two were totally alike in every way, but chiefly in that nothing either said or did made any sense.

So we have this expression that is used when two things are alike, "Tweedledum and Tweedledee," or to describe two different ideas or choices, neither of which matters much. To say that someone is between Tweedledum and Tweedledee is to say it doesn't matter much which way he goes.

Lewis Carroll wasn't the first to use these names in this way, but he was the first to give them characters. Earlier, to "tweedle" was to play or make noises randomly or carelessly upon a musical instrument. During the lifetimes of Handel and Bononcini, each composer had a large following of loyal fans, and the two groups often feuded with each other. Observing the fight, many felt it much ado about very little, some cynics holding that both men were mere "tweedlers" anyway, and that therefore it made little difference whether one favored tweedler one or tweedler two, "tweedledum" or "tweedledee."

Jezebel   *See* DRIVE LIKE A JEHU.

Jingoism   As the fourteenth century began, the Basques were a rugged shepherd people who occupied the Pyrenees Mountains at the boundary between France and Spain. In England, King Edward I was having considerable difficulty subduing another rugged mountain people, the Welsh. To aid in this effort, the king imported a substantial number of Basques, who brought with them their culture and language.

A word commonly used in their expression of religious faith was *Jainko*, probably their way of saying *Jesus*. Like many other names or words having to do with divinity, this one was soon in use in England as a swear word, its pronounciation Anglicized to "jingo." And so it remained.

In 1877, war broke out between Russia and Turkey, a conflict known as the Russo-Turkish War. It appearing to the English that Russia posed a threat to Constantinople, and upon the advice of Prime Minister Disraeli, they sent their naval fleet into the Dardanelles. The result was a tense standoff.

In England, at this time there was a popular singer, a fellow known as the Great MacDermott, who did what popular entertainers are generally inclined to do: He picked up and used in a song a major theme of the time—the war fever with which many were preoccupied. The song MacDermott popularized was built around this refrain:

We don't want to fight; but, by Jingo, if we do,
We've got the ships, we've got the men, and got the money too.

Because this refrain so pointedly (and so singably) caught and expressed a prevailing mood of the moment, the warmongers of that day were soon known as jingoists, and their view of international relations was called jingoism. The word was used in this way by the English, and it was inevitably so applied elsewhere; a jingoist became any intense patriot with a brash readiness to fight. And that is how we use it today, as well. Thus the story of how a colloquial word of religion became a swear word, and that swear word a part of a popular song, and the word from that song acquired a meaning far removed from the original.

John Hancock   The thirteen fledgling colonies of Great Britain decided to unite to create a new nation. It was a daring and dangerous move, as Great Britain was the most powerful nation on earth.

Colonial leaders were aware of the peril in which they placed themselves. Patrick Henry had already stood in Britain's governing assembly in Virginia and shouted, "Give me liberty or give me death," and, "If this be treason, make the most of it."

Then on September 5, 1774, leaders of twelve of the thirteen colonies met in Philadelphia in a convention they called the Continental Congress. They resolved to allow no importation or use of British goods, and the Colonial Association was formed to see to that. This was in response to the Intolerable Acts by which Britain had imposed severe trade restrictions upon the colonies, including the closing of the Port of Boston. On October 26, the Congress adjourned to meet next on May 10, 1775.

Tensions increased, and on April 19, British redcoats and colonial militia clashed at Lexington and Concord in Massachussetts. When the Continental Congress reconvened in May, the atmosphere was electric.

By June 7, 1776, the assembly was ready for a resolution offered by Richard Henry Lee of Virginia calling for a declaration of independence from Britain. Four days later, a committee composed of John Adams, Benjamin Franklin, Thomas Jefferson, Robert R. Livingston, and Roger Sherman was formed to draft such a resolution. The committee selected Jefferson to do the actual writing.

Seventeen days later, on June 28, Jefferson's draft of a resolution was reported to the Congress. On July 2, the Congress declared by vote that, "These United Colonies are, and of right ought to be, free and independent states." Jefferson's document underwent several revisions, and on July 4, 1776, the revised document, the Declaration of Independence, was adopted. It was a dramatic and important moment.

Signing of the Declaration commenced on August 2. Aware of the awful struggle that lay ahead, and with no assurance of its outcome, the act of signing stood, no doubt, as a profound and personal act of commitment on the part of each man. The concluding words of their

Declaration were these: "We mutually pledge to each other our lives, our fortunes, and our sacred honor."

As for the honor they considered sacred, no one could rob them of that; but by their signing that paper, their fortunes and their lives were placed in jeopardy, and they knew it. Yet, man by man, all fifty-five of them signed the document after John Hancock, for he was president of the Congress.

A prosperous Boston merchant, Hancock stood to lose all he had, and for all he knew, he would. Yet with no qualms or quavering he signed. With firm hand and bold strokes, he wrote his name much larger than necessary. Then, as tradition has it, Hancock commented, "There, I trust King George III will be able to read that without his eyeglasses!"

So singular was that signature that it became metaphoric for any signature. A signed name is a John Hancock.

Judas' Kiss   For about three years, Jesus of Nazareth was an itinerant teacher, going about the small country of Palestine advocating justice, preaching love, and proclaiming the advent of a kingdom where righteousness and peace would forever prevail. Priests, lawyers, and other civil and religious leaders perceived his teachings as a threat to their vested interests and were generally annoyed and often angry with him.

While many common people heard him gladly and hopefully, their leaders—the religious ones in particular—sought to discredit or destroy him. They tried again and again to trick him into some violation of their law or prove him guilty of some heresy.

But it was difficult for even his enemies to find much fault in Jesus. Even their own henchmen, when they were able actually to see and hear Jesus, were often convinced of his authenticity and integrity.

The time came at last, however, when the issue reached its inescapable climax. It was in Jerusalem, where Jesus was for the week of Jewish Passover. The authorities were determined that, if at all possible, this would be the week when they would terminate the disturbing career of Jesus.

During his three years of teaching, Jesus had assembled a large number of followers, or disciples, as he called them. Twelve of these constituted an inner circle who were especially close, and one of these twelve was a man named Judas Iscariot. This Judas had perhaps become somewhat disillusioned or impatient with Jesus. Jesus' promised kingdom of righteousness and peace had not yet come, and Judas could see no evidence that it was imminent.

Perhaps Judas had given up on Jesus, or maybe he was trying to force Jesus to do something drastic quickly, but for whatever reason, Judas went to the authorities, offering to help them capture him. Judas told the officials he knew of a time when Jesus would likely be alone with just a few of his disciples. For a price, he was willing to reveal this. They paid him his price, thirty pieces of silver; and a little later Judas led them by torchlight into the midnight shadows of a garden called Gethsemane.

Here in this garden, the posse of priests and soldiers came upon Jesus and the small company of disciples with him. But which of these men was Jesus? Judas had prearranged a signal by which he would let them know, saying, "He whom I kiss; this is he." Now, he rushed forward, and approaching Jesus, he loudly said, "Hello, Teacher!" Then Judas kissed Jesus, and the soldiers took Jesus away, and the next day they killed him.

"A kiss of betrayal," "a kiss of death," and "a Judas kiss" all derive from this biblical story and indicate the kind of treachery that exposes a trusting person to serious jeopardy.

— K —

Kamikaze Commitment   When Kublai was the khan of Mongolia and, looking for new worlds to conquer, he set his avaricious eye upon an island across the sea, Japan. Around the year 1274, he launched an attack against the Japanese, sending a strong naval fleet across the Sea of Japan. But the Japanese were ready, and Kublai's forces were sent home in total defeat.

He then sent envoys to the Japanese demanding that they pay him homage. They refused to do this, and beheaded the envoys.

The Mongol warlord then began to prepare an invincible armada to sail against Japan. The fleet was immense, its very size terrifying, and in 1281 it sailed. Reaching Japanese waters, it encountered a fierce and furious defending force. Although the Japanese faced a superior enemy, the battle raged for weeks, and the Mongols were held to their positions offshore.

Then came a devastating storm, and savage winds whipped the sea into torrents of churning salt water. The invader's boats were splintered, and, water-filled, they sank. When the storm cleared, the war was over. The Japanese had been saved by a wind, a wind God-sent, they thought. They honored that wind and named it. They called it the Divine Wind, the Kamikaze: *Kami* being the word for "God," and *kaze* meaning "wind." The memory of that event became indelible in the Japanese mind, and the cherished legend was told and retold as the centuries passed.

Then came 1941 and the Second World War. The Japanese were not now defending their island, but attempting to conquer the territories of others. They believed their emperor was divine, and with their nationalism and their religion intertwined, they went about their fighting with fanatical passion.

Remembering the mighty Kamikaze of seven centuries earlier, it was easy for these warriors to think of themselves as the divine wind let loose to wreak vengeance or work justice in the world. Thus, an air force flier who was so committed as to load his plane with explosives, dive into a designated target, and die with the explosion became known as a kamikaze pilot. Considering it an honor to die in this way, hundreds of young men did—at Leyte, Okinawa, and elsewhere throughout the Pacific arena.

The word *kamikaze* lives in our language. A kamikaze commitment is a total commitment, the utter and complete giving of one's self to a purpose or cause. To have a devotion that is kamikaze-like is to be unfalteringly loyal, prepared to endure any hardship rather than surrender the ideal.

Keep the Ball Rolling   In terms of sheer buffoonery, the 1840 presidential campaign has never been excelled, and hopefully it never will be. It pitted the aging William Henry Harrison against the luxury-loving incumbent, Martin Van Buren. To make their case against Van Buren, Harrison's handlers pictured their candidate as a down-to-earth, grass-roots, home-spun, back-woods type of American.

Their logo was the log cabin, although Harrison wasn't born in one and didn't live in one. In pointed contrast with the imported wines common at the White House, they made a symbol of hard cider (although Harrison never drank the stuff). Harrison himself spoke of the campaign as "log cabin, hard cider, coonskin humbuggery," but it got him elected.

Banners and slogans and gimmicks of all assorted kinds abounded. One was the rolling of huge balls over long distances, each emblazoned with its own set of campaign graffiti. These balls, usually eight or ten feet in diameter made of paper covered with buckskin, were rolled by relays of excited men over hundreds of miles along city streets and country roads. One was rolled from Cleveland, Ohio, to Lexington, Kentucky; another from somewhere in Kentucky to Baltimore, Maryland; another from Baltimore to Philadelphia, where it fell apart during a parade on Chestnut Street.

Amid all the other slogans and sayings, the prevailing battle theme of these ball-rollers was "Keep the ball rolling—on to Washington!" One roller, being replaced by another, would likely urge his successor to keep the ball rolling. Newspapers along the route followed the progress avidly, reporting it day by day and week by week. Thus the enterprise got considerable attention, and the injunction became well fixed in the public mind—and there it has stuck. When we manage to get something good going, we're apt to say, "Now, let's keep the ball rolling!"

(Mercifully, the actual ball rolling thing pretty well petered out with this one campaign and the one following. It did experience a brief revival in 1888 when William Henry Harrison's grandson, Benjamin, ran for the same office. Incidentally, he also was elected.)

Kilkenny Cats   A person of quarrelsome disposition who appears to relish conflict may be referred to as a Kilkenny cat. We may say that someone is as cantankerous as a Kilkenny cat, or that two or more people fight like Kilkenny cats.

A bit of Irish history is involved here. Kilkenny County was embroiled for nearly 300 years in a bitter border dispute with a neighboring municipality. Through the fifteenth, sixteenth, and seventeenth centuries the struggle was so wasteful of their resources that both were virtually ruined by it.

But the Irish have a charming ability to laugh at themselves and are among the greatest of storytellers.

Fully aware of the ruin they (and their neighbor) were bringing upon themselves by this conflict, they began telling and retelling a story about two of Kilkenny's cats that were tossed together into a saw-pit. Being cats, they fell to fighting with one another. They fought so viciously, scratched, bit, and clawed so violently, that they finally chewed up each other totally, each devouring the other, until nothing was left but their tails!

Kiss of Death   *See* JUDAS' KISS.

– L –

Labor, and Bring Forth a Mouse   Long before people understood volcanoes and earthquakes, the inhabitants of a certain village were once greatly distressed by the behavior of a mountain. This towering mass stood majestically in the midst of a vast plainland, and beside it these people had established a community.

One day, a deep rumble was heard from within the mountain. As the people gathered at the village edge and watched, the mountain trembled, large stones loosened and thundered down the slopes, and great fissures opened as though the mountain were about to shake itself apart.

To the watching villagers, it seemed that inside the mountain there must be some monstrous giant trying to get out. The groans and trembling stones convinced them that an awful struggle was going on inside. At any moment, they expected the mountain to split like a hatching egg and some immense creature to come out of it.

Presently, there was a sharp, convulsive tremor, and just then a mouse was seen to run out from the bottom of the bottommost precipice and scamper away. Then, seeming to heave a great sigh, the mountain subsided into silence, and all was quiet. The villagers returned to their homes and shops and fields, amazed that the mountain had made such a big fuss just to produce one tiny mouse!

Once again, we are indebted to Aesop for the story idea that gives us a picturesque way of saying a rather simple thing. When with much effort we accomplish little, we are likely to say that we have labored and brought forth a mouse.

Law of the Medes and Persians   The law of the Medes and Persians is a law that cannot be changed; there is no way to amend or revoke it. Such laws are certainly rare in the world, if indeed any exist at all. Once, however, they did: It was in the realm of ancient Persia where Darius was the king, and it was in the time when many of the people of Judea were exiles there. Among these exiles was Daniel, an intelligent, talented individual, utterly devoted to the Jewish faith.

By knowledge and skill, though, Daniel had risen to a position of considerable importance in Persia, becoming one of three presidents who managed segments of the Persian empire. When Darius announced plans to make him regent over the entire kingdom, the other presidents and sundry officials, who were wildly jealous of Daniel's success, looked for some way to bring him down. Finding in him no grounds for indictment, they devised a scheme they hoped would bring about his downfall.

These schemers, never mentioning Daniel, proposed to the king that he issue an edict prohibiting for thirty days any person in the kingdom to pray to any god other than the king himself. Not immune to flattery, the king issued the edict, giving it the force of law.

The schemers insisted that the edict be immutable, and Darius, thinking how nice it would be to have a thirty-day monopoly on divinity, fell into their trap. At their behest, he even accepted their recommendation that any violator of the edict be thrown into the den of lions, this being the Persian mode of capital punishment.

Daniel's enemies knew his practices and waited to find him praying aloud to the God of Israel. The conspirators gathered outside Daniel's place, listened to his praying, and went straightway to Darius.

The king was deeply distressed to learn of Daniel's violation of the law, and the committee of schemers was quick to remind him that the law could not be changed. Darius spent the whole day trying to find some way to keep Daniel out of the lions' den, but he failed to find one.

That evening, therefore, the king being powerless against the inflexibility of his own law, Daniel was thrown to the lions. All that night, the severely troubled monarch paced the corridors of his palace. Early the next morning, he appeared at the lions' den, calling out as he approached, "O Daniel, servant of the Living God, has your God been able to deliver you from the lions?" The king, obviously, was hoping it might be so, and apparently he believed it possible.

From the pit came back the clear voice of Daniel, "O king, live forever! My God has sent his angel and shut the lions' mouths, and they have not hurt me." Whereupon Daniel was brought out from the den, and his enemies were thrown in. The lions were not so kind to them.

Often, when it is being suggested that something be changed, someone says, "Why not? After all, this is not the law of the Medes and Persians."

Leak in the Dike   A much loved legend of the Dutch Lowlands, notably recounted in verse by Phoebe Cary, is the story of the heroism of a small boy who saved his country from total ruin. Over centuries, the industrious Netherlanders had reclaimed huge land areas from the sea. Erecting reinforced earthen dikes to hold back the water, they had developed the sea's floor into farms and villages, and here, well beneath sea level, thousands lived and labored. All that stood between these people and the waters of the fierce North Sea were those walls they had built. These walls were diligently watched and maintained with extreme care. The smallest leak could quickly grow into a raging flood that would overwhelm their land.

Near the close of an autumn day, a peasant mother sent her small son on a neighborly errand to a home some distance away. The boy was to deliver freshly baked cakes to a blind old man and return before darkness came. The lad went happily on his way, delivered the cakes, and started out alongside the dike on the path that would take him home.

Near sunset, though, a strong wind arose, and the sea's waves crashed thunderously against the dike. The lad was unafraid, for he had often heard the sound of storms, and he had heard how strong the dikes were. But then he heard a different sound, not the noise of waves and wind, but the trickling sound of running water coming from somewhere on the dike's sloping side not far from where he stood. Almost instantly he saw it: a finger-size mud-laden stream flowing from a tiny opening in the wall. Under the mammoth pressure of the sea, the water had carved through the dike a narrow tunnel for itself, and having now made an exit, it would wash the tunnel wider moment by moment, until soon a great chasm would open, and the whole dike would dissolve into mush.

A leak in the dike! The boy knew the meaning of this. He shouted, but no one heard. He thrust his finger into that opening, and the flowing of the water stopped. He continued to call out, but wind and water made more noise than he.

The sun went down and darkness came. Shivering from the cold and terribly afraid, yet determined to do what he was sure must be done, the brave little fellow never moved from that place. It was nearing dawn when they finally found him, with that small fist and that extended forefinger still firmly fixed like a seal, holding back the sea.

A leak in the dike is any small fault or flaw that will have disastrous consequences if left unattended.

Second: A finger in the dike is a solution too small for a big problem, a stopgap measure which is likely to prove inadequate in the long run.

Left Holding the Bag   One who has been promised something and doesn't get it, or one who has had expectations that never materialize, may be said to be left holding the bag. Likewise, it can be said of one who has failed to receive due share of the proceeds, dividends, or benefits of some venture or undertaking, or one who has been duped, tricked, or swindled out of something expected or promised. The intended victim of a scam or confidence scheme may be identified as a person given the bag to hold.

The expression is of longtime usage, dating from colonial times in America or before. It comes from a trick that has from time to time been played on the gullible. The following is a typical story of such a game.

In an Appalachian community, a group of local men invite the visiting city slicker to go snipe hunting. Being ignorant of snipes, the visitor doesn't know that snipes are water-loving birds that have no hankering after mountain habitats. Neither does this fellow know anything about catching snipes, even if they were in the vicinity.

So these mountain fun-lovers, feigning full seriousness, assemble about 9 P.M. with sticks and clubs and various farm tools, such as rakes and hoes. Also they have one large burlap sack.

With lighted lanterns, they all head into the hills, advising the visitor that the snipes are to be found in the remote, higher elevations. At last reaching the desired place, they reveal the battle plan. The visitor (victim would be a better name) is to stand at this preferred spot, very carefully and quietly holding the open sack with the open end toward the hilltop.

Having extinguished all lights, the men will fan out on both sides, forming a huge semicircle on the hillside, and when the circle is complete, they will close in, forcing the snipes to run straight into the sack. They tell the sack holder that his role is the privileged one, that he is being highly trusted, and that his job is to be performed with extreme care.

The men then disappear into the darkness on both sides, as though going to their assigned positions. The poor victim stands holding his open bag, waiting for snipes to come. They never do, of course. Nor do the men. They all slip away into the darkness, and reassemble at one of their homes for a few swigs of mountain moonshine, a swapping of yarns, and a lot of laughter. As for the poor fellow up on the hill, he is left holding the bag.

Let George Do It   Louis XII, the king of France from 1498 to 1515, doesn't stand triumphantly atop one of history's higher peaks. An ordinary sort, he left no spectacular record of achievement or service to humanity. He did, quite unintentionally, make one lasting contribution. It is remembered—whether he is or not—in the expression, "Let George do it."

The story that made George a scapegoat comes from the reign of Louis XII. When he came to the throne, he brought into his administration a remarkably gifted Frenchman named Georges d'Amboise. Something of a prodigy, Amboise had become a Roman Catholic bishop at age fourteen. Now, as the king assumed power, Louis made Amboise his prime minister. For the next dozen years, the versatile Amboise was to serve France and the king in many ways. Adroit in domestic affairs, skilled in international relations, competent in military operations, and driven by a gigantic personal ambition, the man was a workhorse who always performed well. Until the death of Amboise in 1510, Louis relied heavily on him.

Louis was a ruler who generally meant well, but his abilities were somewhat limited. Often bewildered, even overwhelmed, by affairs of state, the king was in large measure aware of his limitations. Implicitly trusting Amboise, he turned frequently to him for counsel.

Now, when confronted by some difficult problem, the king habitually solved it by turning the matter over to his friend George. When informed of some issue requiring action, the king often responded, "We'll have George see to that." Sometimes he manifested a kind of resigned annoyance, saying, "Let George do it; it's he who is the man of the hour." But, one way or another, when facing a problem to be solved, an action to be taken, an issue to be settled, a need to be met, or something to be done, the king almost always responded by saying, "Let George do it."

The expression is often used; and by using it, we mean to put the doing of our duty on somebody else, or simply to shirk it, leaving it undone. Sometimes we actually say, "Let George do it," and sometimes we simply leave it to George without really saying so. Whichever, George is overworked.

Lilliputian   *Travels into Several Remote Nations of the World by Lemuel Gulliver* was written by the English-Irish author Jonathan Swift (1667–1745). In the land of Lilliput, the people are only six inches tall, with everything else of proportionate size. Since Lilliput first broke upon the literary scene in 1726, small things have been known as lilliputian.

Witty, whimsical, and humorous, the tale is nevertheless a satire, caustic, cynical, and a merciless indictment of human faults and foibles. Gulliver, a ship's physician, makes four voyages. On the first of these, after being shipwrecked, he awakens from exhausted slumber to find himself tied securely to the ground. By stakes and cords and strands of his own hair, the Lilliputians bound him while he was sleeping. Attempting to break free, he is shot by tiny arrows that cannot penetrate his clothing, but sting his face and arms like needles.

When he relinquishes his struggle, his captors prove to be curious and cordial.

Friendship develops easily. Lilliput's largest building, an abandoned temple, becomes Gulliver's residence—an entry two by four feet in size and inside barely enough space for his body. He is with the Lilliputians nine months and thirteen days, and in this time he learns their language and figures largely in their public affairs. He is known throughout the realm as "Man-mountain."

It is soon apparent that Gulliver's presence is a drain on the Lilliputian economy. The labor of 200 seamstresses and 300 tailors is required to make his clothing, 300 cooks prepare his food, and at mealtime 120 waiters serve him, 20 of these working before him on the tabletop. Consuming enough food to feed 1,728 Lilliputians, one of their turkeys is for him only a mouthful.

On the other hand, Gulliver serves the Lilliputians well. In the known universe, there is but one other nation, Blefuscu; and between Lilliput and Blefuscu a state of war has existed for thirty-six moons. The issue is ancient and critical: whether eggs shall be broken from their large or their small ends.

Over time, this controversy between the Big-endians and the Little-endians has cost one emperor his crown and another his life. During the last thirty-six moons, Lilliput has lost 30,000 seamen and soldiers and forty capital ships. Now the Blefuscudians are launching yet another fleet.

Wading in water up to his neck, Gulliver approaches the Blefuscudian vessels. Terrified upon seeing that mountainous human head before them on the water, the sailors abandon their ships; and attaching strings, Gulliver tows the entire fleet to Lilliput. Afterward he negotiates a treaty of peace that ends the conflict.

During his months among the Lilliputians, Gulliver learns a great deal concerning their laws and customs. If one accuses another of a wrong, and the accused is found not guilty, the accuser is then put to death. This, of course, tends to discourage unnecessary litigation. Fraud is a crime worse than theft because due care and diligence can provide some protection against thievery, but honesty has no defense against superior cunning.

Their legal system, based on the principles of reward and punishment, provides not merely for the punishment of an offender but also for rewarding the law-abiding citizen: If for a period of seventy-three moons a citizen has violated no law, he or she is given certain honors and privileges.

In choosing public servants, more emphasis is placed on morals than ability, for public affairs should never be so great a mystery as to require some sublime genius to manage them; the Lilliputians prefer the mistakes honest men may make through ignorance over the deeds evil men do intentionally.

There are strict laws concerning the bearing and rearing of children, for the Lilliputians consider nothing more unjust than for men and women to bring children into the world and leave on the public the burden of supporting them.

Well, in course of time, two influential Lilliputians who resent the presence of Gulliver conspire to destroy him. One is Shyresh Bolgolam, a naval admiral, whose glory has somewhat diminished since Gulliver single-handedly captured the Blefuscudian fleet. The other is the national treasurer, Flimnap, who believes (rather ridiculously) that there's some hanky-panky between his wife and Gulliver.

At last, between wading a lot and swimming a little, the Man-mountain makes his way to Blefuscu, where he is assisted to complete his escape.

Lion's Share   There are several versions of the ancient fable from which this expression comes. The one following is typical.

Lion, Fox, and Ass went hunting together. Coming upon the trail of a fine, fat stag, they stalked him until they brought him down. While Ass made a horrible ruckus with his braying and did a little damage with his kicking, Fox and Lion did the really bloody work. The victim was at last quite dead, and it was time for the victors to divide the spoil.

Since Ass hadn't contributed much to the battle, he was asked to make the division. To the very best of his ability, he did so, carefully separating the carcass into three equal parts. Lion, however, looked upon an equal division as an insult to him. Feeling that his great size, strength, and dignity entitled him to more than a third, he broke into a rage, fell upon Ass, and killed him instantly.

Lion then turned to Fox and said, "Okay now, little buddy, while I rest a bit, you make the division." Fox had a problem: He was tired and he was hungry and he wanted a good portion of that luscious meat, but he was scarcely prepared to die for it. One quick glance in the direction of the dead ass helped him to a prompt decision in the matter. Being a wiley fellow, and of pragmatic mind, he separated only a tiny morsel for himself, leaving all the rest as the lion's share.

Observing this approvingly, his mountainous ego agreeably flattered, Lion said, "Little Fox, you did this perfectly, right down to the smallest fraction. Who taught you the art of division?" And Fox politely replied, "Your Majesty, sir, I learned it from the ass!"

Generally, the lion's share is the larger part of anything. Sometimes it is the superior portion that the one who has greatest power is able to take by force or coercion. Sometimes, but not always, it is that which comes as a result of skill, talent, or just plain hard work. And sometimes, too, it is the gift of someone who has the power to give. But it is always the largest amount.

Lothario   It is the morning of his wedding day, and Altamont is happy. He has reason to be: Calista is a beautiful and intelligent woman, and her father, Sciolto, is one of the richest and most powerful men in Genoa. Besides, Calista's father is a real fan of Altamont's and is very pleased with the marriage.

Calista, however, is living with a secret neither man knows anything about. Lothario knows about it, though, and rather than keep the secret, he is inclined to talk about it, even to boast of it. Having recently and very deliberately seduced the woman, he bragged later to one of his cronies that the experience was all a "luscious banquet." He coldly describes how "the guardians of her honor were charmed to rest," vainly applauding himself for being so irresistible a charmer. He declares unabashedly that in the morning "cold indifference came," and adds,

> I hastily took leave and left the nymph
> To think on what was past, and sigh alone.

Archetypical of the love-'em-and-leave-'em type of rake who uses women and then, passion spent, callously turns and walks away, Lothario's name has become an appellation by which every such man is known. The foppish character has long been a figure in English language and literature.

The story of Altamont and Calista is from *The Fair Penitent*, a poetic drama by Nicholas Rowe, first played in England in 1703. In this tragic tale, Lothario is the spoiler who lays waste the contentment and happiness of all concerned, the central theme being the turmoil in the troubled soul of Calista.

Although about to marry Altamont, she is strongly attracted to Lothario, despite his snide indifference and brutal treatment of her. She sends a letter begging him to give her true love and devotion, signing it "the lost Calista." This he scorns. Inadvertently, he drops the letter and it is picked up by Horatio, friend and brother-in-law of Altamont. At first, Horatio believes the letter is a forgery contrived by Lothario to cause trouble in the forthcoming marriage.

Gradually, though, the truth comes out; in a series of scenes, full disclosure is made. In the process, the guilty Calista is sharply stung when Horatio trustingly declares to her that "to be good is to be happy." A further twinge is felt when her father swears that he will disown her should she ever prove dishonorable or unchaste. She at last perceives something of Lothario's inhumanity when, complaining that he has ruined her, he unfeelingly replies, "Do you call it ruin to love as we have done?"

The inevitable happens at last: Altamont and Lothario fight, and Lothario is killed. Calista snatches the dying Lothario's sword to kill herself, but Altamont interferes. Her father appears and, learning what has happened, draws his sword to kill her himself, but again Altamont interferes. Because Lothario has met his death in Sciolto's house, a gang of Lothario's cronies very nearly kill the old man, inflicting wounds that are eventually fatal.

The final scenes are at Lothario's funeral bier. Here, Altamont finds Calista; knowing it's over between them, they grieve for what might have been. He stands numb from shock, she still strangely under the spell of the man who lies dead before them. Though sorry for the deep hurt felt by Altamont, nevertheless she says,

> "O, Altamont, 'tis hard for souls like mine,
> Haughty and fierce, to yield they have done amiss."

Horatio comes with word of her father's sad misfortune at the hands of Lothario's ruffians, saying, "The great, the good Sciolto dies this moment." Not yet dead, however, but pale and bleeding, Sciolto enters the room. Before his arrival, Calista stabs herself and is now dying. She begs him to forgive her, and he does, saying, "Die, and be happy." She dies, and then he does. Fainting, Altamont is carried away. . . . All this heartache because of Lothario.

Lotus Eaters For ten years the armies of several Greek kings were engaged in the siege of Troy. When Troy eventually fell, these armies were demobilized, and their warriors were allowed to go home. One of the kings involved was Odysseus (Latin: Ulysses), king of Ithaca. With a portion of his army and twelve of his ships, Odysseus set out for his homeland.

To reach Ithaca, it was necessary to cross the Aegean Sea. The voyage would normally have required only a few weeks, but for Odysseus, as things turned out, it took ten years. He suffered many hardships, confronted innumerable perils, and fought countless enemies. By the time he finally reached home he had lost all his men and all his ships.

Of the many encounters along his way, none is of greater interest than the second encounter of this series. Driven for nine days by a raging storm, his ships were at last thrust onto the shore of a strange country. Here, as the storm subsided, the weary travelers stopped to rest and take on fresh water.

Odysseus sent three of his men inland to see what kind of people lived there, and he almost failed to get them back. This proved to be the land of the Lotophagi, the lotus eaters. The three scouts were well received by these natives, who magnanimously treated them to the fruit of the lotus plant. Having eaten a little of the lotus, the scouts lost all interest in ever reaching home, or in anything except eating more of the lotus. Odysseus had a drug problem on his hands.

He finally rounded up the three, forced them weeping and screaming back onto the ships, and tied them under the benches. Odysseus realized that without such drastic measures, he would likely lose his whole crew. He quickly ordered all the men onto the ships and started them rowing at once.

Odysseus rarely ran away from anything, but he ran from this. He usually stood and fought, but here was an enemy he couldn't fight. The lotus eaters were an idle and indifferent lot who lived for nothing but to eat the paralyzing plant.

From this story our language receives a vivid expression. One who lives in a state of carefree indifference is said to be a lotus eater. To live on lotus is to be indolent, nonproductive, an idle day-dreamer. To go about blithely in a make-believe world of casual isolation is to feed on lotus.

– M –

Maginot Line Mentality   If the purpose of walls is to keep people apart, historically they have proved somewhat less than successful. And if walls are built to keep enemies out, they usually don't. What they do is generate in the builders a feeling of security and complacency that renders them more vulnerable than they would have been otherwise. The French found it so.

Theirs was a wall so sophisticated they didn't even call it this; it was a "line"—the Maginot Line. More belowground than above, this elaborate bulwark of defense stretched along the entire French boundary with Germany, all the way from Switzerland on the south to Belgium on the north. A massive structure of concrete and steel, it featured underground railroad lines, living quarters, recreational areas, altogether "more comfortable than a modern city," they said. Bristling with powerful guns, the line was considered impregnable.

This state-of-the-art fortification, constructed between 1930 and 1940, was a direct consequence of the First World War. Having then suffered the disaster of German invasion, the French undertook to fix things so such an invasion could never occur again. Named for politician André Maginot (1877–1932), their defense line was both an engineering marvel and a defense masterpiece. Believing that no enemy could ever come through it, and feeling utterly secure behind it, the French became complacent.

Although Adolf Hitler was gaining power in Germany, and although that nation was arming mightily for conquest, the French were so confident of their Maginot Line that they went about their affairs indifferently. The prevailing attitude was that whatever is about to happen in Europe, it can't affect us; we are fully protected; nothing else is necessary.

Then came May 10, 1940. Hitler's panzer divisions roared into Belgium. Within less than three days, they had made an end run around France's magic line and were sweeping westward toward Paris. The guns of Maginot were never fired; the enemy simply went around and came in another way.

Maginot Line mentality is an attitude of smug indifference, a posture of complacent self-indulgence, that sees itself as secure against all intrusions. It's the self-deceptive aplomb that enjoys at-easeness behind protective walls not nearly as strong as they are believed to be. Whoever and whatever the comfortable haven, the discovery is made at last: No wall is so strong it cannot be breached, and there is ultimately no defense against the inevitable.

Make Bricks Without Straw   A little less than 4,000 years ago, the land of Canaan was stricken by drought and famine. The inhabitants of the land, the Hebrews, compelled to flee for their lives, made their way southward and westward, across the Red Sea from Asia into Africa, and there they became refugees in Egypt. Gradually, these people were forced to become servants and slaves of the Egyptians. Generation after generation came and went, until almost 400 years had passed.

Egypt was in the midst of an immense building boom, requiring massive quantities of building materials, among these bricks by the millions. So it was to the task of making bricks that most of the Hebrews were assigned. It was slave labor, and hot, hard work.

To make bricks, two main ingredients were needed, mud and straw. On the Nile delta, mud was available in unlimited supply, but straw was scarce. If the brickyards were to produce properly, it was necessary for the Egyptians to scour the countryside for straw, and deliver it to the workmen.

Into this situation came Moses; his purpose was to liberate his fellow Hebrews and return them to Canaan. His first move was to go to the Pharaoh, king of Egypt, asking for a three-day leave for the Hebrews to go into the wilderness for a special time of worship and sacrifice.

The Pharaoh firmly refused this request. Instead, the Pharaoh said,

"These Hebrews aren't working hard enough; they are idle. They are even asking for a vacation, and they are not going to get it." So the Egyptian ruler gave the Hebrews' taskmasters an order: Don't ever again go searching for straw for these people; let them go get their own. But see that they make the same number of bricks they were making previously.

So the Hebrews' burden was enormously increased, the requirement impossible to meet. And from this unbearable circumstance our speech is enriched by the expression "to make bricks without straw." To demand that another perform an impossible task is to require that person make bricks without straw. When one, on his or her own initiative, embarks on an undertaking that is clearly doomed because the resources for success just aren't there, it may be said that he or she is trying to make bricks without straw. The expression, in a broader sense, may denote an attempt to do anything that is extremely difficult.

To complete the story: The Hebrew people did, at last, make their exit from Egypt, and eventually made their way to their ancestral homeland, leaving the Egyptians to gather their own straw and make their own bricks.

Malapropism Lydia Languish was young, beautiful, unmarried, and rich. Having read a great many romance novels, she wanted to make an adventure of love and marriage. To do this, she thought she would do something not commonly done in her circles: The man she married must be of an economic and social rank below her own.

Knowing this, Captain Jack Absolute, son of the wealthy and socially prominent Sir Anthony, posed as an ensign named Beverley, a social nobody, and set out to win the heart of Lydia. He succeeded very well, although Lydia's aunt, Mrs. Malaprop, looked with grave disfavor upon these developments.

Mrs. Malaprop, a widow, had herself fallen hopelessly in love with an Irishman named Sir Lucius O'Trigger, with whom she carried on a romantic correspondence—O'Trigger all the while believing he was in communication with the lovely Lydia.

Bob Acres, a well-to-do neighbor of Sir Anthony Absolute, was also trying to win Lydia, but without much encouragement from her. Jack Absolute's friend Faulkland was courting Julia, Lydia's cousin, but because of a peculiar jealousy on his part, this pursuit wasn't going anywhere either.

Sir Anthony, knowing nothing of his son's interest in Lydia, dropped a bomb into all this complexity when he announced that he had selected a bride for Jack. Jack visualized his father's choice as some repulsive female, and besides, he loved Lydia; therefore he vowed he would never marry the woman of his father's choosing, no matter who she was.

Jack didn't know that his father had actually selected Lydia, this in collusion with Mrs. Malaprop, who, of course, didn't know that the so-called Ensign Beverley was actually Sir Anthony's son.

When Jack's father arranged a meeting, in his presence, between his preselected bride and groom, the truth had to come out, and it did. Learning that this fellow with whom she had fallen in love was not, after all, some poor ensign in the king's army, but was instead the cultured and well-heeled son of Sir Anthony Absolute, she turned from him in total rejection.

Previously, believing Jack Absolute to be Ensign Beverley, the frustrated Bob Acres had challenged him to a duel, this showdown to occur in the city of Bath (where all this was happening) at King's-Mead-Fields on a certain day, Sir Lucius O'Trigger to serve as his second. Now, Sir Lucius challenged Jack to a duel, and since he planned to be at King's-Mead-Fields anyway as second for Bob Acres, this contest was also scheduled for the same place and time.

They all then met as planned, the result being that Acres immediately recognized his opponent not as some stranger named Beverley but as his own acquaintance and friend Jack Absolute. By this time, Lydia had learned Jack was fighting a duel over her, and having second thoughts about her rejection of him, she, along with her aunt, rushed to the scene at King's-Mead-Fields.

No duel was fought; instead, everything fell into place. Of course, Sir Lucius was most chagrined to discover that all this time he had corresponded with Mrs. Malaprop, not Lydia. Lydia was reconciled to marrying a man more highly placed than an ensign and realized at last that Jack was her man. Faulkland and Julia got their problems worked out. And Bob Acres, happy the duel was called off, arranged a gigantic party for all the elite of Bath.

This story is a plot outline of *The Rivals*, one of the more popular of the eighteenth-century English comedies. Written by Richard B. Sheridan and first played in 1775, the drama's characters were vividly depicted, including Mrs. Malaprop. A unique characteristic of hers was the manner of her speaking: In an effort to be impressive, she was inclined to use the wrong word.

Wanting to use pretentious, high-sounding language, Mrs. Malaprop had a way of using sound-alike words meaning something other than what she intended. Once she spoke of someone as a "progeny of learning." Someone else was "as headstrong as an allegory on the banks of the Nile." She urged Lydia to "illiterate" Ensign Beverley from her memory. She hoped that a cultured young woman "might reprehend the true meaning of what she is saying."

Oblivious of her mistakes and vigorously defensive, she once declared, "If I reprehend anything in this world, it is the use of my oracular tongue, and a nice derangement of epitaphs!" Her name, appropriately, was an adaptation of the French *mal à propos*, meaning "inopportune" or "not appropriate."

Man Friday   The story is by the British writer Daniel Defoe in 1719, entitled *Life and Strange Surprising Adventures of Robinson Crusoe*. A high-spirited, restless youth of York, Crusoe wants to go away to sea. His father objects and his mother grieves, but he goes anyway. At Hull, he joins the crew of a ship bound for London, but the vessel is lost at Yarmouth Roads and the kindly captain urges the young man to give up his seafaring notions. He persists, nevertheless, having occasion later to say, "I was born to be my own destroyer."

Out of London, Crusoe ships out on one or two successful voyages, but then is captured by pirates off the coast of Morocco and made a slave to the pirate captain at Sallee. After two years, he takes his master's boat out one day for fishing and makes off with it down the African coast. After several weeks, turning westward, he intercepts a Portuguese trader bound for Brazil, is taken aboard, and is treated generously by the ship's master.

In Brazil, becoming a landowner and planter, he does well. Neighbors who grow sugar cane and tobacco, as he does, need laborers for their fields, as he does also. So they form a company, and aboard a large and well-supplied vessel, sail for Guinea, hoping there to purchase slaves. This voyage, however, is never completed. Severe storms take the lives of six of the seventeen men aboard; then the ship runs aground on an unknown island, and all hands are lost except Crusoe, who manages to swim ashore.

When the storm abates, he observes that the wrecked ship lies aground not far off the beach, and he is able to transport from ship to shore a great deal of equipment and supplies. He improvises a dwelling place, part stockade and part cave, provides storage for his salvaged materials, and settles in to survive until some ship may pass this way.

To keep track of passing time, he daily carves a notch in a large post, with a longer one for each seventh day, the first one representing September 30, 1659. For companionship, he has from the ship a dog and two cats, and other animals he domesticates from the native population, especially goats. As far as he can tell, the island is totally void of human inhabitants.

Fifteen years pass, and then one day the castaway finds a human footprint in the sand! Knowing now that he is not alone, he is at first seized by panic, but then cautiously begins to explore areas he has not seen before. He is horrified to discover that his island is periodically visited by cannibals, who bring prisoners, kill them, and ceremoniously cook and eat their flesh.

After another eight or nine years, a party of cannibals beach their canoes on his side of the island, and as they are preparing for their gruesome festivity, Crusoe is able to rescue one of their prisoners. The primitive young islander, in deepest gratitude, signals that he will be Crusoe's slave forever, which is precisely what Crusoe wishes for. The youth proves to be intelligent, agile, sensible, and in every way faithful and helpful.

Because his rescue was accomplished on a Friday, Crusoe names him Friday, and afterward refers to him always as "my man Friday." Friday is a willing learner and always eager to please. With his help, Crusoe is able to do many things previously impossible. He says, "Never was a more faithful, loving, sincere servant than Friday was to me."

Other years go by, and at length comes another contingent of cannibals. This time, one of their captives turns out to be Friday's father, who Crusoe and Friday snatch from their hands, along with another victim, a man from Spain.

At last, an English vessel appears, anchoring offshore. The crew has taken over the ship and made a prisoner of the captain and a few others. These prisoners are brought ashore to be left stranded, while the mutinous crew sails away. But Crusoe and his growing little army interfere with this plan, overpowering the mutineers and assisting the ship's master to reclaim his vessel. In it, the party sails away to England.

Crusoe had been away from his homeland for thirty-five years, having spent more than twenty-six of these years on an uncharted island somewhere in the western seas.

Out of this adventure tale, Crusoe's man Friday stands forth as a symbol of any loyal and faithful friend or helper. His name is often heard as representing some person whose devotion to another amounts to a willing and congenial servitude.

Mantle of Fidelity   King Arthur and the knights and ladies of his court were in festive mood in celebration of Christmas, when into their midst came a strange and cunning boy. Elaborately and expensively dressed, the strange youth carried various exotic items, including a magic wand. Declaring to the men that he was about to test the fidelity of their wives,

> Lest what ye deem a blooming rose
> Should prove a cankered weed,

he took from among his stuff a remarkably beautiful mantle such as a woman might wear, announcing that only wives faithful to their husbands were able to wear it.

At the stranger's suggestion, Arthur's Queen Guinevere was the first to try the mantle. When put on her, the thing literally fell apart! After she furiously stormed away, Sir Kay said to his wife, "If you're guilty, please don't try this thing." But, laughingly, she tried it, and the mantle, shrinking up to her shoulders, left her backside bare. To the tune of raucous guffaws, she also promptly disappeared from the scene.

Next, an aged knight summoned his wife, who, as aged as he, seemed a grandmotherly and saintly type. But once on her, the mantle must have remembered things she may have long since forgotten, for it shrank until nothing was left but a tassel and a thread.

Sir Craddock confidently addressed his spouse, saying, "Come, win this mantle, lady." She came, and she won it; but before she put it on, she confessed aloud that once, before she and Craddock were married, she had kissed him on the lips. But, apparently finding no great harm in this, the mantle caressed her approvingly. The only woman present who could wear the mantle, she wore it well.

The strange boy then pointed to the great boar's head, prepared for eating and garnished with bay leaves and rosemary, which stood at the center of King Arthur's table. He announced that the head could not be penetrated by the knife belonging to any man whose wife had committed adultery. While some men frantically sharpened their knives and others threw theirs under the table pretending they had none, Sir Craddock easily plunged his straight and strongly into the skull.

The youth with the magic wand then brought forth a peculiar-appearing drinking cup, an animal's horn with a gold band about it. He said that no man whose wife had been unfaithful could drink from this horn. Indeed, no man could—not until Sir Craddock tried, and he could and did. Concluding the matter, and pronouncing the queen a bitch and a witch, the mantle-bearing lad then said to the king, "In thine own hall, thou art a cuckold."

That Christmas festival was, no doubt, one always remembered in King Arthur's England. A time of revelation, it disclosed the promiscuity of a whole passel of women. It had nothing to say about the men; but for each promiscuous female there probably was approximately one promiscuous man!

The mantle has earned a place in speech as a way of describing people. Of an obviously profligate individual it may be said that he or she "isn't exactly wearing the mantle of fidelity." Or, of someone it may be said, "The mantle of fidelity just doesn't fit." Or, how about this—"He wears everything well, except the mantle of fidelity."

Dating from an episode of the Arthurian legend, this story is best told in a poem of unknown authorship entitled "The Boy and the Mantle," and included in 1765 in Bishop Thomas Percy's *Reliques of Ancient English Poetry*.

Marathon   The word *marathon* in the English language is virtually a synonym for whatever is long—a long time, a long process, a long distance, a long continuum of anything. The meaning of this word comes to us from a dramatic and decisive moment of world history.

Ancient Greece was the cultural and philosophical center of the world. Its apex was reached in the era of Socrates–Plato–Aristotle, during the century ending with the death of Aristotle in 322 B.C. That mighty intellectual upsurge, however, came within a hairbreadth of never happening. Here is the story.

Darius I had conquered almost all the known world. In that year his huge army (by some accounts 100,000 strong) crossed the Aegean Sea from Asia and quickly subdued Thrace and Macedon just north of Greece. Turning south, this vast horde reached the plain of Marathon between the sea and Mount Pentelicus, just twenty-six miles northeast of Athens, only a day's march away.

The Athenians had mustered every able-bodied man for the defense of their treasured city, and they did not wait for the Persians to come. Under leadership of their commander Miltiades, they marched north, leaving their aged and their women and children to await the outcome. Apparently, the Persians outnumbered them ten to one, and for the Athenian defenders the prospects were dismal.

Arriving at Marathon on that September day, the Greek forces launched an immediate assault on the Persians, making a running charge directly into the main body of the Persian army. The Persians so vastly outnumbered them that they believed the Greeks to be out of their minds to do a thing so foolhardy, and at first, seized by surprise and perplexity, they made no defense. They soon realized, however, that they were being slaughtered right and left.

Quickly then, the Persians rallied and began to fight back, but it was too late. In a series of brilliant military moves, and with heroic displays of courage, the small Athenian troop put the Persians to flight, even capturing seven of their ships before the Persians could board them. That day the Persians lost 6,400 men and the Greeks lost 192. The battle of Marathon was decisive; historically, it meant that the Persians would never conquer Greece and that Greek thought would have its chance to flower.

What a victory! But back in Athens that day, thousands of anxious eyes were turned toward the north: Which army would come marching down from Attica—Persian or Greek, invader or defender?

Old folks, women, and children expected to see their city burned and to be burned with it.

What they saw instead was a lone runner coming toward them, a messenger and heroic Athenian patriot named Pheidippides. Staggering into the city, and summoning all his strength to draw one last breath, he shouted a single great word, "Victory!" and there on the pavement fell dead. At maximum speed this courageous man, who was already exhausted from the fighting, had run that twenty-six-mile distance from the plain of Marathon, anxious to let his Athenian friends know that their city was saved and that the freedom they cherished was still theirs.

Meddlesome Matty   In 1804 in England a small book appeared entitled *Original Poems for Infant Minds*. These poems were written mostly by the family of an engraver named Isaac Taylor. His daughter Jane wrote "Twinkle, Twinkle, Little Star." Daughter Ann contributed a short narrative poem entitled "Meddlesome Matty."

These fifty-four simple lines tell about the humorous and instructive misadventures of a girl named Matilda. Delightful in every other way, the child was ultra-inquisitive. She was a compulsive snooper, forever prying into matters of no concern to her.

One day in a room alone, Matilda saw her grandmamma's eye-glasses and brightly colored snuff box on a table. Of course, she had to put the glasses on. Then, wondering what was in the box, she tried to open it. But the lid was stuck and she had to pull and tug to get it off. Finally, though, it popped off quite suddenly, and

> *All at once, ah! Woeful case!*
> *The snuff came puffing in her face.*

She instantly discovered what it is like to have a lot of powdered tobacco in the nostrils and the eyes. Running around the room in pain and panic, she gave a frantic swipe at her eyes and knocked off her grandmamma's glasses, which broke into smithereens on the floor. Just then Grandmamma appeared, and Matilda

> *Made many a promise to refrain*
> *From meddling evermore.*

Well, this poem was no great literary gem, and Meddlesome Matty (the character) would probably have perished from memory soon after Ann Taylor created her had it not been for an American named William Holmes McGuffey. During two generations this man probably exerted more influence over the American mind than any other person in our history.

Between 1836 and 1857, he published a series of school textbooks commonly called *The McGuffey Eclectic Readers*. These six volumes, for grades one through six, taught more than reading; they also taught manners and values. So McGuffey had to carefully select the material for his books from many sources. Included in his *Fourth Reader* was the little poem about Meddlesome Matty. More than 122 million copies of McGuffey's readers were sold and used in American schools. Millions of children carried the memory of Meddlesome Matty with them into adulthood, causing her name to become a household expression. Many a child caught interfering in other's business was admonished with the words, "Don't be a Meddlesome Matty!" Unfortunately, her name is not heard much anymore.

Meet Your Nemesis   The early Greeks had vivid and virile imaginations. In this fertile and well-cultivated soil many novel ideas took root and grew. Astute observers of the way things worked, these ancient people were keenly aware of cause and effect in human affairs.

Tending to personalize everything, they generally saw human behavior and world events as powerfully influenced by personal beings with specialized interests. Hence the elaborate pantheon of Olympian gods and goddesses, the various classes of demigods and of miscellaneous creatures inhabiting the mystic world somewhere between the divine and the human.

Especially noted by the Greeks was the pervading presence of some power of retributive justice. Somehow, something saw to it that things were kept in some measure of control, that excesses and extremes were held in check. They needed an explanation for this, and, as was their wont, they sought a personal one. In this way they invented Nemesis.

To start with, Nemesis was a quite normal person. But the roving eye of the highest god, Zeus, fell upon her and he began a long period of hot pursuit. To evade his advances, Nemesis changed herself again and again into many different forms, last of all a goose. But Zeus countered this by changing himself into a swan; then he raped her.

After the rape, while still a goose, Nemesis laid an egg. It was picked up by shepherds who gave it to a woman named Leda, and from it Helen was born, whose unstable love life later was a cause of the Trojan War.

Following the rape, Nemesis became extremely vindictive, wreaking her frustration upon everyone within reach. She brought misfortune to everyone who did anything improper; whoever took a wrong turn could expect to meet Nemesis head-on.

In course of time, her mood softened somewhat. While continuing to dispense justice, she developed a concern for keeping things in balance, presiding over the equilibrium of all things in the world. In matters of gaining wealth or power, she was forever saying, "This far and no farther." Thus, for the Greeks, Nemesis became the goddess of limitations, of equilibrium and fair proportion. She continued, however, to hold the scales of justice in her hand and carry the sword of retribution.

As used in our language, to meet one's nemesis is to suffer defeat, to be stopped from further pursuit of a chosen course. A nemesis, of course, is whoever or whatever brings about the defeat or causes the stoppage.

Meet Your Waterloo   Napoleon Bonaparte lived for less than fifty-two years. From his humble Corsican beginnings, riding on the currents of the French Revolution, he rose rapidly to high positions—dictator of France before age thirty, and at thirty-five the emperor (or so he called himself).

Napoleon stands as one of history's enigmas. He has been described as both kind and cruel, beneficent and despotic. But whatever he may or may not have been, he was a strong leader of men. Attempting to expand a nation into an empire in ten fast-moving years, he led his loyal troops to victories over most of Europe, making vassals of nation after nation.

Between 1800 and 1810, he managed to consolidate almost the entire continent under his rule. But in the East was Russia, vast, mysterious, and as yet unconquered. Given the Napoleonic mind, the invasion of Russia was inevitable.

In June 1812, the largest army ever yet assembled in Europe marched across the Russian border. The Russians retreated, mile by mile, and by the hundreds of miles; but as they went, they stripped the country bare, leaving little food or supplies for the invaders.

On September 14, Napoleon entered Moscow, found it almost depopulated, and, like the rest of the conquered country, it was devoid of all supplies and food. The next day, mysterious fires broke out, which burned for four days; Napoleon's expected winter quarters were decimated. He asked for terms of peace, but the Russian czar refused. Having no choice but to retreat, Napoleon did; but the retreat became a rout, with hungry, freezing soldiers scrambling for home, many dying on the way. Only one in five of this army who went into Russia ever came out.

Napoleon's stranglehold on Europe was broken, or so it seemed. The subjugated nations began to rebel; Prussia, England, Sweden, Austria, and others formed an alliance against the French leader, and the War of Liberation commenced. In March 1814, these allies took Paris, and Napoleon abdicated and was exiled to a Tyrrhenian island called Elba.

But the wily Boneparte wasn't through. Less than a year later, he disembarked with a small band of followers from a boat at the French port of Cannes and again rallied the French around him. In less than four months he was in command of an army of 105,000 men. Then he launched an all-out assault against the British and Prussians in a field not far from Brussels, at a place named Waterloo.

Here, on June 18, 1815, with 25,000 men killed and 9,000 captured, Napoleon suffered one of history's most devastating and decisive defeats. Four days later, for the second time he abdicated and was again exiled, this time to Saint Helena. After six years on this island prison, he died of cancer.

On that day at Waterloo, the mighty Napoleon's tower of power came tumbling down. He had seemed invincible and had achieved what seemed impossible, yet he was abruptly defeated.

As this event at Waterloo has a significant place in history, so does the word *Waterloo* in our everyday speech. The expression often used, "meet your Waterloo," means to encounter final defeat.

Mending Fences   In 1829 in Lancaster, Ohio, a family of eleven children was left fatherless by the early death of Charles Sherman. A citizen of modest means, he was unable to leave much for the family's support. One of these eleven children was William Tecumseh, who was nine years old when his father died; another was John, age six. In spite of their hardships, the family turned out well.

William Tecumseh Sherman became famous as a Union general in the Civil War and maintained national prominence until his death in 1891. His younger brother, John, became a lawyer, served six years in the U.S. Congress and thirty-two years in the Senate, was secretary of the Treasury under President Hayes, and secretary of state during the first portion of the McKinley administration. He was responsible for formulating many of the basic laws still significant in American government, including the Sherman Anti-Trust Act of 1890.

But enough about John Sherman and his life in general. Let's go on to look at one small episode in the man's rather preeminent career. At one point as he was completing a term in Washington, there was speculation about his next political move. He traveled from Washington to a farm he owned in Ohio, where he was approached by news reporters who suspected he would again be a candidate. Their questions regarding his intentions yielded no great amount of information, and one reporter asked why he was in Ohio. Sherman replied, "I have come to look after my fences."

In those days, fences were important on farms, and being difficult to maintain, they did indeed require a considerable amount of looking after. And, of course, so did a politician's connections, relationships, and standings with the voters.

Ohio newspapers reported that Sherman had come home to "mend his fences." Because most people had a good idea what politicians normally do when among their constituents, they assumed that Sherman was not really patching holes in farm fences but was patching up his relationships with the voters and local leaders. (He probably was.)

Anyway, that is how this new expression came bounding into our language. To mend one's fences is to straighten things out with others, to smooth out any rough spots in relationships, create good feelings, build confidence, and establish rapport.

Mentor   The cast of characters for this story consists of Odysseus, king of Ithaca, a good man and devoted husband and father; Penelope, his wife, who is intelligent, loving, and faithful; Telemachus, their son and only child, who is bright, alert, and promising; and Mentor, their trusted friend, who is loyal, helpful, and giving.

In ancient Greece at the time of the Trojan War, Trojan prince Paris had absconded with Helen, wife of Menelaus, king of Sparta, and had taken her to Troy, a heavily fortified city across the Aegean Sea. Menelaus wanted his wife back and he recruited kings of the other Greek states to help him retrieve her, Odysseus among them.

Odysseus didn't want to go, but felt it was his duty. In his absence he wanted Telemachus to have good care, wise counsel, and above all, a father figure in whose likeness the child might be inspired to grow. Odysseus chose Mentor, and to this most trusted friend he committed his son and the affairs of his household. Odysseus knew his absence would be long, but he probably never imagined it would stretch to twenty years—ten at the siege of Troy and ten in a horrendous struggle to reach his home.

A lot happens to a baby in twenty years! But Mentor was there to see Telemachus through all of it. In the drama of Greek mythology, he doesn't stand as one of the giants, but he played his role so well that his name is proverbial for a wise counselor. A mentor is the more mature or more experienced person who assumes a responsibility for the less mature or less experienced to direct that person toward some goal or achievement.

The original Mentor faced numerous and serious problems, not that Telemachus was a difficult pupil, for he was an apt and willing one, and the relationship between teacher and pupil was warm and close. The difficulties arose from circumstance. Odysseus wasn't long gone when a whole flock of male vultures of the human variety descended upon his palace, making themselves virtually resident, plundering his estate, and becoming generally obnoxious to Penelope.

After Odysseus was gone a long while, with no word of his whereabouts, many of these characters tried to convince Penelope that Odysseus must surely be dead. They used every argument and every trick to persuade her to marry one of them, but she refused.

Reaching the age of seventeen or eighteen, and considering himself a man, Telemachus resolved to rid his mother of these pests. His first move was to make a long journey in search of his father or news of him. While failing to find Odysseus, he did learn that somehow Odysseus had angered Poseidon, god of the sea, and that this vindictive deity had made the voyage to Ithaca as difficult as possible, but that now, after many delays, his father was somewhere nearing home.

Shortly after his return to Ithaca, Telemachus and the ever-faithful Mentor learned that a lone stranger had appeared on the outskirts of the realm. Setting out promptly to investigate, they found the stranger to be the long-absent Odysseus, traveling in disguise. Having heard rumors of conditions at his palace, the shrewd Ithacan king had returned incognito, the better to deal with what problems he might find.

Here in this meeting at a shepherd's hut, the mighty Odysseus, the wise Mentor, and Telemachus decided what they would do. With the aid of two other men, they fell upon that passel of palace leeches, slew them by the score, and so scared the rest that they never dared return.

Father, son, and mother were together again, and the son was all the father had hoped to make him. Mentor had served well. (See also ODYSSEY; WEAVE A PENELOPE SHROUD.)

Merlin's Magic Mirror   In Arthur's time in England, the best and bravest men were knights who carried long lances, wore heavy armor, and rode powerful battle mounts. But not all who did so were men; some were women, often the young and the beautiful. One of these was Britomart, the daughter of King Ryence, who, spurning the womanly arts, set out "to hunt out perils and adventures hard."

Merlin, a master of the magic arts, had given a magic mirror to Britomart's father as a means of defense against all foes, as it revealed all of their hostile schemes and plans. In its strange globular shape one could see whatever one wished of faraway affairs and future events.

One day, by chance, Britomart wandered into the closet where the mirror was stored and observed herself as she looked into it. Then, very maidenlike, she asked it to show her the man she would one day marry. Instantly, in the mirror a heroic knight appeared, his crest and shield and armor all clearly seen. The man in the mirror was a stranger to Britomart, and although she liked what she saw, she thought little of it at the time.

But Cupid's arrow had been fired and had found its mark, but "so slyly that she did not feel the wound." That night, though, she felt it, and so it was night after night, as sleeplessly she wrestled with these new emotions.

Britomart's distress was correctly read by her aged maid, who well understood the telltale signs of a girl in love. But the old one's attempts at comfort brought no relief. The best she could do was hold out to the love-stricken girl the hope that Cupid had fired a second arrow—one straight to the heart of the man in the mirror.

But who was this love and where was he? A visit to the church brought no help; neither did a ghastly potion made from milk and blood and three hairs from Britomart's head, together with sundry other ingredients. The girl desperately moaned, "Neither God of love, nor God of sky, can do that which cannot be done." But the old woman, devastated to see Britomart suffer so, vowed that they "by wrong or right" would go forth "and find that loved knight."

And so they went. First they went to Merlin, maker of the mirror, feeling, no doubt, that the magician had some responsibility in the matter. They found him in his deep cavern where few people ever dared to go. Braving the eerie environs of his hideaway, they approached the wizard among the strange lights, shapes, smells, and sounds that are a wizard's wont.

Before the women told him, Merlin knew the purpose of their visit, and he smiled. Then, going into a long discourse, he told Britomart what children she would bear and how her progeny would be important in the world. The old woman, however, had a more immediate matter on her mind: "How shall we know him, and how shall we find the man?"

Merlin's reply was concise and to the point: "The man whom the heavens have ordained to be the spouse of Britomart is Arthegall." Britomart, clad in an armor her father had taken from a Saxon queen, set out then to find her man; at last she found him, or he found her, or the two of them found each other, and the magician's prophecy proved true in the end. But this is another story.

Now, we sometimes speak of wanting Merlin's magic mirror to see into the future and find answers to our questions. One further word in regard to this tale: It's one of a great number from the long, Old English poem of Edmund Spenser, *The Faerie Queen*, written in 1596.

Midas Touch   Back in the days of primitive Greece, a fellow named

Midas was the king of Phrygia, and he was very rich. But like many people who have a lot of something, Midas wanted more gold.

The god Silenus was a lesser deity in the court of Dionysus, a king among gods. One day while out in his realm, Midas came upon Silenus sleeping under a tree, drunk. When Silenus was somewhat recovered from his inebriation, Midas asked that the god teach him wisdom.

In response, Silenus told Midas of two cities somewhere in another world. One of these was Eusebes, a city of great piety, where the inhabitants were always so happy that even when they died they were laughing. The other was Machimus, a city prone to warfare, whose citizens were born fully armed and spent their entire lives fighting. Although these cities were so different, they had one thing in common: Both were very rich. In both cities, gold was as common as iron is in most places.

Without a doubt, Midas was impressed with this, especially with the part about the gold. Later, Silenus again came wandering through the kingdom of Midas, and this time the king's minions arrested him for vagrancy and brought him in. Midas recognized Silenus and ordered that he be returned to the court of Dionysus.

In gratitude, Dionysus offered to grant any wish of Midas. Very little time was required for Midas to decide to take advantage of this golden opportunity: He wished that everything he touched would turn to gold. Dionysus smiled a bit upon hearing this request, but he had promised, so he granted the wish.

Elated, Midas believed he now had everything going his way; merely by touching it, he could change the most worthless trinket into precious, gleaming gold. However, along about dinner time, he made a disturbing discovery: The food he tried to eat turned into gold before he could swallow it. He was afraid to touch his wife or children, and with good reason. That night he went to his bed hungry, lying sleeplessly on a pillow of gold and under a blanket of the same stuff.

As soon as morning came, and Dionysus had opened his office for the day's business, Midas was knocking at his door. "Please take away this awful gift," he begged. Dionysus did, and one suspects he smiled again, a knowing kind of smile that said, "I hope this character has learned something."

Often in our day we speak of the Midas touch, referring to one's ability to accumulate a lot of money with apparent ease, meaning usually that one just can't miss, that every venture turns out successfully.

Millennium   *See* ARMAGEDDON.

Monkey on Your Back   An offending or handicapping condition is commonly referred to as a monkey on your back, especially if you can't get rid of the problem. A shortened form of the expression may be heard as one impatiently or angrily says to another, "Get off my back!"

Where does this expression come from? From Aesop and one of his many fables. The story begins with a sailor who started off on a long voyage, taking with him a monkey whose antics would provide amusement for him and the ship's crew. As the vessel approached the shores of Greece, a violent storm arose, the ship sank, and all on board were forced to swim for their lives.

Monkeys aren't known as swimmers, and this one was no exception. As he was splashing about in the water, in terror of drowning, a gentle, friendly dolphin came swimming by. Believing the monkey a man, and always ready to befriend humans, the dolphin dived under the struggling creature and surfaced with the monkey safely atop his back.

Heading for shore, the dolphin was compelled to listen to the monkey's prattle about what a fine fellow he was and how very important a personage. Growing weary of all this boasting, the dolphin began to wish himself free of the insufferable bore.

As they neared the Grecian coast, the dolphin politely asked, "Are you an Athenian, sir?" The monkey replied that he was indeed, descendant, of course, of one of the most noble families of that fine city. As the monkey continued in pursuit of this new line of self-praise, the dolphin broke in with a second question. "Do you know the Piraeus?" he asked. The monkey heartily replied that certainly he did know him, that the Piraeus was a splendid citizen and a good friend for many years.

What the lying braggart didn't know was that the Piraeus was not a person at all, but the name of the harbor at Athens. The dolphin, of course, knew this; he now knew that he had not only a bore and braggart on his back but a liar as well. Completely fed up with this ungrateful pretender, the dolphin was now more than ever eager to be rid of him. But there was that monkey, hanging on as though his life depended on it, which it did in fact.

While monkeys aren't good swimmers, dolphins are, and they swim equally as well underwater as on top of it. So down went the dolphin, diving deep into the sea, taking the monkey with him. In due time, the dolphin came up, but not the monkey. The dolphin had found a clever way to rid himself of the unwelcome burden on his back. Fortunately, we don't currently use this expression with such a final intent in mind.

Musical Charm of Orpheus   Reference is often made to the musical charm of Orpheus. One may wish for his skill or to be able to do with music the kinds of things he did. That music has power is a fact long known, and for 3,000 years Orpheus has stood as the classic embodiment of this truth.

Ancient Greeks looked upon their gods and demigods pretty much as oversized humans, as having ordinary human qualities of personality and character while possessing extraordinary powers. Orpheus was one of these, a son of Apollo, himself a divine musician and possessor of a golden harp. In early childhood Orpheus manifested musical talents in keeping with his family heritage.

Frequently he would go out for long periods of time and play his lyre among the fields and grasses and rocks and hills. Here the birds stopped their songs to listen to his. The bees sat still among the flower petals, listening. Ants paused in their running about, and spiders ceased their spinning. No creature had ever before heard a lyre played so beautifully. As Orpheus became older, other creatures gathered round to listen—wolves, bears, lions, owls, and eagles. Even trees uprooted themselves and came to stand around him.

And the nymphs came. One of these, enchanted by the music of Orpheus, was Eurydice, and she later became his wife. As time went on, Orpheus used his musical skill to help many people. Among these were Jason and his Argonauts, who had to sail their ship close by the island where the Siren sisters operated a deadly scam, singing so enticingly that passing sailors were lured to their island and then destroyed. Jason took Orpheus with him on this voyage, and as they passed the Sirens' island, the music of Orpheus was so beautiful that the sailors chose not to hear the songs of the Sirens.

In time, though, tragedy came to Orpheus and his beloved Eurydice. She was bitten by a cobra, and the poison was so powerful that she had to leave this life and go down into the Underworld. Orpheus missed her, and with help from all the nymphs, searched everywhere for her. Exhausting all other possibilities, he concluded at last that she must have gone to the Underworld. No one who went there ever returned; but Orpheus so much desired to rescue his beautiful wife that he resolved to go anyway.

His music was so moving that the hard-hearted Charon forgot to charge his fare and ferried Orpheus across the River Styx into the Underworld, Hades. Playing his lyre, Orpheus made his way ever deeper into those dark regions. Souls in the terrible torment of their assigned punishments got a brief respite from their everlasting misery. Sisyphus had been condemned to roll a monstrous stone uphill forever, but he stopped to listen as Orpheus passed, as did the daughters of Danaus who had been doomed to the eternal task of drawing water in a sieve.

King Pluto and his queen Proserpina were the administrators of that horrible place and were known to be cruel and unrelenting in their judgments. But even their hearts were softened by the music of Orpheus. They agreed to permit Eurydice to return with Orpheus, provided that she would follow him and that, until they were completely out of Hades, he would never turn and look back. He had to believe she was following him, and this was hard for him to do.

But he did it—almost. When in sight of the world of light and freedom, hearing no sound behind him, and overwhelmed by anxiety and doubt, Orpheus could bear it no longer and turned. Eurydice was there; for an instant he saw her, reaching out to him, but then she faded into the darkness. She was gone; he had lost her. Heartbroken, he made his way out of the place.

From that time, it was only sad music that came from the lyre and voice of Orpheus, heartbreaking to all who heard it. He retired into the mountains. And some said that ever afterward, when the wind blew from the summits, they could hear the wailing, mourning sound of music. (See also SIREN SONGS.)

My Name Is Mud   "If I go golfing with Jim, my name will be mud," says Joe, knowing he promised to bring his kids to the playground. And Johnny, after school, says to Marianne, "If I don't go straight home, my name will be mud." The meaning is obvious: When in disfavor, one's name is mud. But why mud? Why not some other disagreeable thing? Well, partly, at least, because of Dr. Samuel Alexander Mudd, a physician. The expression had a limited use before Dr. Mudd came on the scene, but it was his involvement that gave it household status and a permanent place in our common speech.

The story begins just five days after General Lee's surrender at Appomattox; Americans, South and North, were breathing their first sighs of relief that the horrible struggle was over. It was the evening of April 14, 1865, and the weary president, seeking a small respite from the awesome burdens of his office, sat in a balcony box at Ford's Theater in Washington. A frustrated actor named John Wilkes Booth sneaked in behind Mr. Lincoln and shot him in the head. Leaping from the balcony and breaking a leg in the leap, the assassin managed to escape. At 4:00 the next morning, he and a fellow conspirator were at the farmhouse door of Dr. Samuel Mudd near Bryantown, Maryland.

As any good physician would, the doctor set the stranger's broken leg, and later that day the two men rode away. Within a few days, it became known that the doctor's patient had been Lincoln's assassin. Together with many others, Dr. Mudd was arrested and charged with involvement in the murder plot. In the hysteria of the time, the fact that Mudd had been a Confederate sympathizer was enough to condemn him in the minds of many people.

Although no evidence was ever presented that the doctor was in any way implicated in the plot to kill Lincoln, a military tribunal declared him guilty. Sentenced to life imprisonment, he was incarcerated at old Fort Jefferson in the Gulf of Mexico. Feelings of hostility were so strong against him, especially in the North, that his very name became an epithet denoting disfavor.

The popular attitude toward the man was wholly unjustified, as was clearly indicated by passing time and subsequent events. During an epidemic of yellow fever at Fort Jefferson, the prisoner exhibited exceptional heroism. At risk of his own life, he ministered selflessly to the ill and the dying. Falling victim to the fever himself, he survived;

but with his health gravely impaired, he was later to die at age forty-nine from effects of the disease.

Because of the physician's unselfish service during this crisis, and because of increasing doubts concerning his guilt, Dr. Mudd was granted a presidential pardon by Andrew Johnson in 1869. Over the ensuing years, numerous legal measures have been taken to clear his much-maligned name. Tragically, though, in those first awful years the damage was done—his name is still "Mudd."

– N –

Naboth's Vineyard   See DRIVE LIKE JEHU.

Namby-Pamby   Over the centuries, some raging battles have been fought in the arenas of literature and art, not with spears and swords but with tongue and pen. Eminent creative individuals, in many instances of the jealous or picayunish types, have often quarreled with one another in spiteful controversy.

One such fracas provided a stimulating topic of conversation in the literary circles of early eighteenth-century England. Mostly, it pitted Alexander Pope (1688–1744) against Ambrose Philips (1674–1749), with Pope on the offensive.

Philips, Cambridge-educated and ambitious, won early acclaim for his poetry. In time, finding a better market for the more frivolous material, he largely abandoned the erudite for the popular, turning out a great deal of the insipidly sentimental, including a considerable amount for children. The public loved it and purchased it. Sales soared, and this stirred considerable resentment among other writers whose works weren't selling nearly so well.

One of these, a close associate of Pope, was Henry Carey, who, in mockery of Philips, published a parody of Philips' rather infantile verse. He even came up with a burlesque on Philips' very name. The name *Ambrose* in common speech often shortened to *Amby*, Carey gave that contraction a sort of baby inflection resulting in *Namby*. *Namby* Philips? No; *Pamby* went well with *Namby*, so Pamby it was— "Namby-Pamby." Carey wrote:

Namby-Pamby's doubly mild,
Once a man and twice a child.

Alexander Pope, reigning sovereign of English literature at the time, arose to his full four-foot-six and joined in the fray. He thought Namby-Pamby a fit appellation for Philips, and for years used it often with all the stinging force of his notoriously vitriolic pen.

Thus, Namby-Pamby, first applied derisively as a man's contemptuous nickname, quickly became identified with the man's work—insipidly nice, nauseatingly sweet, and childishly affected—and then, of course, with anyone or anything of similar character—indecisively weak, wishy-washy, and slushily sentimental. So, a namby-pamby person isn't exactly the most vital or vigorous citizen on the block.

Narcissism   Out of early Greek mythology comes the intriguing tale of Narcissus and Echo. Narcissus was a remarkably handsome young man, a real heartthrob for all women. Echo was a nymph, once a servant of the goddess Hera, but having displeased her mistress, she had been deprived of all power of speech except to repeat words already spoken by someone else.

Many young women were strongly attracted to Narcissus, but their attentions were always spurned by him, and usually quite rudely. He was passionately stuck on himself, preoccupied with his own appearance, his own good looks. Numerous women's hearts were irreparably broken by his callous indifference to their feelings.

Echo, like many others, became a casualty of the attention that Narcissus lavished exclusively upon himself. Out in the forests and mountain wastelands, she pined away for him until nothing was left of her but her voice.

Then one day it happened: Narcissus saw his own face. Mirrors were not common in those days, and until that point Narcissus had only imagined what he looked like. On this fateful day, though, he stopped to drink at a clear, still mountain pool. There, looking up to him from the water, was a face, his own, to him the most ravishingly beautiful face he had ever seen. "Oh you beautiful creature," he whispered, "I love you."

Narcissus reached out his hands, but the instant his fingertips touched the water the image became distorted and disappeared. As the water became quiet again, the face reappeared, but then vanished each time Narcissus tried to touch it. In extreme frustration and confusion, the young man stood above the pool, and the image he loved was distorted by his own falling tears.

He cried out, "Alas! Alas!" and from somewhere in the distance he heard Echo answer, "Alas! Alas!" As she had pined away for him, now there by that pool he pined away for himself. Then by that pool he died, and in that place a flower sprang up and bloomed. It was called the Narcissus.

The final picture we see of this vain youth is that of his soul traveling to the Underworld, crossing the Stygian River, leaning over the edge of the boat, trying to catch a look at himself in the water.

Narcissism is an overindulgent self-love. A narcissistic approach to life is characterized by an utter preoccupation with oneself, especially with one's form or appearance.

Never Never Land   Never Never Land is a fantasy world. It's the land where most of the action occurs in the story of Peter Pan, the 1904 creation of J. M. Barrie. Initially, Barrie's mythical land of nowhere was simply "Never Land"; the second "Never" was added later. The tale is a highly imaginative venture in whimsy.

On the day of his birth, Peter heard his mom and dad discussing what they'd like him to be when he became a man. But Peter didn't want to be a man, not ever. So, on that very day he ran away and went to live with the fairies; their mailing address was Second to the Right and then Straight On Till Morning.

Although a resident of fairyland, Peter did some rambling about in the grown-up world. Loving stories, he often visited the home of Mr. and Mrs. George Darling, for here he could listen in as Mrs. Darling told bedtime stories to her three children, Wendy, Michael, and John. But one night the maid slammed the window shut so quickly that it caught his shadow on the sill, and he had to leave without it. Sure that the intruder would return for his shadow, the maid rolled it up and put it in a dresser drawer.

Well, Peter did return, along with Tinker Bell, an ordinary fairy of the jealous type whose job in fairyland was to mend pots and kettles. They rescued Peter's shadow at last, but in the process awakened the three Darling children. Quite ready for an adventure, the children excitedly accepted Peter's invitation to go away with him, for he promised to show them how to fly.

In Never Never Land lived the Lost Boys, all of them children who had fallen from their baby carriages and had gone unclaimed for seven days. (There were no girls, because they were too smart to fall from a carriage.)

Also in Never Never Land lived a nasty band of pirates under the leadership of Captain Hook. One of the Lost Boys had chopped off one of Hook's arms and fed it to a crocodile, who liked it so much he salivated hungrily for the rest of Hook. In addition, there were the Red Indians; these were friendly men who guarded and helped the boys in many ways.

After a long time and many adventures, the little Darlings decided it was time to go home—after all, mom and dad might become worried about them. Homeward bound, the party was captured by Captain Hook; but Peter came to the rescue, Hook jumped into the sea, and the crocodile got him.

Home at last, Wendy, Michael, and John were joyously welcomed, and Peter, who always looked upon Wendy as mother, was urged to remain with them. But flying away, he proclaimed to Mrs. Darling, "No one is going to catch me, lady, and make me a man!"

So today we often speak of someone who has impractical or fanciful ideas as living in Never Never Land.

Niobe's Tears   To speak of Niobe's tears is to speak of perpetual weeping. A reference to the tears of Niobe suggests a grievous sorrow undiminished by passing time. Niobe, a personality of Greek mythology, was a daughter of Tantalos, the wife of Amphion, and the queen of Thebes. And, as it turned out, she had a lot to cry about.

Niobe was the proud mother of seven sons and seven daughters. Although many mothers are proud of their children, Niobe was proud of herself for having them. Because on fourteen occasions she had given birth, she vainly vaunted herself as a person to be esteemed above others. It was this vanity that brought her an awful grief and a flow of tears that never ceased.

The goddess Latona was the mother of only two children, Apollo and Diana, and because Niobe was the mother of seven times as many, she thought herself superior to the goddess.

At an annual celebration honoring Latona, Niobe appeared among the celebrants, shouting to them, "Why all this attention paid to Latona and none to me? I have fourteen children and she has only two. I am rich with a great abundance of everything, and I shall remain so. I am too strong for ill fortune ever to put me down. I deserve your worship more than Latona ever can!" Niobe soon learned, however, that goddesses do not look kindly upon competition.

Niobe's haughty challenge greatly angered the goddess. A little while afterward, giving vent to her anger, she called her two children and sent them to Thebes on a mission of revenge. From their mother's abode high in the Cynthian mountain, Apollo and Diana flew fast through the air to Thebes. Here they alighted on the towers at the palace courtyard. From these towers they carefully aimed their arrows and fired down among the people until all seven of Niobe's sons lay dead.

As the seven daughters then gathered around in mourning, seven other arrows came streaking from the towers, each finding its mark, and the seven daughters joined their brothers in death. Sitting there among the bodies of her slaughtered children, Niobe began to weep and to rail vehemently against Latona. This wailing and railing continued unabatedly for many days. Then, at last, deciding she had heard enough, Latona turned Niobe into stone.

But the tears continued to flow; the railing had stopped, but not the tears. Much later, a powerful wind lifted the stone and carried it away to a nearby mountainside, where today there is a stone from which drops of water always flow. Some say these drops are the never-ending tears of Niobe.

Not Worth a Continental   For a century and a half, a few thousand Europeans had tenaciously clung to the eastern shoreline of North America. A spirited and adventurous people, they had gradually increased in number over the years and acquired an identity all their own. Increasingly weaned from the motherlands, they drew closer to one another. They considered theirs the wilderness they had struggled to tame.

When these colonists organized themselves to make their bid for independence, their organization was expansively named the Continental Congress. To finance the struggle for freedom, the Continental

Congress issued paper money, although there was nothing more tangible than the commitment and resolve of the people to back it up. This money, issued in the amount of $200 million, was called continental currency. Inevitably, it rapidly declined in value. To make matters worse, a Tory sympathizer named Isaac Clements became quite proficient at counterfeiting "continentals." Soon, $40 of continental were required to purchase one silver dollar.

Among colonial folks, the near-worthless money became something of a byword. Whatever was considered of little value was said to be "not worth a continental." One wishing to express indifference might say, "I don't care a continental," meaning not at all. This phrase expressing worthlessness has survived for more than two centuries, and we still use it.

By the end of the Revolutionary War, the American colonies and their Continental Congress were virtually bankrupt. With a debt of $44 million borrowed from the citizens and $10 million owed to Holland and France and no power to collect taxes, the infant nation was at the point of dying. But what the new nation lacked in economic assets it had in people and personal commitment.

There was, for example, Alexander Hamilton. Treasury secretary in the administration of President Washington, this zealous patriot negotiated the payment of all debts and even arranged for the reimbursement of individual states in the amount of $20 million.

Well, as we know, the infant republic eventually grew up to become a giant among nations, with currency highly valued everywhere in the world. Their legacy, however, lingers in our English speech. Although their money was weak, the people were strong.

– O –

Odyssey A long journey of the wandering or rambling variety is an odyssey. The journey may be geographical or it may be mental or philosophical. But any kind of travel, especially if the itinerary is involved or complicated, is commonly known as an odyssey.

Why? Because approximately 3,000 years ago a remarkable literary craftsman created an epic poem that was known in ancient times and is a classic today. This master storyteller was Homer, and his epic is a story in two parts, *The Iliad* and *The Odyssey*, the former being the story of the Trojan War and the latter the story of one man's struggle to reach his home when the war was over.

This man was Odysseus, the Latin Ulysses. Following the ten-year war at Troy, Odysseus spent another decade in a passionate struggle against awesome odds to reach Ithaca, his home. He was an important person, the respected king of Ithaca.

Odysseus began that homeward trek with twelve ships and their crews, traveling across the Aegean Sea, a voyage that usually took only several weeks. But Poseidon, god of the sea, did everything possible to prevent his passage, and Odysseus had to suffer through harrowing disasters and trials of every kind.

Having lost all his ships and men, and now floating on a makeshift raft, Odysseus was caught in a frightful storm and driven to the shore of a land unknown to him. It proved to be the land of the Phaeacians where Alcinous was king. The king's daughter was a helpful friend, finding the exhausted Odysseus at the shore and taking him to her father. It was Alcinous who assisted Odysseus finally to reach his home.

While Odysseus was the guest of Alcinous, the host arranged an elaborate banquet in his honor. At this banquet Odysseus was invited to tell the story of his journey. He did so, and this first-person account (running to about 25,000 words) constitutes the main body of Homer's magnificent poem.

Thus, in Homer's telling of it, the long and convoluted wanderings of Odysseus is *The Odyssey*. And such travels are odysseys still.

Open Sesame   As this yarn develops, it would appear more appropriately entitled *Morgiana, Heroine of Ali Baba's House*. Instead, it is named *Ali Baba and the Forty Thieves*. From *The Arabian Nights*, this is the story.

Ali Baba's brother Kasim had married wealth and was therefore well-to-do; but Ali Baba was a poor man. However, he discovered the cave where a band of forty thieves stashed all their loot, and learned the password by which the entrance door could be opened. Using the words "open sesame," he was able to steal from the thieves two ass-loads of gold.

Mrs. Ali Baba, agog over all that gold, rushed over to Kasim's house to borrow a scale to weigh it. Her sister-in-law, being instantly curious as to what her poor relatives could possibly have that would require weighing, was determined to find out, and so she put a bit of wax in the bottom of the scale pan. Of course, in the weighing some of the gold stuck to the wax, and when the borrowed scale was returned the secret was revealed. His dear, loving brother threatened to turn him in to the authorities unless he shared the secret, so Ali Baba complied.

Promptly, Kasim sought the cave, and finding it unguarded, spoke the magic password, and the great stone door opened. He entered and the door closed behind him. In frenzied excitement, he gathered huge amounts of gold and stacked it near the cave's entrance; but when ready to open the door, he was unable to remember those two critical words. "Open barley," he cried, but nothing happened. Desperately, he called out the names of many small grains—all he could think of—but never *sesame*.

The thieves found Kasim in their cave when they returned. They killed him, of course, then quartered his body and hung two quarters on either side of the entrance. These were found by Ali Baba on his next visit and delivered to the grieving widow, who hired a local tailor to sew them back together and fit the reconstituted corpse with a funeral garment. After the official mourning ritual, Ali Baba married the widow, and moved himself and his other wife into Kasim's fine domicile.

From here on, the plot becomes really involved. Let it simply be said that those thieves thought it advisable to eliminate the prying snoop who had discovered the secret of their cave, namely Ali Baba. Ali Baba's slave girl Morgiana, by her wits, saved his neck (literally) on numerous occasions.

On one of these occasions, she scalded to death thirty-seven of the thieving fellows by pouring boiling oil into the thirty-seven jars in which they were lying in wait for the signal to pounce on her master. In the end, she got the robber captain himself by interrupting her after-dinner dance long enough to stab him to death. This gave her master sole access to that cave. And thus did Ali Baba come away from the fracas with millions in gold and one additional wife.

Quite a tale, with virtually no evidence of honor or integrity to be found. But those two words, *open sesame*, have long occupied a place of respectability in our language. We are likely to speak of any unfailing means of achieving an end as an open sesame.

– P –

Pandemonium The story is *Paradise Lost*, (1667), by John Milton, an epic poem and an all-time classic. Vivid in its description, dramatic in its action, and powerful in its imagery, the poem was a blockbuster in its time and has stood ever since as one of the giants of literature.

There was a rebellion in heaven led by Satan with Beelzebub. Heaven's forces were led by Michael and Gabriel. But it was heaven's Prince, God's own Son, who at last threw the rebels out.

Down they fell, "hurled headlong flaming from the ethereal sky," into "loss of happiness and lasting pain." It was dismal there. "One great furnace flamed, yet from those flames no light," "where peace and rest can never dwell [and] hope never comes."

Here Satan rallied his defeated horde, talking still of their "glorious enterprise," vowing never to bow or "sue for grace," but "to wage by force or guile eternal war." He proclaimed, "To do ought good will never be our task, but ever to do ill our sole delight." Vowing "it better to reign in Hell than serve in Heaven," he set about to reign.

So Satan called a strategy session of all his slimy, sleazy hosts. The word went out of a "solemn Council forthwith to be held at Pandemonium, the high capital of Satan and his peers." Prior to Milton's writing of this line, the word *pandemonium* had not been seen or heard. He invented it, assembled it of three parts, the Latin *pan* meaning "all," and *demon* meaning "evil spirit," together with the suffix *ium* indicating place or location. Hence, *Pandemonium* became "a gathering place of all demons."

Occupied as it was by incorrigibles, the place Milton described was one of discord, chaos, confusion, and therefore with the noise of every horrendous thing. It was inevitable, given the state of human affairs, that Milton's new word would enter permanently into the language. So it did; pandemonium is any state of chaotic uproar, whether among demons or otherwise, most commonly otherwise.

The Pandemonium conferees made a momentous decision. Realizing that war could never be won in heaven, they declared war on earth, and Satan was assigned to lead the attack.

Pandora's Box   Among the personalities that run through Greek mythology, it is often hard to know where the divine ends and the human begins. To complicate matters even more, between the two extremes there is a whole gamut of intermediate creatures whose status is open to interpretation.

Prometheus, although earth-born, appears to have been a god, but his brother Epimetheus was unquestionably human. Another difference between these two was that Prometheus was very wise and his brother rather stupid.

Prometheus was sympathetic with humanity and tried to do nice things for humankind. Zeus, the high god, however, did not wish humankind to achieve too much or to become too godlike, and Zeus was angry with Prometheus for being so friendly with the humans. So he devised a plan to hurt Prometheus and to produce havoc among humans. To achieve his purpose, Zeus ordered the creation of a woman, asking several of the lesser gods each to contribute some quality of character or personality.

The woman's name was Pandora, the name meaning "all-gifted," for the gods had put some of almost everything into her when they made her. When she was all finished and ready to go, Zeus sent her to Epimetheus, that slow-witted brother of Prometheus. Prometheus had warned his brother never to accept any gift from Zeus; but Pandora looked pretty good to him, so he took her in and made her his wife.

As part of his plot, Zeus sent along with Pandora a certain mysterious box. It was tightly sealed, and Pandora had been warned to never, never open it. Zeus had loaded that box with all kinds of evils, plagues, pestilences, and calamities—things that up until that time had never afflicted humanity.

Well, one of the ingredients one of the gods had put into the makeup of Pandora was curiosity, and no doubt Zeus was counting on that, for it was important in his plan. Being curious about its contents, Pandora had a strong yearning to find out what was in that box. Pandora begged her husband for permission to open the box, and Epimetheus let her do it.

Instantly, all sorts of shadowy shapes came flying out; all the problems, disasters, conflicts, and hatreds known now to humans came out of that box. Realizing that something was amiss, Pandora quickly slammed the lid, but it was too late, for all those evils were already released into the world.

Then from inside the closed box Pandora heard a voice, the voice of yet another begging to be let out. Hope, you see, had been packed at the very bottom of the box, and before Hope was able to get out, Pandora had closed the lid. Now Hope was clamoring to be set free. Pandora had a decision to make: Would she let Hope out? Looking back through history, some say Pandora let Hope out, some say she didn't, and the tale is variously told.

But what is most notable about that box is all the other stuff that came out of it, making the box a lasting part of our language. To open a Pandora's box is to set in motion a connected series of misfortunes that can be neither controlled nor terminated.

Pantagruelian *See* GARGANTUAN.

Panurge Question To ask for information intending to argue with the answer or to ask advice merely to contradict the one who gives it are Panurge questions.

This Panurge character was a brainchild of François Rabelais, creator of the Gargantua stories. Gargantua had a son, Pantagruel, and Pantagruel's companion was Panurge. In their many and varied adventures, Panurge proves himself a jolly rascal, a licentious, intemperate libertine, a braggart, and a coward.

Always in debt, he knows 63 ways of making money and 214 ways to spend it. He is an insufferable know-it-all. There is one question, though, for which he doesn't know the answer or pretends not to: Should he marry?

He is forever pestering everybody for opinions and advice on this critical issue. Seeking his answer, he casts lots and tries to interpret dreams; he consults a theologian, a poet, a philosopher, a physician, a court fool, and a varied mix of others. He argues vigorously that no means yes and yes means no.

In a typical conversation between Pantagruel and Panurge, Panurge will ask, "Should I marry?" Pantagruel will answer, "Yes," but Panurge will offer some strong objection, to which Pantagruel will respond, "Then don't marry." Panurge will then say, "I had my heart set on it," and Pantagruel will reply, "By all means, then marry." So the exchange continues, for every "yes" a rebuttal offered, and for every "no" some reason why marriage will be best.

As a last resort, Panurge, accompanied by Pantagruel, makes the perilous trip to her distant island to consult the Oracle of the Bottle. With all the importance of bottles to these two, they feel there ought to be some wisdom there somewhere. But there isn't; even the answer of the Oracle, like everything else, is inconclusive.

The whole story seems to be much ado about very little, a vague venture into a wilderness of uncertainties. But this is not frivolous literature; it was written as a burning and bruising satire on the life and customs of sixteenth-century France, with its emptiness, futility, and hypocrisy. (See also GARGANTUAN.)

Patience of Job   "The patience of Job" comes from a remarkable story in the biblical book of Job. The central character is the man whose name is also the book's title. We do not know when Job lived. He lived in the land of Uz, but of its whereabouts we know nothing. Job was a mighty Mideastern patriarch who had seven sons and three daughters, 7,000 sheep, 3,000 camels, 500 yoke of oxen, and many other possessions. And he was a righteous, good man.

There came a time when the "sons of God" presented themselves in heaven, and among them was Satan. God said to Satan, "Where did you come from?" A good question, since obviously Satan was out of place in such company. Unabashedly, though, he replied that he had come "from going to and fro on the earth, and walking up and down on it." Cynically, Satan saw himself as master of all he touched and boasted that the whole world was subject to his command, everyone pliable in his hands.

God asked, "Have you considered my servant Job?" Satan shrugged, smugly confessing, "Yeah, I have, and I'll admit he's still serving you, but not for nothing. He expects to get a lot out of it, and he does, because you are protecting him. If you took all he has away from him, he'd curse you to your face."

But God had confidence in his man. So God said, "Satan, you are free to do as you will with everything the man has. Only don't touch him personally." Gleefully, Satan went to work on Job, in fiendish delight, stripping him of almost everything. The Sabeans stole all Job's oxen and killed the drivers; lightning burned up all his sheep and the shepherds; the Chaldeans made off with all 3,000 of his camels; and then a windstorm brought down the house where Job's children were gathered, and all ten of them perished. Through all this, Job was unwavering in his faithfulness to God. He calmly said, "Naked I came into the world, and naked I shall go from it."

Again, there came a time when the "sons of God" were assembled before him, and again Satan was there. God said to him, "Satan, have you noticed that my man Job still holds fast his integrity?" Always ready with a glib reply, Satan said, "Yes, because everything a man has he will give for his life; but only touch Job's flesh and bone, and he will curse you to your face." Still having an unfaltering trust in Job, God said, "Okay, you may work on his person. Do anything to him—only do not kill him; don't take his life."

So, once again, Satan did his satanic thing, and Job was afflicted with awful sores from the soles of his feet to the top of his head. He sat in ashes and scraped his body with pieces of broken pottery. His wife said to him, "Curse God, and die." But curse God he would not, and die he did not, not then anyway.

Job bore his losses and sufferings with supreme patience and the best of good grace. Patiently, he endured the doubt and despair of his wife. When three opinionated friends came and burdened him with their own misguided notions as to the cause of his suffering, he bore this also with a patient fortitude.

And so it was throughout, until eventually the storm passed, and Job was restored to health and good fortune. Job's manner of moving through his long, dark valley of distress has earned for him a topmost position in the ranks of all who have endured trouble patiently. And people with similar temperaments are now said to have the patience of Job.

Pay the Piper   The town is real: Hamelin, on the River Weser in the northernmost quadrant of Germany. The story is legend: Dating from the fourteenth century A.D., it's a tale that has been told and retold from then until now, most impressively in a poem by Robert Browning.

Hamelin was overrun by rats. They ate the people's food, chewed up their clothing, harrassed them while they worked, and annoyed them unbearably when they tried to sleep. Nobody ever had the opportunity to do anything but fight rats.

The town council met in deliberation of the crisis. All were stymied, from the fat mayor to the last rat-bitten urchin in the streets. Nobody knew what to do. Just then, there was a knock at the council chamber door, a timid-sounding knock—or was it perhaps the scratchings of another rat?

When someone finally opened the door, a man came in. He was a strange fellow, tall, thin, and gimlet-eyed, dressed in a clown suit of red and yellow. He said he was the Pied Piper, and everybody could see that suspended from a scarf around his neck was a strange pipe made of reed. He said, too, that he could rid the town of rats; for, after all, in other places he had eradicated swarms of gnats and vampire bats, and a town full of rats would be an easy chore for a talent such as his.

"How much," the mayor asked, "will you charge to rid our town of rats?" "A thousand guilders," the stranger said. And everyone agreed they would gladly give even fifty thousand to have this done.

This decided, the stranger stepped into the street and commenced playing on that pipe. Strange sounds came out, but so did the rats. Out of the alleys and the houses, up from the burroughs and down from the attics, by the dozens they came, and then by the hundreds and the thousands, a seething black sheet of them, covering the cobbles and the lawns, screeching and squealing, following that piper as he piped, along the streets and across the fields, all the way to the deep, black water of the River Weser! And in they plunged, where they drowned. The exterminator had done his work; the rats were gone.

And now it was payday for the piper; those thousand guilders were now due. The mayor said, "Won't fifty do?" "All the rats are gone," he said, "and you are only a traveling clown; we pay you a thousand guilders? No, and there's nothing you can do about it!"

Again the piper stepped into the street and put the pipe to his lips, and again the strange notes came. But they were different this time. And this time it was the children who came to him; laughing and shouting, running and leaping, 130 of them. And so they followed the piper along the street all the way to the Weser.

Dumbstruck, the people saw the procession approach the water. At the last moment, though, the piper turned and headed straight toward the side of Koppleberg Hill. "This will stop him," the people thought. But no; as he drew near, a great cavern opened in the hillside, and, following the piper, the children all gleefully marched in, all but one, that is. The portal closed behind them, and no one ever saw the piper or the children again.

Oh yes, the piper must be paid, or else! The moral of this story is that nothing comes without a cost. If an opportunity seems too good to be true, it probably is. Remember that the piper who comes piping so enticingly today will come collecting tomorrow.

Peeping Tom   In the middle portion of the eleventh century A.D., a nobleman named Leofric was the Earl of Mercia and Lord of Coventry in Anglo-Saxon England. His wife's name was Godiva. We know very little about these people, but they are the chief figures of an engrossing legend that may or may not be fact.

On one occasion Leofric levied an exceptionally high tax upon the people of Coventry. Already an impoverished population, these peasants and tradesmen were now laden with an unbearable burden. Leofric's wife, a lady who kept in touch with the common people, was sympathetic with them in their plight. She approached the Earl with the suggestion that he reduce the tax, but with a shrug of unconcern, he refused—probably telling her that he would run the country and that she should stick to her household chores.

Godiva was not one to give up easily, however; she looked on these people as her friends and was quite willing to stand with them in their trouble. A champion of their cause, she became a mediator on their behalf, and they knew it. Persistently, she kept pestering her husband until eventually he grew a bit weary of it. One day, with the intent of terminating the matter, he said, "I'll never do this, never, until you ride naked at noon through the streets of Coventry."

If Leofric thought this would finish the issue, he didn't know his own wife well enough. She passed word to her friends all through the city, requesting that on a certain day at noon everyone remain in their houses with their shutters closed. Respecting the lady's wish, the people did this, and on that day Godiva mounted a snow-white horse and rode naked through the city, from end to end and back again. Incidentally, according to the lady's request, the tax was reduced!

There was one problem that day, though. A tailor whose name was Tom sneaked a peek through a knothole in his shutter and made the mistake of bragging about what he had done. He promptly lost his eyesight. Some said his blindness was a divine judgment. Others said that the divine action was assisted somewhat by local citizens with red-hot stove pokers.

Anyway, the infamous Tom is still remembered: Any man can be called a peeping Tom if he sneaks a lecherous look at a woman when she doesn't want to be seen. Someone who surreptitiously spies on another—for whatever reason—can also bear this same name. Remembered, too, is Godiva, too much perhaps for her famous ride and not enough for the fact that she was an early activist who passionately believed in getting things done.

Philadelphia Lawyer   A year before the birth of George Washington, a conniving bureaucrat named William Cosby was appointed governor of the British province of New York, replacing an industrious, strong-willed Dutchman named Rip Van Dam. The contrast between an honest government and the corrupt administration that followed it was all too apparent to the good citizens of New York province.

One of those citizens was a printer named John Peter Zenger, a man of conscience and courage. He had learned his trade under William Bradford, publisher of the *New York Gazette*, and during the tenure of Governor Cosby he was associated with James Alexander as publisher of a small rival newspaper, the *New York Weekly Journal*. The *Gazette* spoke for Cosby and his clique; the *Journal* dared to oppose him. The underhanded shenanigans of the governor, never mentioned by the *Gazette*, were faithfully reported by the *Journal*.

Cosby had Zenger arrested and imprisoned for libel, and Cosby's crony, Chief Justice James Delancey, refused to grant release on bail. Zenger was in prison nine months before finally being set free by verdict of one of the most important courtroom trials in American history.

Two local lawyers who undertook the defense of Zenger were promptly disbarred by action of the Chief Justice. As the months went by, the Zenger case became widely known and was discussed by many along the Atlantic coast.

In Philadelphia there was a lawyer, an elderly gentleman now retired from the practice of law, who learned of Zenger's plight. His name was Andrew Hamilton (not to be confused with Alexander). This venerable man offered himself as Zenger's defense attorney, and his offer was accepted. Then, without charge, he saw Zenger through more than a month of intricate courtroom drama.

It was a jury trial with the Chief Justice presiding. In those days, under British law truth was not an issue in cases of libel. The only issue was whether the accused had written or said the offending words.

Hamilton's first move was to admit that without question the defendant had written and published that with which he was charged and to suggest that therefore all witnesses be dismissed. This being done, the whole proceeding became a matter of legal argument. Attorney General Richard Bradley, acting as prosecutor, argued that even if Zenger's writings were true, they were not less libelous, but even more so according to British law.

In response, Hamilton declared that by this rationale "truth is a greater sin than falsehood." "There is heresy in law as well as religion," he said, and when such is brought to light, correction must be made. From August 4, 1735, until mid-September the arguments went doggedly on. Despite the Court's prejudice, Hamilton forcefully drove home the point that "free men" are "entitled to complain when they are hurt," that they are free to speak, that they cannot be impugned for speaking, but only for speaking *falsely*.

Arguments at last completed, the jury's decision came quickly; it was short and to the point: "Not guilty!" That day a new legal principle was established—the freedom to speak or write anything, as long as it is the truth. And fifty-two years later, that principle became a cornerstone in the constitution of a new nation, the United States of America. A cherished freedom, we call it the freedom of speech.

Well, Zenger was released from prison, Cosby's stranglehold on New York was broken, Hamilton was hailed as a hero, and out of this historic episode a new expression came lastingly into our English speech. A Philadelphia lawyer is a smart person. Facing a complex problem, people may say, "It would take a Philadelphia lawyer to figure out this one."

The expression has, however, suffered a perversion by some who think of lawyers as tricksters. For these, regrettably, a Philadelphia lawyer, instead of being a person of superior ability, is a shyster and a charlatan. Both historically and actually, the perversion is unfortunate.

Philippic   A philippic is a long, harsh, and hostile speech directed against one person. It is sometimes said that instead of addressing the issues, candidates for public office may degenerate into delivering philippics against one another.

The expression is a linguistic holdover from some of the world's more significant history. After the death of Julius Caesar, Rome became embroiled in domestic strife as powerful men struggled for control. The astute and articulate Cicero launched a series of verbal attacks on Marc Antony, and these volatile speeches eventually cost him his life.

At Rome in Cicero's time were many students of Greek history. Being fully familiar with events of three centuries earlier, they put a name to the vitriolic orations of Cicero, calling them philippics.

Why? Because of Demosthenes, Greek patriot of the fourth century B.C. In his time, the Greek city-states, usually in competition and conflict with one another, were threatened from the north by Philip II of Macedon. The Macedonian, a master strategist, had a way of playing the states against each other, causing devastating effects on Greek morale.

Enter Demosthenes, an irrepressible Athenian lawyer who overcame crippling speech defects to master the art of public speaking. In 351 B.C., he delivered an historic oration against Philip, warning the people of the threat he posed to Greece and calling for their resistance. Over a ten-year period, Demosthenes continued to deliver vehement speeches against Philip.

At last, largely through the efforts of Demosthenes, Athens and Thebes joined forces to oppose the Macedonian, but they suffered decisive defeat at the battle of Chaeronea in 338 B.C. Two years later, Philip, falling victim to an assassin, was succeeded by his more famous son, Alexander the Great, who continued to dominate Greece. Upon the death of Alexander in 323 B.C., a far lesser light named Antipater came to power in Macedon and completed the subjugation of all the Greek states.

In the process, he demanded that Athens surrender its patriots, that is, all leaders who had opposed the Macedonian takeover. Yielding to this pressure, the Athenian Assembly voted for their condemnation. Demosthenes fled to the island of Calauria where in 322 B.C. he committed suicide. (For a century and a half then, the Macedonians controlled Greece—until the Romans came.)

Philistine   More than 3,000 years ago, the Israelites escaped from Egypt and finally arrived in Canaan. At about the time of their arrival, another group of wanderers also came. Coming from across the Mediterranean, these people settled close to the shore on the plains of Philistia; coming from the east across the Jordan, the Israelites mostly occupied the hill country. Their territories abutting and to some extent overlapping, these two peoples commingled somewhat and were often at war.

The Israelites considered themselves a special people, chosen by God as his representatives on Earth, and they saw the Philistines as an uncouth gang of rustics and uninitiated outsiders. As the records of ancient Israel were read and reread over the centuries, appearing in both Jewish and Christian literature, the reputation of the Philistines became well established; their name became virtually synonymous for the coarse and loutish.

The word *Philistine* is variously employed today, ranging from a spirit of good humor to that of outright derision. The people of ancient Philistia are long gone, but their name is still with us, and just maybe we unjustly malign them in its use. They had a fairly sophisticated form of government and they created beautiful pottery; but then, too, they had no compunction about punching out the eyes of a captured enemy.

Phoenix-like   We deal here with a legend that was ancient even in the time of ancient Egypt, a legend known and seriously regarded, not merely in a single culture or country but in many—the legend of the phoenix. The phoenix was a bird, not a family of birds or a member of one, but one bird—without ancestry, without progeny.

One of the most compelling concepts in mythology, the idea of the phoenix has a mystic aura about it and stands as a tantalizing synthesis of the primitive and the mysterious that can exercise the mind to the very limits of reason.

The bird was a noble creature, more like the eagle than any other, with the colors of red and gold. Herodotus, the Greek historian who is considered "the father of history," wrote that he saw the phoenix once—at Heliopolis in the sixth century B.C. But the bird's home was somewhere in Arabia, or so it was commonly believed. Here it built its nest of the limbs and leaves of spice trees, and from here it roamed about the world, its eerie presence felt in many places.

The phoenix had a life span, most believed, of 500 years. As its life cycle was drawing to a close, by the powerful fanning action of its wings, it set its nest ablaze and burned itself to death in the flames.

But this was not the end. From the ashes of its own burned body, the creature arose to live again, a new phoenix, commencing yet another cycle of 500 years. So it was, cycle after cycle, from the beginning of history until the fourth or fifth century A.D. About this time, the fabulous creature faded from the human consciousness, remaining only as a memory and subject of speculation.

And there has been much speculation. The phoenix has appeared in literature over the centuries, including one of Shakespeare's more applauded and puzzling poems, "The Phoenix and the Turtle."

Anciently, the phoenix was the Egyptian symbol for the sun, moving as it did in daily cycles, going down only to rise again. More recently, it has stood as a symbol of immortality, the doctrine that life survives death. Early in the Christian era, monastics often wrote of Christ as the "Phoenix of God," for, as was believed, he who had died was risen from the dead. Some scholars and philosophers have variously attempted to trace what has been called the phoenix cycle in world history, believing that at critical times and places this mystic creature has made its presence known.

Like the bird itself, its name has had remarkable power of survival. It can be found today on maps in various locations as the name of cities and towns; astronomers have given it to one of the constellations; airmen during World War II gave it to one of their planes (which, unfortunately, crashed mysteriously and did not rise again).

The name survives in our speech. To say that anything or anyone is phoenix-like is to say that thing or person has risen or has demonstrated the ability to rise from defeat or recover from adversity. Thus it may be said that, following the Second World War, Japan arose phoenix-like from the ruins of defeat.

The other use of the name results from a different aspect of the story: That bird was the only one of its kind. When we say of something that it is the phoenix of its kind, we mean that it is the only one, that there is no other like it.

Pollyanna   This delightful, irrepressible, freckle-faced little girl appeared first in 1913 when Eleanor Porter wrote the novel that bears her name. Pollyanna's parents both deceased, she came to the small town of Beldingsville to live with Polly Harrington, her middle-age aunt. The woman, although well-off financially, was withdrawn, austere, and bitterly negative about life. Her only guide for living was to do her duty, and this she did grimly.

It was this sense of duty that moved Miss Harrington to accept the care of Pollyanna, to whom she assigned a dark attic room and gave orders in the tone of a military disciplinarian. A woman with a chronic dislike for the company of others, she certainly didn't take well to having a child in the house, but duty demanded it. The newcomer found warm friendship, however, in Nancy, the housemaid, and Old Tom, the gardener.

Pollyanna, as her aunt would later say again and again, was "an extraordinary child." She loved people and she loved life; she had a caring heart, a hyperactive mind, and a tongue that wouldn't quit— she was a chatterbox. Hers was not, though, an idle chatter; it had purpose and was always well intentioned.

Pollyanna's father, a clergyman, had been deeply loved by his adoring daughter. From him, she had learned a kind of game she loved to play. It had come about when the little girl, wanting a doll, had been disappointed when no doll appeared. Instead, the one item from the barrel of used goods sent to the "home missionary" that no one else needed, and therefore Pollyanna might have, was a pair of crutches. To get crutches when she had hoped for a doll had been a bitter pill to swallow.

But Pollyanna's father had shown her that in this there was something to be glad about: She didn't *need* the crutches! Here had begun the "glad game" that she and her father had played together as long as he lived, and now that he was gone, she sought others with whom to play it. As Pollyanna saw it, in every situation, however disagreeable, there was always something to be glad about, and the game was to find it.

Having mastered the art of playing the game, Pollyanna brought it with her when she came to Beldingsville. Soon the outgoing, radiant, happy child had almost the entire community playing that game with her—and some of the residents played it among themselves! Mrs. Snow, the invalid; John Pendleton, when he was laid up with a broken leg; Paul Ford, the pastor in a time of deep discouragement; Jimmy Bean, a homeless boy; and others all around had found their spirits lifted, their skies brightened, and their zest for living restored when they played Pollyanna's game.

Then came the accident by which Pollyanna was temporarily paralyzed, and it was believed she would never walk again. It was hard then for her to play the game, but finally she could and did. Her invincible confidence that something of beauty and good could be found in every experience touched the lives of many people. Because of it, the lonely Dr. Chilton and the bitter Miss Harrington were brought together in joyous reunion, healing a lovers' quarrel that had parted them fifteen years before and had turned the woman into an embittered person.

In less than a year, the town of Beldingsville was dramatically transformed because one little girl had been steadfastly convinced that, if one looked hard enough, something good can be found in everything.

Pollyanna's creator later wrote another book, *Pollyanna Grows Up*. This unique character, though, has given her name a lasting place in our language. A dictionary will say that a Pollyanna is an excessively or persistently optimistic person.

In its common use, however, Pollyanna's name is given quite another twist. In a world where force is often more popular than love, a Pollyanna is usually seen as a person who is naive and unrealistic. In circles where the code word is power, the term *Pollyanna* is often used as a derogatory reference to a person who wishes to get things done in some kinder and gentler way. Too bad, really, that the child's good name should be so unfeelingly maligned!

Potemkin Front and Village   A Potemkin front is a false one. A

Potemkin village is an illusionary one. A Potemkin covering of any kind is intended to conceal the ugly, the evil, the offensive, or the otherwise undesirable. To give something a Potemkin cloak is to make it appear as what it is not. And the expression can relate to people as well as things.

Grigori Potemkin was one of the many lovers of Catherine II, empress of Russia. One of the last of a long list, many other men had preceded him to the royal bedroom. To start things off, although married to Emperor Peter III, Catherine was amorously involved with a fellow named Grigori Orlov. The two of them led a conspiracy to overthrow Peter. This was accomplished in June 1762, and Catherine replaced her ousted husband as the supreme ruler of Russia. A few days later, Peter was murdered, and thus began the thirty-four-year reign of Catherine the Great.

Toward the end of her reign came Potemkin, a field marshall of the Russian army. Largely through his efforts, the Crimea was conquered and in 1783 annexed as a part of Russia. Four years later, Potemkin arranged to have the empress make an inspection tour of her newly acquired territory.

The result was a spectacular road show. Traveling in royal splendor, the empress was accompanied by some of Europe's most important people—the king of Poland, the emperor of Austria, and diplomats of status from many countries. One of these was a Saxon named Helbig who afterward reported on the journey with somewhat exaggerated descriptions.

Helbig said that Potemkin had made extensive preparations for Catherine's visit, contriving at every point to impress the empress with the beauty and prosperity of the conquered land. According to his account, Potemkin had erected colorful facades in front of ugly old buildings to conceal the poverty and squalor that existed. He even constructed facades representing entire villages where there were none. The implication was that Catherine never detected the deception and that she went home believing the Crimea a much greater asset than it really was.

The Saxon's report may or may not have been true. In any case, the story was broadly circulated and widely believed at the time. If true, the high-flying empress would have been somewhat comforted by the fact that, among rulers, she was neither the first nor the last to have been deceived by underlings who have wished to insulate their leaders from conditions and problems in the real world.

Pound of Flesh   *See* SHYLOCK.

Procrustes and His Bed   Travelers in all times and places have been subjected to roadside rip-offs. There have long been those unsavory characters who lie in wait for the unwary. Sundry roadside enterprises have been set like traps to catch the unsuspecting, and many of these have been dens of extreme villainy.

But somewhere between Athens and Megara there was once, according to Greek mythology, a roadside establishment so utterly villainous that most others look like havens of rest by comparison. The proprietor was Procrustes, alias Damastes, meaning "the stretcher." He was a big fellow; in fact, he was called a giant.

His house stood close by the road, invitingly attractive to weary travelers. He always offered a ready welcome to all who came, never turning anyone away. But here the happy part of the story ends and the gruesome part begins.

Procrustes had in his house a massive iron bed, and always insisted that his guests sleep in it. In fact, he insisted so much that he tied them to it. A real stickler for detail, he also insisted that the occupant fit the bed. If the guest was too long, Procrustes cut him off using his big, broad double-bladed ax, removing as much as necessary of the feet and legs. If the occupant was too short, Procrustes stretched him on a diabolical system of racks and pulleys designed for the job.

Such inconsiderate treatment by the host always proved fatal to the guest, whereupon Procrustes tossed the remains out for the wild animals and confiscated all possessions of the deceased. He was, you see, simply a highway robber, although his mode of operation was somewhat unique.

All things, of course, must come to an end, even giants who make people fit beds. Procrustes came to his end when Theseus stopped by one day and decided enough was enough. He killed the grisly wretch by the very means that had been used to kill so many others. But the killer's name did not die with him.

Procrustes' bed has long occupied a significant place in language. One who wishes to speak of extreme ruthlessness may call it a Procrustean brutality. But our chief use of the expression is to denote a compulsory conformity, or an attempt at one. To set up a mode or standard and demand that all others accept it is to make a Procrustes' bed and expect everyone to lie in it. It is a Procrustean motivation that impels one to use drastic or violent means to obtain compliance with some narrow or shallow notion.

So has Procrustes' name acquired a unique place in our language. However, it has a quite limited use: It has not yet been used as the name for a chain of roadside inns (nor is it likely to be)!

Prodigal Son   A certain Mideastern gentleman owned a substantial amount of farmland, a large number of farm animals, and had many servants. More importantly, he also had two sons, both of whom worked with him about the place. The older son was a reliable workman who was usually faithful and punctual. The younger was a rather restless fellow, whose mind seemed to wander afar, and whose work often suffered from inattention.

One day this younger son approached his father with a radical and disturbing proposal. Knowing that he stood to inherit a portion of his father's wealth eventually, he said to his father, "Give me my portion now. I don't want to be a farmer anyway. I want to get what is mine, and go off on my own."

Saddened and troubled as he was, the father agreed to do as the young man requested. A few days later, after converting everything he could into cash, the youth packed his bags, waved a casual goodbye, and walked away. His grieving father, never really saying how deeply saddened he was, watched him go.

For the young man, the next few months were a real blast. He did a lot of things he had never done before, and a great many he perhaps should never have done at all. He made a lot of new friends and got a lot of invitations to all the most exciting places and the most lively parties. He was very popular, but somehow his popularity declined as his supply of money ran low, and by the time it was all gone, so were his friends.

Deciding he needed a job, he looked for one, but the best he could find was with a swine herder, feeding hogs. He had always hated hogs, as had all his ancestors, but there he was, actually caring for the ugly creatures in their pigpen. His pay was so meager he was soon hungry. He would gladly have eaten the husks from the corn the hogs ate, but somebody might catch him.

One day, the very desperate young man was struck by a sudden thought—to return home and become a hired servant in his father's house. So he went. As he approached the house, but was still a long way off, his father saw him coming. The old man shaded his eyes beneath an uplifted hand and strained to see; then his heart skipped a beat. And the old man broke into a run down the path. Meeting his son, he hugged and kissed him. Then calling all the family and all the servants with a great shout that brought them running, the father said, "Look! My son is back; he has come home. Go quickly, get my best robe and put it on him, and put the family ring on his finger."

Every family tried to have always at least one calf fat and ready for butchering for any occasion of surprise or joy. This family was no exception, and certainly this was an occasion of both surprise and joy. So the father said to the servants, "Go, butcher the fatted calf, and prepare a fine feast; for this son of mine who was as though dead is alive again." And it was done.

From this parable, first told by Jesus, we have two English expressions in common use. To "kill the fatted calf" is to go all out to show hospitality. A prodigal son is a wastrel who shows careless disregard for commonly accepted values or family traditions.

Promethean Fire, Power, and Peril   Prometheus was a Titan, as was Zeus, and the two were cousins. The Titans were in general a brutally lawless bunch of hoodlums. Zeus rebelled against them, opposing their oppressive and cruel practices in every possible way. He was later joined by Prometheus, and the two of them, in a major war of rebellion, sent almost the entire band of Titans down into the dark regions of Tartarus. Zeus then became the chief ruler of the universe, especially serving as the god of the heavens, while Poseidon ruled the sea and Hades the underworld.

On Earth, Prometheus took special interest in the affairs of the human creatures who were trying to establish themselves. He taught them useful skills, such as how to make bricks and erect houses and how to build ships and tame wild beasts. He imparted to them valuable knowledge of many kinds and gave them powers far superior to any other of the earthly creatures.

But the more power the humans acquired, the more they seemed to want. Despite their abounding ambitions, Prometheus loved them very much, unselfishly wishing to do his very best for them. In his zeal to be helpful, he perhaps overlooked the dangers involved, for these bumbling creatures were ill prepared to manage the godlike powers they sought.

The ultimate power was fire, and Prometheus resolved to get it for them. So he stole fire from the gods, the very fire of the sun itself, and he brought that fire to the Earth and placed it in the hands of humans. Now men could melt and shape iron to make swords and build chariots, and they did. It was soon apparent that the humans possessed a power that they lacked the wisdom and good judgment to control or use properly.

A serious problem developed: When employed by men, fire always lost its intrinsic and elemental purity, its divine quality. Thus, fire was profaned, this being a major sacrilege that deeply offended and angered Zeus. As punishment for Prometheus, Zeus had him chained to a great rock high in the Caucasian Mountains where for years he suffered the unbearable agony of having a bird each day eat his liver, which would then grow back.

But the harm was done; humans had in their hands the power of fire, whether they were capable of managing it or not. And so we often speak of Promethean fire, Promethean power, and Promethean peril to describe a human ability that is extremely hazardous for humanity.

Prometheus to Epimetheus   Sometimes when we wish to emphasize the vast difference existing between two extremes we may say it is all the way from Prometheus to Epimetheus.

Prometheus and Epimetheus were important people in Greek mythology. They were brothers, the sons of Iapetus and Clymene, and their names mean "forethought" (Prometheus) and "afterthought" (Epimetheus).

The difference in names was by no means their only distinction. Prometheus was intelligent and farseeing, while Epimetheus was dull and slow-witted. As cousins of Zeus, they were gods, sort of. Like all the other gods, they had major assignments in the early formation of the human race.

Epimetheus was given the job of equipping the animals for living on Earth, and in so doing, most people thought he really goofed. Carelessly, he bestowed the best gifts on the animals—fur for keeping them warm, feathers enabling them to fly, and a superior instinct for self-preservation.

Prometheus, who was in charge of equipping humans, had very little left to work with, for apparently his brother had gotten first dibs on the gift bank. Prometheus was able, however, to give humans the ability to stand up on two feet and he stole fire from heaven to put into human hands.

While Prometheus was always a benefactor of humankind, Epimetheus brought awful calamities upon humans. Wishing to release a big box of troubles upon the world, the gods selected Epimetheus as the one gullible enough to help them do it. They sent the box with Pandora, the woman who Epimetheus married immediately upon her arrival. Then despite the warnings of his brother, Epimetheus stupidly allowed her to open that box.

And so it does appear to have been a long way from Prometheus to Epimetheus—from forethought to afterthought.

Prophet Without Honor In His Own Country   It is often said that familiarity breeds contempt, and if not contempt, indifference. We tend to take for granted what is commonly present, even other people.

Here, for example, is the nuclear physicist, known and honored worldwide; but in his own home community he is known only as the head of a family, a good neighbor, and member of his service club and the PTA—and not one citizen in a thousand would walk across the street to hear him lecture on nuclear physics or anything else.

Early in the career of Jesus, he ran head-on into this pervasive trait of the human character. Having grown up in Nazareth, a small Galilean town, Jesus was known throughout the community as a worker in the village carpenter shop and a quiet pupil of the local rabbis. Then came the day, when he was about thirty, that he announced his singular mission and began to go about the surrounding country teaching, preaching, healing sick folks, and doing many remarkable things. His fame spread abroad, and no doubt word of it drifted back to Nazareth.

After a few months, now accompanied by a small band of followers, Jesus returned to Nazareth, not merely to visit but to teach. When he spoke in the local synagogue on the Sabbath day, his hearers were the townspeople who had watched him grow to manhood in their midst. The record says "they were astonished" and "were offended in him." They said to one another, "Where did this man get all this? Is not this the carpenter, the son of Mary, and brother of James and Joses and Judas and Simon, and are not his sisters with us?"

Those people could not entertain the thought that this local boy could possibly be anyone special; as Saint Mark reports, "This proved to be a hindrance to their believing in him."

The response of Jesus to all of this was to say simply, "A prophet is not without honor, except in his own country, and among his own kin, and in his own house." So saying, he summarized a persistent truth about our multifarious nature. Concerning the familiar, we suffer from a strange myopia, as we are unable to perceive the greatness of what is near—the prophet without honor in his own country.

Puck   See ROBIN GOODFELLOW.

Pyrrhic Victory   The ancient Grecian state of Epirus was situated on the Ionian Sea, less than 100 miles from the southern tip of Roman Italy. In the third century B.C., this state was ruled for about twenty-three years by Pyrrhus, a relative of the deceased Alexander the Great. Like his famous relative, Pyrrhus had visions of conquering the world.

In 280 B.C., leading an army of 25,000, he crossed into Italy in a major challenge to the might of Rome. In that year, his forces engaged the Romans under Consul Laevinius at Heracla. In this first large-scale battle between Greeks and Romans, the Greeks were victorious. Rome, however, refused to surrender or agree to any terms of peace.

A year later, at a place called Asculum in southern Italy, Pyrrhus again met the Romans in a major battle. It was a desperate struggle between huge armies, both composed of brave men with the best of training and equipment. Losses on both sides were awesome, but at last Pyrrhus and his Greeks drove the Romans from the field. As the victors counted their dead and wounded, it was apparent that the flower of the Grecian army had perished. When Pyrrhus was congratulated on the victory, his famous response was this: "One more such victory and we are lost!"

A Pyrrhic victory is one that costs too much. It's a bad deal when, in winning, one loses more than the victory is worth. And it happens not only on battlefields but sometimes also in personal relationships.

Four years after Asculum, the Romans decisively defeated Pyrrhus at Beheventom, and three years after that, he died, a refugee at Argos, killed when a woman flung down upon his head a tile from a rooftop. Like his celebrated kinsman, Alexander, his dream of conquering the world turned out to be only a dream.

– Q –

Quisling   A quisling is a traitor to one's country, or to anything else to which loyalty has been pledged. But not all traitors qualify as quislings. A quisling is a betrayer of the very worst kind. Some traitors are guilty of nothing more than giving an enemy information that may be hurtful to their own country. But Quisling, the original, the man who bore this name, was guilty of giving away much more than information: He gave away his country. Actually and physically, he turned it over to the enemy.

A Norwegian, Vidkun A. Quisling, born in 1887, received a military education, and in 1911 entered his nation's military service, taking an oath of allegiance to his country and king. For the next twenty years, he served Norway in various capacities, including positions at the embassies in Russia and Finland.

During the latter portion of this period, Adolf Hitler was rising to power in Germany, and Quisling developed a compelling admiration for the man. Early in 1933, Hitler became chancellor of Germany, and within the year, in imitation of Hitler, Quisling organized a Fascist party in Norway. Retiring from the military, he devoted the next few years to political activity, gathering around him a small group of well-organized Fascists.

By 1939 Hitler's armies had overrun much of Europe. Late that year, the Germans passed secret word to Quisling that Norway was next on Hitler's hit list. Quisling was ready in April 1940 when the Germans made a massive assault on Norway. King Haakon courageously refused to surrender, but Quisling and his cohorts seized the radio facilities at Oslo, declaring themselves in command of the nation. The king and his officers were forced to flee to England, where they established their government-in-exile, and the German conquerors installed Quisling as head of their government in Norway.

Having totally turned over his country and his people to Hitler and Hitlerism, Quisling became a Nazi puppet, ruling Norway while the German dictator pulled the strings in Berlin. Yielding to Hitler's every wish, Quisling obediently instituted his policies.

This continued until April 1945, when Hitler's tyranny came to its fiery end. So did Quisling's. The government-in-exile moved back to Oslo. Quisling was tried, found guilty of treason and the murder of more than 1,100 Norwegian citizens, and on October 24, 1945, was executed by firing squad. His actions were held in almost universal contempt, and the only legacy he left was his name, an odious byword for the most despicable of traitors, the very sounding of which seems to suggest insidious betrayal. Even before the end of World War II, masters of English vocabulary such as Winston Churchill and H. G. Wells were using the name of Vidkun Quisling as a synonym for the worst of perfidy. His name quickly became an afflictive adjective, as pundits wrote of quisling intellectuals, quisling news media, and quisling clergy.

Quixotic   First, to define a few terms: The Middle Ages refers to that period of about a thousand years in European history between ancient and modern times (A.D. 500 to 1500); whatever relates to that period is known as medieval. The medieval system of knighthood was called chivalry. A knight, pledged to courage and honor, always stood ready to redress any wrong, help the weak, and protect women. A knight-errant was one who wandered about seeking ways to serve and demonstrate his prowess. A tilt was a contest in which two knights on horseback thrust with lances, attempting to unseat each other. A squire was a knight's assistant or helper.

Now to the story. In the Spanish province of La Mancha lived a gentle, humble man, an avid reader of stories about chivalry. He read so many of these that he began to imagine himself a knight, a mighty warrior, and a doer of noble deeds. At last, he began to act out his obsession.

Believing himself a nobleman, a don, he assumed the name Don Quixote of La Mancha. In the rusty old armor of his grandfather, wearing a helmet made of paper, mounted on a broken-down old nag he called Rocinante, he set forth to right all wrongs, a knight-errant, so he thought. He persuaded a simple-minded rustic named Sancho Panza to go along as his squire, this fellow riding a donkey named Dapple. A common peasant girl who Quixote idealized and imagined as his Queen of Love and Beauty became the inspiration for his ventures, and to her he gave the high-sounding name Dulcinea del Toboso.

People who knew him and understood his obsession tried to dissuade him, but without success. Attempting to remove the source of his dementia, a local priest burned his library of chivalric romances. The village barber disguised himself as Dulcinea in an effort to persuade him to give up his quest. In the end, it was a neighbor who at last succeeded: Disguising himself as a knight of higher rank, he ordered Quixote to give up and go home, and the old man did. Becoming somewhat more lucid, he willed what remained of his estate to a niece, providing she never marry a man given to reading books on chivalry.

In the long illusionary interval, though, Quixote and Sancho Panza rode about as conquerors, with their two disreputable mounts stumbling along beneath them. Seeking wrongs to right and people to help, Quixote imagined he found them everywhere.

His first encounter was with a score of windmills that he saw as an army of evil giants. Fixing his lance and crouching forward, he drove his spurs into Rocinante's bony body and charged. When a whirling blade knocked him to the ground, he blandly announced that sorcerers had suddenly changed the giants into windmills.

To this day, after nearly 400 years, this outlandish windmill scene is still very much in mind. One is tilting at windmills who fights an imaginary enemy, who flails away at dangers or threats that do not really exist, or who consumes precious resources in misguided conflict with a nonexistent foe.

The story of Don Quixote is the chronicle of one misadventure after another. On one occasion he came upon two friars escorting a noble lady in a coach, and believing she had been abducted by them, he attacked. Once he attacked a funeral procession because he thought it was a parade of monsters. And there was a time when, much to the distress of the shepherds, he saw two flocks of sheep as two opposing armies and decided to intervene. Such encounters with imaginary enemies number in the hundreds.

As word of the old man spread throughout the country, he became the object of much teasing and taunting. It was considered good sport to create conditions to rile him. Considered fair game, he was frequently set up for a fall, but he never seemed to know it. In his distorted mind, there was always some good explanation or reason for even his most outrageous behavior. He continued to be humble and kind, a willing and patient martyr to his cause.

Over time, his name has made a unique place for itself in our language. An absurdly romantic but wholly impractical person is called quixotic. A Don Quixote is enthusiastically visionary, has high ideals and lofty and unselfish sentiments, but is pitifully unaware of the illusionary nature of his or her dreams.

The story of Don Quixote is, of course, the work of Miguel de Cervantes; it is a novel of enormous size, about 461,000 words, featuring 669 characters. It was done as a satire on the whole institution of chivalry as known and practiced in the late sixteenth and early seventeenth centuries.

— R —

Rabelais Dodge   A Rabelais dodge is an evasive tactic, a scheme designed to avoid responsibility or to escape an obligation by pretense. It is to arrange a deception that diverts attention from what ought to be done.

The expression comes from an episode in the checkered career of that enigmatic Frenchman, François Rabelais (1494–1553). Scholar, philosopher, physician, writer, and an erratic, unpredictable, fun-loving man-about-town, Rabelais has been often identified as one of history's great creative minds.

Some of his creations, though, were of rather dubious character.

Once, having stayed for a time at a posh country inn, he realized that he had no money to pay his bill. Never one to be found lacking in imagination, Rabelais rarely missed a chance to do something spectacular or surprising. Thus, here at this inn, he pulled off one of his typical tricks. Concocting a set of circumstances that made him look like a traitor planning to poison all the princes of France, he contrived to get himself arrested.

By the authorities, he was taken away to Paris, where he wished to go anyway. Once in the capital city, he was promptly released, there being of course no evidence against him. In this way, he avoided payment of his hotel bill and got free passage to Paris. (See also GARGANTUAN.)

Raise Cain   To raise Cain is to stir up trouble. The expression arises from the most ancient of stories, the story of the beginnings of our humanity as found in the traditions of the Hebrew, Christian, and Muslim peoples.

The story goes this way: The first babies born in the world were two brothers, Cain and Abel, and a twin sister of each. Cain became a keeper of sheep and Abel was a tiller of the ground. Their father, Adam, wanted Cain to marry Abel's twin sister and Abel to marry Cain's twin. Abel was in agreement with this arrangement, but Cain objected, wishing instead to marry his own twin.

In an effort to mediate the dispute, Adam proposed a trial by sacrifice—both young men were to offer religious sacrifice, and the one whose sacrifice was accepted was to be considered in the right. Cain brought grain from his fields and Abel an animal from his flock. Abel's sacrifice was accepted and Cain's was not.

Cain became angry; a bitter resentment and jealousy of his brother arose within him. One day, he enticed Abel to go with him into the fields, and there Cain murdered his brother. Later, he professed to know nothing of Abel's whereabouts or of his death, saying, "Am I my brother's keeper?"

Thus, as the story goes, did the firstborn child of humanity have within him most of the dark passions that have since afflicted his kind. Cain has become virtually the archetype of an ugly underside of the human character. To raise Cain is to bring this up and stir it into action.

Read the Riot Act   Incredible as it may seem, from 1714 to 1727, England was ruled by a king who spoke French and German, but not English. A resident of continental Europe, and not even a British citizen, the throne of England became his by inheritance (his mother was the granddaughter of James I, British king from 1603 to 1625).

Crossing the English Channel to claim his inheritance, the new king assumed the throne in the name of George I. Their imported sovereign was instantly disliked by the English, and not much respected. The man had already divorced his wife and had her imprisoned, where, incidentally, she spent the remaining thirty-two years of her life. Also it was well known in England that the newly crowned monarch had at least two mistresses on his payroll in Germany.

Understandably, George I didn't go into England on a tidal wave of popularity; neither did he rest comfortably on a solid base of public confidence during his reign. Fully aware of this, the king felt it necessary to protect himself against any plot his subjects might undertake against him. Fearful that plans might be contrived or that popular uprisings might be instigated, he wished to restrict public assembly. Only a few months into his reign, he finagled a law to do just this, an infamous piece of legislation known as the Riot Act.

If twelve or more people assembled anywhere, the act required any public official aware of the assembly to read the act in their hearing. If the assembly failed to break up immediately, each of the people present was automatically guilty of a felony and subject to severe punishment.

This is what an assembled group would hear: "Our Sovereign Lord the King chargeth and commandeth all persons being assembled immediately to disperse themselves, and peaceably to depart to their habitations or to their lawful business, upon pains contained in the Act made in the first year of King George for preventing tumultuous and riotous assemblies. God save the King!" Obviously, by this act, the king was trying to save himself. And he did—at least from any foul play at the hands of the people.

Well, after almost three centuries, the riot act is still read on occasion. For example, if Joe is late to work and his boss has a few stern words for him, Joe is likely to say afterward, "He really read me the riot act!" To read the riot act is to administer a severe scolding or warning with threat of retribution.

Real McCoy   When we want to state firmly that something is genuine, we may say, "It's the real McCoy." We mean that it is not an imitation or a counterfeit, but the actual thing itself. Although there are older, similar expressions such as "the real McKie," which probably originated in Scotland, this one apparently dates from the 1890s and originated in America.

Norman Selby McCoy (1873–1940) was a welterweight boxer who was world champion in 1896. Since any prizefighter with a name like Norman Selby will inevitably require some nickname more in keeping with his profession, this fellow was known as Kid McCoy. It was a time of bare-knuckles boxing and bare-knuckles lifestyles, when the Marquee of Queensberry Rules governing the sport were still considered sissy by most.

Once in a barroom when McCoy was identified, several of the men expressed their pleasure in being elbow-to-elbow with such a distinguished person. One of the patrons, however, in an advanced state of inebriation, refused to believe that McCoy was indeed McCoy. Loudly calling him an imposter and liar, he challenged McCoy to a fight. There was really no fight to it; the challenger never had a chance because McCoy floored him with one convincing punch. Picking himself off the floor and struggling to his feet, the fellow looked incredulously around, rubbed his near-broken jaw, and in a tone of awe and finality, announced to all present, "It's the real McCoy!"

Anyway, this is the tale, true or not, that went the rounds of boxing circles and barrooms. Always good for a laugh, and told with various embellishments, the story was so vivid and its point so clearly put that its punch line (no pun intended) has survived in our language long after the story itself is mostly forgotten. Whatever the truth of the story, it was one much relished by McCoy in his boxing career.

Rip Van Winkle   Rip was not the most illustrious of the Van Winkles. Washington Irving, who invented him, or rather adapted him from a prior incarnation, made him one of the lesser lights in the not-too-well-illuminated Catskill Mountains of New York.

Rip's wife was forever nagging him to do something worthwhile. He much preferred, however, to spend his time with other idlers at the village inn. Even this sanctum of stag camaraderie was not impervious to the intrusions of Rip's domineering wife, for she often sought him out there with some shrill command or strident reprimand.

No great wonder, then, that Rip frequently took his gun and disappeared into the woodlands, to be gone sometimes for days before he showed up again. There came at length a memorable day when he thus vamoosed, not to return at all, at least not for twenty years. He really hadn't planned to stay away so long, but up there in the mystic mountains a strange misadventure delayed him somewhat.

He encountered a group of peculiar little old men, silently and seriously playing ninepins. Of an appearance unlike any Rip had ever seen, these fellows were quaintly dressed and seemed to be involved together in a small world of their own, completely ignoring him. Of special interest to Rip was a keg of some drink unlike any he had ever tasted (and he had tasted many). So when none were looking, he visited the keg time after time, each drink calling for the next one. At last he fell asleep.

He awakened to a beautiful, bright morning, amazed that he had apparently slept there all night. The little old men were nowhere about, and neither was the keg. Rip dreaded having to face his wife, but mustering such courage as he had, which wasn't much, he made his way toward the village. He was puzzled by the presence of an unusual stiffness in all his joints and that his beard had grown to great length.

Coming into the village, he was perplexed even more. Most things were strange to him, and he didn't recognize anyone. His uncouth and unkempt appearance began to attract attention, and soon he was being quizzed as to who he was. In reply, he declared himself a local resident and "a loyal subject of the king." "A Tory!" the people shouted with a hostility he couldn't understand. He didn't know it yet, but he had slept all the way through the American Revolution! King George III wasn't popular in New York anymore, nor were the Tories. After a twenty-year snooze, Rip had awakened to a different world.

He found, to his regret, that most of his old cronies were now dead. It was, though, a sort of relief to learn that sometime earlier his wife had suffered a fatal hemorrhage while screaming at a peddler. He also found his daughter, now married and the mother of a small boy named Rip. In her home he lived to old age, spending most of his time at the inn, telling everyone the fantastic tale of his long, long sleep.

Rip leaves us the legacy of his name, which we use from time to time. We may call a person a Rip Van Winkle to indicate that he or she is blithely unaware of significant changes going on or indifferent to mighty movements sweeping through the political or social scene. A Rip Van Winkle is one who can sleep through a revolution, never knowing that anything has happened.

Robin Goodfellow   Hermia wants to marry Lysander, who loves her deeply, but Egeus, her father, says no; he says she must marry Demetrius. Theseus, the duke of Athens, who has the final say in such matters, agrees with him. The upshot is that Hermia is required either to marry Demetrius or enter a convent and never marry at all. Equally unwilling to accept either alternative, she is joined by Lysander, and together they flee into the forest. They are followed by Demetrius, who also wants to marry Hermia, and he in turn is pursued by Helena, who is desperately in love with him.

In the forest is a kingdom of fairies; Oberon is their king and Titania is his queen. King Oberon has a helper, a sort of errand boy. His name is Puck, or Robin Goodfellow, one fellow with two names. Puck is a lively, fun-loving, impish, mischievous little elf.

Oberon possesses the juice of a certain flower that has a strange effect on people: Placed on their eyelids while sleeping, it causes them to fall in love with the first person they see upon awakening. Observing that Demetrius is inexcusably hostile toward Helena, he sends Puck to find Demetrius, to catch him sleeping, and to anoint his eyelids with this juice. Eagerly, Puck goes—this is precisely the sort of mischief he likes most—but he finds Lysander instead of Demetrius, and so anoints the wrong pair of eyes.

Meanwhile, Demetrius has run away from Helena, leaving her alone in the forest. Searching for him, she comes upon the sleeping Lysander instead, and awakens him. Seeing her, Lysander is of course instantly love-smitten. Now Lysander loves Helena instead of his betrothed Hermia, and Helena loves Demetrius who doesn't love her or anyone else very much.

But the fairies soon take care of this by anointing the eyes of Demetrius and producing Helena for him to see first upon awakening. When he eloquently professes great love for her, she believes he is making sport of her, as his transformation is too hard to believe. Hermia now arrives, and the two women rail at each other, and then the two men likewise.

The men go off into the shadows to find a battlefield where they will fight it out. The good intentions of Oberon and Puck having gone awry, the two sprites realize they must do something quickly, for the night is nearly past. Puck follows the men, and pretending in the darkness that his voice is that of Demetrius, he taunts and frustrates Lysander until, at last exhausted, he falls asleep. Now once again Puck anoints his eyelids.

Thus the story goes, and with a lot of going to sleep and awakening in the woodland this night, at last Puck and Oberon get their scenario straight. Lysander and Hermia are together, and so are Demetrius and Helena. Theseus, the duke of Athens, is himself engaged to be married to the Amazon queen Hippolyta, who he has defeated in battle. In the end, there is a triple wedding at the palace of Theseus.

So goes Shakespeare's comedy, *A Midsummer Night's Dream*, and so comes to us a delightful tidbit of language. A Robin Goodfellow is a spritely, cheerful, fun-loving person, given to mischievous pranks and clever ruses and dodges. Or, call him Puck, if you will. To be "puckish" is to be impish and full of mischief—never malicious, but not wholly to be trusted either, a kind of rascal in the good sense of that word.

Robin Hood   He may be fictional, or he may have once lived. Whatever the basis of his legend, it has thrived for about eight centuries now. Dating from a time when England was young, the legend varies somewhat from telling to telling, but his character is always that of an utterly engrossing and intriguing fellow.

At age eighteen, and already an expert bowman, Robin Hood was on his way to an archery competition when he encountered a gang of fifteen ruffians, one of whom he shot in self-defense. Corruption being rampant in the government, and his chances of getting justice nonexistent in the courts, young Robin fled for refuge into the little-known regions of Sherwood Forest.

Here, within about a year, he assembled around him scores of other men who had been wronged or were about to be. United by this common tie, all stood ready to aid any citizen who might be treated unjustly and to make life difficult for those who treated them badly. The band developed and followed a strict code, specifying that none of them would ever harm a child or wrong a woman. Clad in green for blending into the woodland, they made the forest their base of operation and their home.

They robbed, but they took only from the rich or the wicked so that they could assist the poor, the abused, and the troubled. They were a lighthearted bunch, going about their business mischievously in a spirit of gamesmanship. Their many adventures were attended by much humor; they were lovers of pranks, expert at games of cat and mouse. Always seeking to avoid bloodshed, Robin Hood himself, for example, killed only one man, Guy of Ginsbourne, a sort of general-purpose hoodlum who deserved the blow that Robin dealt him.

The band made great sport of outwitting the sheriff of Nottingham, who tried repeatedly to round up and arrest them. They elected to rely on cunning, not force, and the policy served them well. By unanimous judgment of the common people, Robin Hood and his band were champions of right.

When in 1189 Richard the Lion Hearted came to the throne, conditions improved vastly in England. Due to these improvements, the role of Robin and his men was considerably diminished; but with their record, they were still considered outlaws and they continued to inhabit the wilds of Sherwood Forest.

There came a time when Richard paid a visit to Nottinghamshire. While there, he resolved to meet with Robin Hood, of whom he had heard much, and for whom he held a secret sort of admiration. With the guidance of a go-between, and disguised as friars, the king and his party made their way to Robin Hood's hideout. The upshot of this visit was that the king pardoned the entire band, took Robin, Little John, Will Scarlet, and Alan a Dale with him to London, and commissioned the others as royal rangers. Robin was made earl of Huntingdon and faithfully served England for his remaining years.

He has survived well in legend and literature; his buoyant spirit and passion for justice and his independence and originality have held a continuing fascination over the centuries. Even in our time, any person who takes from one to give to another is likely to be represented as a Robin Hood, the taking being perhaps forcible or illegal and the giving usually of charitable intent.

As for "Robin Hood's barn," it's a term that denotes all the land where the rich and powerful kept their supplies in storage. It is, therefore, a long, long way to "go all around Robin Hood's barn." It isn't the most direct route, nor does it follow an established and well-traveled trail. But neither did the career of this offbeat character.

Romeo and Juliet   This story occurs in the beginning of the thirteenth century A.D. in the city of Verona in Italy. The two leading families, the Capulets and the Montagues, are feuding. The Capulet family leader has a beautiful fourteen-year-old daughter named Juliet; she is being courted by various young men, and Count Paris is the favorite of her doting father. Among the Montagues, the brightest and most handsome youth is Romeo, and Romeo thinks he is in love with a girl named Rosaline.

Masked and disguised as servants, a group of Montague youths crash a formal dinner at the Capulet mansion. Here, Romeo sees Juliet, and all thoughts of Rosaline promptly disappear from his mind. She is as attracted to him as he to her, and before the evening passes each knows the other's name and family. This evening, also, the two declare their love for each other, she from her balcony and he from the shadows of the garden below.

Romeo goes then to his friend and confessor Friar Lawrence, telling of the secret love he and Juliet have for each other. Seeing in this a hope for ending the family feud, the friar gives encouragement. Shortly afterward, with the friar's cooperation, the two are secretly married. Leaving the wedding, Romeo encounters a fight in progress in the public square—between the Capulets and the Montagues, of course.

Here, Romeo sees his good friend Mercutio killed by Tybalt, one of the Capulets. In quick vengeance, Romeo kills Tybalt, a first cousin of the girl he has married earlier this evening. The prince, who rules Verona, comes into the square, and learning what has just happened, summarily banishes Romeo.

Juliet must now bid her young husband farewell, which she does with tears. Immediately afterward she is told by her parents that three days later she is being married to Count Paris. Desperately she runs to Friar Lawrence, presumably to make her confession, but actually to seek his help. The friar gives her a certain medication that will produce all the signs of death, advising her to take it immediately prior to the scheduled wedding. The friar further assures her that he will send word of this plan to Romeo, who will come by night and rescue her from the mausoleum.

All goes according to plan, except that the runner entrusted with this message never reaches Romeo; en route, he stumbles into a plague-stricken house and is placed under quarantine. Word reaches Romeo that Juliet is dead, and full of rage, he rushes from Mantua to Verona, resolved to take his life at Juliet's side.

Romeo, though, is not first to reach Juliet's tomb. Bringing flowers he had planned to give his bride the next day, Paris places them at her bier tonight. Romeo stumbles into the shadowed crypt, the two fight, and Paris falls dead. Romeo drinks the poison he has brought, and within moments, he dies alongside the bier of Juliet and the body of Paris.

Friar Lawrence then enters, Juliet awakens and asks, "O comfortable friar, where is my lord?" Then she sees the bodies of Romeo and Paris next to their blood-spattered swords. Hearing someone's approach, the friar advises Juliet to flee, and he hurries away.

Alone now in the tomb with the bodies of the two men, Juliet attempts to lick enough poison from the lips of Romeo to cause her own death. Failing in this effort, she snatches Romeo's dagger from its scabbard, and saying, "This is thy sheath; there rust, and let me die," she plunges the weapon into her heart. The three bodies are found by the approaching guard. And here, as dawn begins to show in the east, old Capulet and old Montague at last shake hands and declare the old feud finished.

It's a sad, tragic story told by Shakespeare. Its movements and meanings have been pondered for almost four centuries. Out of all this complexity, though, one simple theme stands forth: the passion of young love.

From this story we get a Romeo, a love-smitten young man, and Romeo and Juliet, who symbolize an unshakable devotion.

Rube Goldberg   Something is awkwardly and inefficiently put together in a patchwork sort of manner, and someone pronounces it a Rube Goldberg job. Born in San Francisco and obtaining a bachelor of science in engineering, Reuben Lucius Goldberg (1883–1970) pursued a career in this field for only a few months, as a designer of sewer pipes. Then he was a news reporter and sportswriter. His career actually commenced, though, when he became a cartoonist.

Doing both humorous and serious cartooning, he became famous for both, winning a Pulitzer Prize for the latter. But it is the former for which he is most remembered.

Goldberg created a cartoon character who he called Lucifer Gorgonzola Butts, an eccentric professor who was utterly impractical in all his ideas. Professor Butts invented contraptions to perform simple tasks, such as bringing in the morning newspaper or opening milk bottles, but always in some inefficient and roundabout way.

One of these inventions was an automatic stamp-licker. It was activated by a midget robot, programmed to overturn a can of ants on a page of postage stamps, gummed-side-up. These were then licked by an anteater who had been kept on starvation diet for three days. Another invention was an alarm clock. To build one of these, two cups are counterbalanced, one containing buckshot and the other a precise amount of water. In a given amount of time, the water evaporates, tipping the balance, and spilling the shot into an ice-covered pail. As the ice is broken, voracious small fish leap for bait suspended on a string. This pulls a pin that releases 500 pounds of ball bearings, which roll down a chute striking a brass drum just inches from the sleeper's ear!

Running for years as a feature in the American press, Goldberg's Professor Butts came up with hundreds of needlessly complicated contraptions. Intricately contrived to the point of being ludicrous, his innovations provided a great deal of amusement.

Hence, the artist's name, Rube Goldberg, became a household word for any outlandish apparatus or scheme. A Rube Goldberg device, whether thing or idea, is one so complex as to be impractical, or, worse, ineffective, or, worse yet, wholly unworkable. It should be noted, however, that Rube Goldberg contraptions did work—if one had the patience to set them up, if everything happened as it was supposed to, and if one could wait long enough to see it all happen.

With all the humor involved, there was, nevertheless, serious purpose in Goldberg's work. It was a good-natured lampoon of the American preoccupation with technology and also a satirical commentary on the ever-increasing complexity that seems to afflict every aspect of the social order.

— S —

Say It Ain't So Joe The 1919 World Series pitted the National League's Cincinnati Reds against the American League's Chicago White Sox. The victory went to Cincinnati.

However, serious questions soon arose about the games. It appeared to some who were familiar with the sport that strange things had happened on the playing fields—that on numerous occasions Chicago team members had not performed up to par and that they had made numerous, inexcusable errors. There was an uneasy feeling that something was amiss.

The Chicago manager employed detectives to look into the matter, and what they found rocked the baseball world like a thunderbolt. Gamblers had paid eight of the White Sox players to throw the series. The players had accepted the bribes and had deliberately lost the series.

One of those players was left fielder "Shoeless" Joe Jackson, one of baseball's all-time greats in the batter's box—that season he had had a phenomenal .351 batting average. He had millions of fans and was the idol of almost every sports-loving lad in America. But Jackson was one of the eight found guilty of accepting bribes and banned from organized baseball for the rest of their lives.

As the hearing ended and the men were leaving the room, long rows of spectators were lined up to see them go. At the forefront of these stood a shabbily dressed young boy with tears in his eyes. As Jackson passed, the boy plaintively called out, "Say it ain't so Joe!" Joe Jackson, eyes averted, made no reply.

That child's cry of distress was given a lot of publicity at the time, and the words have become a cliche said in response to any piece of unwelcome news, as a flip reaction to disappointment of any kind, and as a lighthearted way of signifying displeasure.

It must be noted, though, that many have questioned Jackson's guilt in the scandal—as he batted .375 in the series, made no fielding errors, and was later acquitted of the crime.

Scapegoat Moses was the mighty leader of Israel; his brother Aaron served as his first lieutenant. Moses did most of the administrative chores, and Aaron had the priestly duty of representing the people before Jehovah, their God. On one occasion, two sons of Aaron, somewhat wantonly entering their Holy Place, got too near Jehovah and died.

To prevent a repeat of this fatal indiscretion, Aaron was given specific instructions about how he should approach Jehovah, never going at will into the Holy Place, but only with elaborate preparation. After bathing thoroughly and clothing himself in linen, he was required to take with him a variety of animals for sacrifice, among these two male goats.

Between these two goats Aaron was to cast lots. In this way, one was selected to be offered as a sacrifice. The other animal became what was called the scapegoat. Over it, an elaborate ritual was performed. By means of this ritual, the sins of the people were laid upon that goat—transferred from them to it.

This thus-burdened creature was then taken away into the wilderness and there permitted to escape into whatever fate awaited it. The people believed they had sent it away to Azazel, a vague, shapeless, shadowy demon whose haunts were the wilderness wastelands. Whatever became of the goat, the people believed that by it their sins had gone away.

Here we have an expression sometimes used in describing human relationships. A scapegoat is one who is made to bear the burden or blame of others. The scapegoat is in no way a volunteer, but is rather a victim, a person used by others to excuse themselves of responsibility or exempt themselves from fault or failure.

Scrooge   One of the best known and most loved narratives in English literature is *A Christmas Carol* by Charles Dickens, written in 1843. The main character, Ebenezer Scrooge, is likewise one of the best known and most notorious skinflints. Scrooge has long been a synonym for all the stingy and miserly characters who move among us. A Scrooge-ish person is one who is callously selfish.

It is the day before Christmas, but the festive spirit hasn't even touched old Ebenezer's flinty shell. He is still saying no to every charitable idea, and his opinion of Christmas is summed up in two of his own words, "Bah. Humbug!"

As he arrives that night, however, at the lonely fortress he calls home, the face of his late partner, Marley, looks out at him from the door knocker—this despite the fact that Marley has been dead for seven years. Later in the evening, his deceased partner appears to him, bound in heavy chains and saying, "I wear the chains I forged in life." Unnerving as this is, it is mild in comparison with what follows. Before the night is over, Scrooge is visited by three spirits who show him how really horrible he is.

First comes the Ghost of Christmas Past who takes him on a tour through his own yesterdays—his childhood home at Christmastime, the fateful day when his developing love of gold had separated him forever from the youthtime sweetheart he might have loved and married. Reminded of the way things once were, impressed with the great amount of living he has missed, Scrooge begins to wish he hadn't been so unkind to his current business clerk, Bob Cratchit, or so hostile to all appeals for the poor.

Next comes the Ghost of Christmas Present. By this spirit, he is shown the home of the Cratchits, the love that is there, their heroic struggle against poverty, the inspiring courage of the crippled boy, Tiny Tim. He is then taken to look in upon the joyous gathering of family and friends at his nephew's house, and he regrets he had been so rude when the nephew had stopped by his office earlier to wish him a merry Christmas. Scrooge is shown two wretched children, their names Ignorance and Want. Whose children are they? "They are Man's," the spirit says.

As this ghost fades away, the third appears, the Ghost of Christmas Yet to Come, a black-robed phantom who never speaks, but whose long arm and bony forefinger are effective instruments for pointing out the scenes Scrooge is yet to see. These are postmortem tableaux in which Scrooge hears a group of men joking about his death, hears someone say that "Old Scratch" is dead, and sees his old office now occupied by another. Most disturbing, though, is the scene in which he sees that, after he is dead, scavengers have stripped the curtains from around his bed and taken the burial shirt off his body. In a neglected cemetery he sees an unkempt grave, the stone bearing only two words, "Ebenezer Scrooge."

By now, the old skinflint has seen and heard enough. With trembling voice he inquires of the Phantom, "Are these things . . . that Will be . . . or that May be?" There is no answer. He then pleads,

"Assure me that I may yet change . . . by an altered life." But no assurance is given. The Phantom shrivels, dissolves, and disappears.

Awakening securely in his bed, Scrooge feels that several days have passed. But, no; all this has happened in one night, and it is Christmas morning. Scrooge is now seized by an overwhelming conviction: It's not too late! Then a second thought strikes him with compelling force: I will do everything I can to amend my life, and I will do it now!

Suddenly exhilarated, he moves into a frenzy of activity. In joyous excitement, he has the largest turkey in town delivered to the home of Bob Cratchit, he greets everyone in the spirit of the season, he has Christmas dinner at his nephew's home and is the life of the party— and the next day he substantially increases Bob Cratchit's salary. The stingy old Scrooge is a new man.

Scylla and Charybdis   *See* DEVIL AND THE DEEP BLUE SEA.

Scythian Defense   In the sixth century B.C., Darius I of Persia undertook the conquest of Scythia, a predominately rural country near the Black Sea in southeastern Europe. The Persian armies were the largest, best trained, most disciplined, and most powerful military force in the world at that time. Scythia was a nation with no walled cities, no forts, and an army much smaller than Persia's.

Darius, however, failed to conquer Scythia, and the story of his defeat is an intriguing one. Darius could never induce the Scythians to stand and fight. Their strategy was to stay just one days' march ahead of the Persians. Thus they led the exhausted and confused invaders in circuitous routes of their own choosing over much of Scythia. As the Scythian army withdrew in some chosen direction, it systematically destroyed the water wells and drove away the cattle and other livestock, making for the Persians the critical problem of providing food and drink for both man and beast.

In all his forays into foreign lands, Darius had never encountered such strange military tactics. He was perplexed and frustrated, as was his entire army. Eventually, he sent messengers to the Scythian leaders demanding to know their intentions. He received only total silence. At length, however, a lone Scythian courier arrived at the tent of Darius, placing before the powerful king these simple objects: a bird, a mouse, a frog, and five arrows. Then, with no word of explanation, the messenger silently withdrew.

For a time, much perplexity prevailed in the Persian camp. What was going on here? Nobody knew, and the uncertainty produced a most unsettling apprehension that soon resulted in a general breakdown of morale. What sort of enemy were these Scythians anyway? Were they a whole race of crazy people? Or, did they perhaps have some private knowledge the Persians did not have?

It was not long, though, until someone came up with an interpretation of the Scythian tokens brought to Darius: Unless the Persians would fly away like birds, or burrow into the ground like mice, or retreat into the marshes like frogs, they would all become the victims of Scythian arrows. For the Persians, it was an altogether unnerving state of affairs.

So, having never engaged in battle with the Scythians at all, Darius retreated from their land, in baffled perplexity, leading his powerful battalions home to Persia.

Although Darius was the world's most powerful monarch, and his armies the world's greatest, although he was accustomed to getting what he wanted, one silent messenger and his strange message put that mighty monarch's mind into total disarray. His towering self-confidence tottered, his haughty assurance wavered, and his courage faltered.

This strategy of the Scythians, to make this sort of response to an enemy, is known as a Scythian defense, or defiance. It is a nonviolent way by which the weaker confounds the mightier, winning by the power of suggestion.

Seventh Heaven   He has just won the sweepstakes, he just got his first new car, or his girlfriend just said yes to his proposal of marriage—we say, "He's in his seventh heaven!" To be in a state of extreme joy, on some pinnacle of satisfaction, is to be in one's seventh heaven. *Seventh*, we say, because some lesser heaven isn't high enough to say what we want it to; we must go to the top. So what of it, this penthouse place with prospects so pleasing and promising?

Well, in Islam, there are five duties, six beliefs, and seven heavens. These seven are often mentioned in Islam's sacred book, *The Koran*.

It is said here that Allah "created the seven heavens, one above an-other," and that he "is Lord of the seven heavens."

In the first century, the Christian apostle, Paul, wrote of the su-preme ecstasy of having been once "caught up to the third heaven," and there hearing "things that cannot be told." Six centuries later, Mohammed I put forth a system that provided seven heavens stacked one on top of another.

One story, not from *The Koran* but from the Islamic apocrypha, the *Miràj Nàmeh*, relates an experience of the Prophet Mohammed in which he was escorted on a V.I.P. tour of all seven of the heavens. It was on the twenty-seventh of the seventh month, apparently in the year 620, when the archangel Gabriel appeared by night to the prophet and said to him, "Allah commands you to come before His Majesty. The door to the seven heavens is open and the angels are waiting for you. Rise up, O messenger of Allah, and let us go!"

To cleanse the prophet's heart, the angel washed his breast with water from Zamzam, the sacred spring. Then appeared the Buràq, a mysterious and magical sort of horse, on which the prophet was mounted. So the journey began, Gabriel propelled by his 600 mighty wings and Mohammed astride what was, no doubt, the swiftest horse ever ridden by man.

The first heaven was found to be made altogether of turquoise; here the prophet had the opportunity of talking with Earth's first man, Adam, who although he had had all that time to work at it, had gotten only as far as heaven number one. Number two was of white pearl; then, flying over the White Sea, the travelers entered heaven number three, all of red hyacinth, where there were thirty divisions of archangels, with 30,000 ordinary angels attending and serving each one.

Passing quickly through heaven number four, they came into the fifth, made of gold, and here was a great sea of fire, to be poured on the last day into hell to add to the torments of the damned. In the sixth heaven, the prophet met Moses, who wept upon the realization that the Moslem faithful outnumbered his own.

They came, then, to the seventh, and it was made entirely of light. Here, near the entrance, was a creature with seventy heads, each head with seventy mouths, each mouth with seventy tongues, and all of them continually singing the praises of Allah. Here also was an angel of colossal size, having 10,000 wings and eyes so large that all the oceans of the world would not fill one of them.

Eventually, in the tour of this seventh heaven, Gabriel was permitted to go no farther, but Mohammed was allowed to go on, and did. He went all the way to the throne of Allah, a throne of red hyacinth, encircled by 700,000 tents, each as large as the world and spaced 50,000 years apart, and in each tent fifty divisions of angels praising Allah. From his throne, while Mohammed listened, Allah spoke 99,000 words of instruction to him.

In the seventh heaven, the prophet visited paradise, a special department set aside as the habitation of earthlings whose pilgrimage had brought them this far. Here there were beautiful lakes and flowing streams, shaded bowers, and, of course, no sandstorms ever. Here also were the *Houris*, beautiful young nymphs; each human male, arriving in this place, was assigned one or more of these. (In this story, Mohammed had no report of what was done for female arrivals, or even if there were any.)

In the saga of the *Miráj Nâmeh*, all this and much more transpired during the hours of that one eventful night, and by morning, the 600-winged Gabriel and the fast-flying Burâq had the prophet back on earth and safely in his bed. Unlike the apostle Paul, who was unable to tell what he heard in his third heaven, Mohammed was quite prepared to report what he heard and saw in the seventh.

Shadow of an Ass Demosthenes, a Greek patriot of the fourth century B.C. who was generally acclaimed as a most effective public speaker, often drove home his points with the skillful use of stories. Here's the story he told to emphasize the point that it is foolish to quarrel over unimportant matters, or to fight over the shadow of an ass, as it were.

Now, the ass is not notable as a prince among beasts, and his shadow is certainly not a precious thing to be quibbled about. To quarrel over an ass's shadow is about as pointless as anything one could ever do, and as brainless. The story Demosthenes told he had gotten from Aesop, who had appeared on the Greek scene a few lifetimes earlier.

One morning in Athens, a traveler rented an ass to carry him and his luggage to Megara. Paying the rental price, he loaded up his stuff, mounted, and started off, with the animal's owner following on foot so he could claim his property at the journey's end.

The sun was bright, the day was hot, and by noontime the traveler began to look for a spot where he could rest and cool off. Finding no place of respite from the merciless sun, he eventually stopped, dismounted, and sat down in the shadow of the ass.

Soon, the beast's owner arrived, sized up the situation, and finding the weary traveler asleep, seized the ass by his reins and led him a few paces forward. Of course, the animal took his shadow with him.

Soon awakened by the heat, and observing what had happened, the traveler angrily led the ass a few steps farther and defiantly placed himself in the shadow again. Then, between the two men, a storm of angry words began to fly back and forth like sharp-pointed darts.

The traveler protested that, having rented the ass, its shadow was also his to use. The owner argued that he had rented only the ass, not its shadow. Did the shadow go with the ass, or did it not? So the argument raged, quickly degenerating into a screaming match and then into a fight. In the commotion, the ass ran away, and neither man ever saw him again.

But not content to leave the issue there, each man tried to collect damages from the other. Taking the matter to the magistrates, the lawyers on both sides collected fat fees, and neither man had anything left with which to pay damages to the other.

Perhaps both learned the folly of fighting over a shadow. Regardless, today pointless quibbling over nonessential trifles is often expressed as fighting over the shadow of an ass.

Shangri-La   A place of mystery, a hidden paradise, or an imaginary utopia is called Shangri-La. From a novel by James Hilton, *Lost Horizon*, Shangri-La was not a real place at all.

In 1931, Hugh Conway, age thirty-seven, is a diplomatic attaché of the British consulate at Baskul. Because of trouble there, the entire staff is evacuated. Conway departs in a plane with Miss Roberta Brinklow, a Christian missionary, Henry Barnard, an American operator who turns out to be a wanted criminal, and Captain Charles Mallison, another consular staff member.

In flight, it is soon apparent the plane isn't going in the right direction and the pilot is not the man assigned to fly the mission.

Hijacked, the passengers are taken to a remote mountain lamasery somewhere in the Himalayas. It is soon realized that the high lama has brought Conway to him for one reason—the old man is now 250 years old, and feeling he will soon die, he wishes Conway to assume his post.

Here in the lamasery of Shangri-La the aging process is slowed so that all residents are actually much older than they appear; Lo-Tsen, a beautiful Chinese girl, is actually a woman of sixty-five. All residents live well and in contentment, but no person has ever been permitted to leave. The place is benign; all the buildings are modern, fully equipped, and comfortable.

Time passes, and Conway is often called into audience with the high lama; it turns out, he had once been a Capuchin friar who was lost in the mountains in 1734 and rescued by Buddhists and converted to their faith. He then discovered the rare medicinal merits of this location, and established this lamasery, becoming the high lama.

Then comes the day when the old man explains to Conway that, foreseeing world civilization destroyed by war, his plan is to save a remnant of it here, and from here start over. He tells Conway he is about to die and is counting on his guest to take over. And while the two men talk, the old man lies back in his chair and dies.

At this time, porters arrive, and in the confusion following the lama's death, they make possible the exodus of some who wish to leave. Barnard chooses not to leave because he is a wanted man and this is a safe refuge. Brinklow will not go because she has hope of christianizing the place. Mallison is quite ready, provided he may take Lo-Tsen with him, and she wants to leave with Mallison because she believes he loves her. (Mallison will not accept Conway's word that the Chinese girl is actually an old woman and when taken away from Shangri-La will soon die.)

Feeling that Mallison and Lo-Tsen will need his assistance on the trek out, Conway accompanies them. Along the way, Conway becomes ill and is treated for extreme exhaustion. He had been brought to the hospital by a small, aged Chinese woman who then disappeared; when Conway was later released, he also vanished.

And that's the last we know of Shangri-La.

Shibboleth   Forty-two thousand men once lost their lives because they were unable to pronounce a word correctly. It happened more than 3,000 years ago on the banks of the Jordan River in Palestine. This was a time when the Israelites had no strong central government; their kingdom, under Saul, had not yet been established, and each tribe had independent control of its own affairs. There were sometimes problems between tribes, territorial disputes, or other issues that brought them to open war.

At one point, conflict flared between the Gileadites and the Ephraimites, who occupied territories on opposite sides of the Jordan. Jephthah was the leader of Gilead, and the Ephraimites quarreled with him because he had not asked for their aid in a war with the Ammonites. They were so peeved that they raised an army and crossed the Jordan in an all-out attack on Gilead.

In this struggle, the Gileadites were successful, utterly defeating the Ephraimites in the field and taking possession of the fords where the retreating invaders would have to cross the river. Units of Jephthah's army were stationed at these fords, with orders to destroy the men of Ephraim as they attempted the crossings. There was a lot of traffic back and forth across the river, and all the people on both sides were Israelites who looked very much alike and spoke the same language, but only the Ephraimites were to be killed.

Jephthah came up with a clever strategy to distinguish the Ephraimites from the others. While all Israelites spoke the same language, area dialects and accents differed considerably. Jephthah knew of one sound that was practically impossible for an Ephraimite to make, and he instructed his men accordingly.

As a man approached one of the Jordan fords seeking permission to cross, a guard would ask, "Are you an Ephraimite?" If the answer was no, then the guard would order him to say the word *shibboleth* (meaning "an ear of grain" or "a river at flood"). Unable to sound the "sh," an Ephraimite would come out with "sibboleth," and would be killed on the spot—thus the 42,000 deaths.

A shibboleth is a kind of catchphrase or password identified with a clique, an organization, or a point of view that stands as a test of credentials or loyalty. Shibboleths are a kind of parrot-talk, words to be said with a rote correctness, even though not understood. We are uttering shibboleths when we say all the right things, whether or not we know what we are saying, or, if knowing, mean it.

Shirt of Nessus In Greek mythology, a Centaur was a creature having the head and shoulders of a man and the body of a horse. Nessus was a Centaur, and he and Hercules had fought on two or three occasions, and there was a deep animosity between them.

Hercules married a princess named Deianeira and was taking his bride home when they came to a swollen river. As Hercules wondered how to get his bride across, Nessus came galloping up and offered to carry her across on his back. Hercules let him do it, but when the Centaur reached the opposite side he started to run away with the girl, and Hercules shot him with a poisoned arrow.

As Nessus was dying, he gave Deianeira a package containing a quantity of his own dried blood, telling her that if she should ever lose the love of Hercules, this charm would restore it. Later, when Hercules took Iole as his mistress, Deianeira believed she had good reason to use the blood of Nessus on him.

About this time, Hercules went to Mount Oeta to offer a sacrifice to the gods. When the altar was ready, he sent his friend Lichas for the ceremonial robe needed for the ritual. Seeing this as a good chance to use the charm Nessus had given her, Deianeira dissolved the dried blood in water, saturated the robe with that solution, and sent it to Hercules.

Receiving the robe, Hercules threw it on in preparation for the ritual of sacrifice. But this was a sacrifice he was destined not to perform. Immediately the robe, or shirt, began to burn into his flesh, as the poison of his own arrow was in the blood of Nessus, searing its way into him.

Frantically attempting to tear the shirt from his body, he found this impossible, for great pieces of seared flesh loosened and came with it. In unbearable pain, he flung his friend Lichas into the sea. Then he converted the altar into a funeral pyre, climbed onto it, and ordered his servants to set it afire. After some hesitation, one of them did, and that day the career of the mighty Hercules was abruptly terminated. His wife, realizing what she had done, then took her own life.

To give or receive a shirt of Nessus is to deal with a gift that is fatal, or, at least, brings consequences of disaster. To wear a shirt of Nessus is to be in a position of inescapable misfortune.

Shoulder to the Wheel One of Aesop's many stories had to do with a countryman, a rather simple fellow, who was driving his heavily loaded cart along a muddy and deeply rutted road. The crude vehicle was pulled by a pair of oxen whose powerful bodies leaned hard into the rugged wooden collar they wore. Although the faithful, plodding creatures labored with all their might, the cart eventually stalled and they were unable to move it.

The carter was angry, and he prodded and whipped the poor beasts violently, all the while calling loudly for Hercules to come help him. By some miracle, the mighty Hercules did indeed appear. And he spoke to the carter: "Foolish man and stupid, you expect your oxen to do everything for you, and when they fail, you call upon me. But what have you done? Nothing. Don't ask me to do anything for you until you have done your best to do the thing yourself. Put your shoulder to the wheel, and use what strength you have to help those oxen move this load along."

As a figure of speech we sometimes use, to put one's shoulder to the wheel is to do one's absolute best to get something done. It is to bring to a task every resource of ability and energy.

Shylock   As Shakespeare tells it, Antonio is a successful merchant of Venice, by nature a melancholy fellow, but well known in the Rialto, Italy's chief marketplace. His friend Bassanio would like to go to Belmont to court Portia, a beautiful, intelligent, rich, highly gifted young woman. But Bassanio has a problem: He is broke. He asks Antonio for a loan of 3,000 ducats, but at the moment Antonio doesn't have the cash on hand because he had invested heavily in merchandise now aboard three ships somewhere on the high seas.

Antonio is willing, however, to stand as security for any loan Bassanio may obtain. So they approach Shylock, a Jewish money-lender. In spite of the deep tensions that exist between Jews and Christians, Shylock agrees to make the loan, even without interest; but in pretense of good-natured banter, he says he will cut off a pound of Antonio's flesh if Bassanio fails to repay the money. With equal banter, and not realizing that Shylock is deadly serious, Antonio agrees, and the contract is made a matter of public record.

Bassanio sets out jauntily for Belmont, but word is soon received that all of Antonio's ships have been sunk, and in the Rialto it is believed that the merchant is financially ruined. At Belmont, Bassanio is successful in his wooing of Portia, but word soon arrives of Antonio's misfortune. After she and Bassanio are hastily married, he hurries away to Venice to be with his stricken friend, who must now appear before the duke for a final judgment in the matter.

Portia, a resourceful and determined young woman, goes to her cousin who is a lawyer, and from him she obtains certain documents and legal information. Then, disguising herself as a lawyer, she also rushes away to Venice. Her identity unknown to anyone, she appears in the duke's courtroom to plead the cause of Antonio. Shylock is determined to have that pound of flesh; he would rather have this than twenty times the amount owed him. He sees this as a chance to strike back at Antonio and all non-Jews for all past insults and abuses.

But Portia proves herself a clever and competent attorney. She pleads for mercy, justice, and charity. But a contract is a contract, and the decision is that Shylock may have that pound of flesh. At length, the victim stands bare-chested with Shylock before him, knife in hand. All are aghast at the horrible thing that is about to happen. And Portia, pretending acceptance of the inevitable, is saying over and over in a dozen different ways that what must be must be.

Suddenly, though, just as Shylock is about to apply his knife, Portia turns abruptly to him, saying in a commanding voice, "Tarry a little; there is something else." She tells him to go ahead and take his pound of flesh if he wishes, but to be sure there is no bleeding, for with the shedding of even one drop of Antonio's blood, all of Shylock's possessions will be confiscated. Startled, Shylock asks, "It that the law?" It is, says Portia, and furthermore if he should try to take that pound of flesh and actually slice off an ounce less or an ounce more, he would be in serious legal trouble.

Shylock backs off. But Portia isn't finished with him yet. Because taking that pound of flesh would also have taken Antonio's life, he now stands guilty of attempted murder, and therefore, under law, half of all he possesses is forfeited to the state and the other half to the intended victim. Shylock leaves the duke's courtroom in total devastation. All the others are happy; even Antonio's ships are safe, for the report of their loss was false.

In the four centuries since Shakespeare, many others in their writing and speaking have used his material liberally. From *The Merchant of Venice*, a shylock is an avaricious, acquisitive, greedy, grasping individual. A pound of flesh is that one final morsel of advantage that one can ruthlessly squeeze out of another. It is what a man exacts simply because he can. It is what is taken, after everything else, as an ultimate indignity.

Simon-Pure   If something is genuine, why do we sometimes say it's simon-pure? A person of impeccable character may be described as simon-pure. Or, of some well-known philanderer it may be humorously undersaid that he or she isn't exactly simon-pure.

For the answer we go back to 1718 and to British poetess and dramatist Susan Cantlivre. In that year, her comedy entitled *A Bold Stroke for a Wife* was first produced at Lincoln Inn Fields in London.

In the play was a character named Simon Pure, who is the play's only person of integrity and complete sincerity. At the time, names of play's characters were usually chosen to reflect the personal qualities of the characters to whom they were given, and so it was with Mr. Pure.

Ann Lovely stood to inherit the fortune of 30,000 pounds from her deceased father. But there was a catch—the eccentric old man had assigned four men to serve as her guardians, and, to receive the inheritance, Ann must marry, with full approval of all of the guardians.

The problem was that these four men were as unalike as four men could possibly be, and the prospects were dim indeed that all could ever agree on any man as a suitable husband for Ann. Frustrated by the constraints of their control of her life, Ann summed up their respective characters: "Foppery, folly, avarice, and hypocrisy are by turns my constant companions."

Colonel Fainwell wanted to marry Ann, and she was quite willing, but not so willing as to forfeit her fortune to do it. She stated her view of such matters in these words: "Love makes a slovenly figure in that house where poverty keeps the door." Fainwell, equally concerned about those thousands of British pounds, enlisted the services of two cronies, Freeman and Sackbut, in an elaborate campaign of deception to obtain consent of the four guardians by representing himself differently to each of the men.

In borrowed clothes and with borrowed footmen, and pretending to be a french dandy, he quickly obtained the enthusiastic approval of the foppish Sir Philip Modelove. Then he cozied up to Mr. Tradelove in the guise of a Dutch business tycoon, conned him into a bad wager that left Tradelove owing him 2,000 pounds, a debt Fainwell would be willing to forgive if Tradelove would agree to his marrying Ann, which Tradelove gleefully did. Number three among the guardians was Periwinkle, an impractical virtuoso who had visions of easy money, and so was easily deceived into an agreement. These successful manipulations left only one of the four, Obadiah Prim, a very proper Quaker.

Fainwell and his co-conspirators intercepted a letter intended for Prim. From it, they learned that a Quaker gentleman named Simon Pure from Pennsylvania was soon to arrive at Prim's and was to be welcomed in brotherly love. Resealing the letter and sending it on, Fainwell, having already operated in the disguise of a French dandy, a Dutch trader, and a magician, now disguised himself as a Pennsylvania Quaker and approached the Prims at their home.

Fully convincing Prim that he was indeed the good man from America, he obtained Prim's signature on a document consenting to his marriage to Ann. Then the real Simon Pure arrived, as did the other three guardians, all of whom had signed similar statements of consent. All quickly realized they had been conned by the same man, all were embarrassed for having been so gullible, but all were able to laugh about it—even Prim, although he found it necessary to say, "I am sorry the maiden has fallen into such hands."

The girl got her 30,000 pounds, and Fainwell got the girl. The American Quaker got nothing—except his name into the language, where it has persistently remained.

Siren Songs   The word *siren* comes to us from a story loved by the ancient Greeks. It takes place on an island somewhere in the eastern Mediterranean where there lived three female creatures who had the faces of beautiful women and the bodies of scaly, misshapen birds. Their mission in life was deception and seduction, and they were good at it.

Together, these sisters comprised a spectacular ensemble of music-makers. One played the lyre, another made music on the flute, and the third sister sang. They performed near the seashore, sitting among the growing plants, flowers, and trees in such a way that only their heads and shoulders were visible. By all accounts, their music had an almost irresistible appeal; it was bewitching, beguiling.

But they weren't there to make music for the fun of it or to entertain passers-by: It was to entice sailors to their island not for romance but for murder. The sailors they successfully lured were killed and eaten. Their subterfuge deceived many, and it was said that beneath the fronds and flowers among which they sat and sang were stacks of their victims' fleshless bones.

Listening to them, the Sirens sounded wonderful, but seeing them was a horrible experience. They had fetching voices and repulsive bodies. The problem was, however, that when a man got close enough to see what they really were, it was too late for escape. The word *siren* means "entangler," and this they were!

Two intrepid traveling groups, nevertheless, did not succumb to the sisters. One was Jason, sailing by with the Argonauts on his search for the Golden Fleece. He had on his boat an especially gifted passenger, the divine singer, Orpheus, with his lyre. The music made by Orpheus was so enchantingly beautiful that the sailors never heard the music of the Sirens. Protected by the power of a greater attraction, the fatal allurements had no appeal to them.

The other who outwitted the Sirens was Odysseus (Latin: Ulysses) on his long voyage home following the Trojan War. As a preventive measure, he stopped the ears of all his crew with wax, so they were unable to hear. And then he had them bind him securely to the vessel's mast, so he was unable to get himself free. It was said that after the Odysseus episode, the Siren sisters either drowned themselves or flew away to some unknown place. (Rome maybe? for the Siren story later appears also in the literature of the Romans.)

So, on our English-speaking tongues, the word *siren* may do far more than identify a noisemaker on an approaching motor vehicle. A siren song or sound is any alluring attraction drawing someone away from a worthy purpose or a charted course. And, of course, an alluring and dangerous woman can be described as a siren. (See also Musical Charm of Orpheus.)

Size of MacCool's Baby   On the coast of northern Ireland where County Antrim abuts the North Channel, one may see a strange natural formation known as the Giant's Causeway. A long, narrow mass of basaltic stone extending far into the sea, the formation is composed entirely of some 40,000 columns standing on end as though some prehistoric pile driver had sunk them deep into the ocean floor. Between one and two feet in diameter, these stand at places to a height of about twenty feet above water level. Prismatic in shape, each having four to ten sides, they fit so precisely together that when viewed from above, they form a gigantic mosaic. Across the channel, seventy-five miles away, stands a similar formation at the Scottish island of Staffa.

Geologists say these formations are the result of volcanic activity occurring some fifty million years ago. For centuries, though, Irish folklore has insisted on a different explanation.

Finn MacCool, a legendary folk hero, was the subject of many stories the Irish loved to tell. This fellow was a giant, who was so enormous that it may be said he was a giant's giant. In Scotland, he had an enemy named Finn Gall, also an oversized chap.

To get at his adversary, Finn MacCool constructed a causeway stretching from shore to shore. In one long day, he drove huge stone columns into the ocean floor, with their tops protruding above the water so that one could cross from coast to coast. Being at the day's end a bit tired, and postponing his fight with Gall, he decided to go home and rest.

Discovering the structure MacCool had built, and wondering what sort of man the builder might be, Finn Gall came across to have a look at him. Arriving before MacCool awakened, he stared in awe at this mountainous hulk of sleeping man. Much impressed with the giant's monstrous size, he was even more impressed when MacCool's wife cleverly lied, "That? That's not my husband; that's our baby!"

Gall thought, "If that's their baby, what must the father be like?" In much haste he withdrew, retreating as rapidly as possible across the causeway, destroying much of it as he went. And the ruins of MacCool's workmanship stand today pretty much as Gall left them.

To this day, when we want to say that something is big, we may say, "Oh, it's about the size of MacCool's baby!"

Slough of Despond   *The Pilgrim's Progress* is a story that gives us three oft-used expressions. It was written by John Bunyan (1628–1688) mostly in Bedford Prison, England, where Bunyan was held for more than twelve years for preaching the Christian gospel without a license.

The Pilgrim's Progress is an allegory of a Christian's life. The hero is

Christian, who makes his much-troubled way from the City of Destruction to the Celestial City. Evangelist advises him that there is indeed a Celestial City, and to reach it, he must first pass through Wicket Gate.

Christian thinks he knows the location of the gate, but cannot see it, and he travels by a light that is dim. Before reaching the gate, he stumbles into the Slough of Despond, a deep boglike, marshy place, and because of a heavy burden he carries, he has awful difficulty getting out. He does at last, though, with the aid of Help. The slough of despond has become proverbial for a time or experience of hopelessness, dejection, and discouragement.

Christian does in due time pass the Wicket Gate, beyond which he climbs a hill to the place of the Cross, where the heavy burden falls from his back, giving him greater freedom to travel. So he does, struggling against this adversary or that, and assisted in various ways by others offering aid.

Traveling at one point in the company of Faithful, the two of them come to the village of Vanity. Here, Beelzebub, Apollyon, and Legion have established a marketplace where items for vain people are sold. Here in Vanity Fair the two travelers refuse to buy anything, although the urge to do so is strong and the sales pressures are great.

Their refusal angers the merchants who then excite the people, and the pilgrims are arrested. Faithful is condemned to be burned at the stake; afterward, though, a heavenly chariot carries him away. Finally, Christian is able to make his escape.

Vanity Fair is symbolic of all worldly enticements that would draw aspiring persons away from higher motivations and more noble actions.

Following his escape from Vanity, Christian is joined by Hopeful, and the adventure continues. Walking in the Narrow Way, they stroll alongside a pleasant river for a while, but within a short distance, the path turns away from the river and becomes rough. They then take an easier path nearby, and as night falls, they become lost. When morning dawns, they find themselves near Doubting Castle, home of the Giant Despair. They are captured by the Giant, who locks them in a dungeon, cruelly mauling and beating them. Christian remembers at last that he carries a key called Promise, and with this key he unlocks the dungeon door, and the two are free again.

Doubting Castle, as the name is now used, refers not to a place or a building, but to a state of mind. It is a name for that timidity of spirit that makes prisoners of pilgrims, that faithlessness that paralyzes and halts all further forward progress.

Having gotten free of the Giant's castle, Christian and Hopeful again find the Narrow Way, follow it to the Delectable Mountains and on to the Celestial City.

Snafu   During wartime, soldiers develop a sort of subculture of their own. Away from their homes, and thrown together in situations for which past experience has not prepared them, they are soon joined in a certain bond that has a character of its own—its own philosophy, ethic, and language.

In the Second World War, conditions were extremely complicated with many nations involved on many battlefronts. In communication, logistics, and general organization, there were staggering difficulties, frequently confusion, and often foul-ups of various kinds. It seemed sometimes to the service people that if anything could go wrong, it usually did. And, inescapably, they developed their own way of talking about it.

In the British Army, the phrase was "situation normal, all fouled up," or, more commonly perhaps, with a sexual vulgarity in lieu of the word *fouled*. Gradually, the saying became condensed even further, as they began using only the first letters of these five words, this coming out "snafu." Things got snafued, or somebody was in the process of snafuing something.

The expression spread to the other British services and to the Americans, and soon it was common lingo in wartime communication.

And its use didn't end with the war—there seemed to be considerable need for it even afterward. So aptly does it indicate ineptness and concisely depict the foul-ups that result from bungling, that the expression survived the war and continues as a commonly used word in our vocabulary.

Something's Rotten in Denmark   Suspecting acts of trickery or skulduggery, one may say, "There's something rotten in Denmark." The expression assumes a variety of forms, but in whatever form, it owes its existence to the tragic story of Hamlet by William Shakespeare.

A brilliant youth, Hamlet has been studying at the university in Wittenberg. He is now at home in Denmark, due to the sudden death of his father, the king. His father's brother Claudius has already assumed the throne. He has also, in violation of law, married Hamlet's mother, the lately bereaved widow, Gertrude.

Events have moved at a dizzy pace. In these bewildering circumstances, young Hamlet is comforted greatly by the presence of his university friend, Horatio, a young man of philosophical inclination.

As the play opens, sentries keeping watch on the palace walls see something more terrifying than an invading army—a ghost. It is the ghost of the deceased king, clad in full armor, strolling silently through the night, again and again, night after night.

This is made known to Horatio, who is not a believer in ghosts, but upon seeing the apparition, he is totally convinced. He tells Hamlet, believing that the ghost, thus far silent, will speak with Hamlet if it has the opportunity.

It is then with a sense of grim foreboding that on the following night Hamlet, Horatio, and the soldiers of the watch keep their apprehensive vigil. As before, the specter appears, this time beckoning Hamlet to follow it. As Hamlet moves to do so, the others, fearful for his safety, attempt to restrain him. So determined is Hamlet that he draws his sword against his friends and then walks away with the ghost. As he leaves, one of the soldiers says to Horatio, "Something is rotten in the state of Denmark."

His father's ghost reveals to Hamlet that his recent death was murder, that the murderer was Claudius, that Claudius and Hamlet's mother have been having an affair, and that Claudius has committed the murder to make himself king and to make Gertrude his wife.

A great deal being very rotten in Denmark, Hamlet is deeply troubled by the offensive stench of it. He feels he must avenge his father's death. But how? Making matters more complicated, his father's ghost has forbidden him to harm his mother. Knowing that his homeland is in evil hands, he cries out,

> The time is out of joint, O cursed spite
> That ever I was born to set it right!

Well, he tries. But Hamlet is not a fighter; he is a thoughtful, introspective young man, an idealist really, and circumstances have cast him in a role for which he is ill suited. In the final struggle, death is the only winner: Claudius, Gertrude, Hamlet, and a great many others are dead.

Sour Grapes   When we cannot have what we want, and excuse our failure to get it by saying we really didn't want it anyway, we are exemplifying the sour grapes syndrome. The story is from Aesop, the well-known fable of the fox and the grapes.

The fox was a hungry vixen. For some time, she had been unsuccessful in her hunting for hares and other small game and had been unable to find any fruits or berries. Famished for want of food, she came upon a garden where grapes hung ripe and red on the gardener's trellis. Looking at them, she could almost taste their juicy goodness.

Being a fox, and therefore not a climber, she could only reach the grapes by leaping, but the luscious clusters were beyond her reach. Try as she would, she was unable to jump high enough. As she frantically repeated her efforts, she became tired and her leaps grew shorter and shorter, until eventually she could scarcely lift herself off the ground.

At last, having failed completely to taste even one of the grapes, she stuck up her nose, assumed an air of casual indifference, and, hoping no one had seen her, turned and walked away. Her parting words were, "Oh well, they were sour anyway!"

Sow Dragon's Teeth   To sow dragon's teeth is to make problems for oneself or to stir up contention. The story source of the expression has two main characters, Cadmus and Jason.

The first is Cadmus, a character in Greek mythology, who wandered into the area of Thebes before there was a Thebes. There was, however, a spring of fine water guarded by a fierce dragon. Cadmus killed the dragon and, at the suggestion of the goddess Athena, sowed some of its teeth, like corn, in the ground. Immediately there sprang up from the sown teeth a whole army of hostile, armed men.

Cadmus tossed a stone into the midst of them, and, each suspicious of the others, they began fighting among themselves, killing one another until only five remained. These became servants of Cadmus and helped him build the city of Thebes.

Now comes the Jason part of the story. Sometime subsequent to Cadmus, Jason and his Argonauts, searching for the golden fleece, found it at last in Colchis where the cruel Aeetes was king. The fleece was guarded by a never-sleeping dragon, and the king was in no mood to give it up. Rather than fight Jason and his men, however, Aeetes devised a scheme to get Jason killed. He told Jason he would give him the fleece if he could plow a field using two fire-breathing bulls and sow the field with some dragon's teeth Athena had given him (these being the remainder of the teeth from the dragon Cadmus had killed).

Aeetes was sure the bulls would kill Jason as he tried to yoke them to the plow. And he knew from Athena that an army of armed men would arise from the ground where those teeth were sown. Aeetes reasoned that if Jason should avoid being done in by the bulls, these armed men were then sure to get him.

Jason proved Aeetes wrong on both counts. Successfully managing the bulls, he plowed the field and sowed the teeth. As for the armed men who sprang up—well, Aeetes had a daughter, Medea, who had fallen in love with Jason, and she confided to him the secret means of dealing with them. So when those men popped up out of the ground ready for attack, Jason hurled a stone into their ranks and got them to fight among themselves.

Quickly killing one another, these ground-born fellows soon eliminated themselves. Then, with the assistance of Medea, Jason seized the fleece and made off with it—and the girl.

Sphinx   It is sometimes said that someone is a sphinx or is sphinxlike, meaning mysterious or enigmatic. We are usually saying the person is a riddle, obscure, or noncommunicative.

Sphinxes abound in mythology and the legends of antiquity. A famous one, or a monument thereof, can be seen yet today near the pyramid of Kahfre in Egypt. But this sphinx has nothing to do with the way we use this word in our language. For our story, we go to Greek mythology and the primitive city of Thebes.

Here, King Laius and his Thebans had gravely offended the gods. Hera, wife of Zeus, sent a sphinx to punish them. This sphinx was a sort of monster, having the head and breasts of a woman, the body of a lion, the wings of a bird, and the tail of a snake. Looking at her, if one could bear to do so, one would probably ask, "What is this anyway?"

Her distinguishing characteristic, though, was not so much her bad looks as her bad habits. Among others, she had the habit of killing people—not for any reason in particular (no discernible reason anyway). On Hera's mission to Thebes, this horrible creature took up residence in the mountain pass above the city, confronting all travelers who came that way. To all people she posed a riddle, always the same one, and all who failed to solve that riddle were hurled over a precipice to their death.

To make matters worse, the riddle was one nobody could solve: What creature walks on four legs in the morning, on two at noon, and on three in the evening?

Finally, when Oedipus approached Thebes and met the monster, he heard the riddle and solved it. His solution: The creature is man, who crawls on two hands and two feet as a baby, walks upright in his prime, and leans on a staff in old age. Hearing the answer by Oedipus, the sphinx let out a blood-chilling scream and threw herself over the precipice to her own death.

The sphinx did not merely pose a riddle; she was one. Why, for instance, was that riddle of hers so important to her? Why did she make the solution of that riddle the criterion of life or death for all who heard it? What was so devastating about the eventual solution of the riddle that she destroyed herself?

You see, she was a mystery. She was beyond understanding. She was an egnima. She was . . . well, she was a sphinx—the original.

Spoonerism   William Archibald Spooner (1844–1930) was a British scholar, and from 1903 until 1924 he was the warden of New College, Oxford. By all accounts, he was your typical absent-minded professor, a master of mix-up.

One evening an acquaintance encountered Spooner wandering in bewilderment about the streets of Greenwich. He said, "I've been here for hours. I had an appointment to meet someone at 'The Dull Man, Greenwich' and I can't find it, and the really strange thing is that no one seems to have heard of it." Later that evening when he returned to Oxford, his wife set him straight: "It wasn't 'The Dull Man, Greenwich' you were to go to, but 'The Green Man, Dulwich.' "

Not merely in his thinking but also in his speaking, Warden Spooner was given to transposing the initial sounds of two or more related words. In a New College chapel service he once attempted to announce a hymn that included the words "conquering kings," but it came out, typical Spooner, "kinkering congs."

Once he severely reprimanded a student for "hissing his mystery" lecture. On another occasion, in a public address, he tried to say that something was a half-formed wish, but it came out "half-warmed fish." In Spooner's way of saying it, a reference to God as a "loving shepherd" came out "shoving leopard," and a "well-oiled bicycle" became a "well-boiled icicle."

In rhetoric, such transpositions are known as methesis. But this word is not often heard; instead, we call them spoonerisms and they can sometimes be riotously funny.

Stolen Thunder   In the early years of English drama, the creation of sound effects was a difficult aspect of presenting a play. In the absence of sophisticated mechanical and electronic devices, the production of sound was very much a problem and was regarded as a major element in the dramatic art.

In the first third of the eighteenth century, John Dennis was a principal critic and dramatist in England, but more notable as a critic than successful as a dramatist. The plays he wrote were generally not well received. One of these was a tragedy entitled *Appius and Virginia*, produced in 1709, generally spurned by the critics, and so severely criticized by Alexander Pope that it sparked a lifelong feud between the two men. In the face of all the criticism, the play had a very short run, being quickly withdrawn.

Dennis had invented a new and improved way of producing thunder, probably an arrangement of wooden troughs and hollowed logs. This device was first used during the brief run of *Appius and Virginia*. Soon after the closing of the play, Dennis had occasion to be present for a performance of Shakespeare's *Macbeth*. During one of the scenes, there suddenly came the loud rumble of thunder. Dennis instantly identified the sound as coming from the device he had made. Angrily, he leaped to his feet and shouted, "Damn them! Not content to stop my play, they now steal my thunder!"

The story of this outburst went quickly through the literary and cultural circles of England. Almost immediately, in those circles stolen thunder was often heard in humorous reference to anything one might have taken from another. The expression soon spilled over into general use, and there it has survived for almost three centuries.

When one is about to say or do something deemed significant, and another says or does it first, it is often said, "You have stolen my thunder." A reference to stolen thunder is frequently heard when one's unique or special way of saying or doing things is picked up and used by others.

Stone Stew   The vagrant fellow was shabbily dressed, his dark old suit somebody's castaway, his toes showing through holes in shoes long overworn; but he was clean, and there was on his face the hint of a grin and a twinkle in his eye. Approaching the manor house, he didn't turn in at the front door, but went around back to the place servants usually go, and there he knocked.

When the servants opened the door, he said what vagrants usually say: "Can you please give me some food?" They looked at one another and shook their heads and said no. And then he asked what vagrants usually don't ask: "Can you make a stew from a stone?" Again they said no, but he said, "I can." And then they noticed that in his hand he carried a clean, smooth, small stone. Holding this forward for them to see, he said, "Here, let me show you how," and he walked into their kitchen. There was the great cooking stove and lots of pots and pans, and the cooks and servants gathered around.

Taking a pot from a shelf, the stranger put in the stone, and said, "I'll need some water," they brought it, and he poured it into the pot with the stone, and cheerfully chattering all the while, he cooked it until it boiled. Delicately dipping a little, blowing to cool it slightly, he sipped reflectively, paused a wee bit, and then said, "It needs a little salt, I think." So the salt was brought, and later likewise the pepper; and then tasting again, this culinary genius announced, "It's almost ready now, but for better flavor, it needs a little fat meat." Then afterward the fat meat needed some potatoes to absorb the grease, and then some vegetables to provide just the right flavor.

So it went, tasting after tasting, ingredient after ingredient, until eventually all the miscellaneous leftovers from the past three days were simmering in the pot. Announcing finally that this novel culinary creation was finished, the fellow ladled out a bowlful for each member of his enthralled audience and a large one for himself. All pronounced it good, very good.

Nobody present had ever before eaten a stone stew, or even heard of one, for that matter. What an innovative idea, they all thought—to make stew from a stone! And it never dawned on any person present that that small round rock had nothing at all to do with the making of that stew—except in their minds, that is.

As a result of this old tale, stone stew (or maybe stone soup) refers to a miscellaneous concoction, a hodgepodge of things or ideas without much to hold them together.

Strength of Atlas   Strength and physical prowess were esteemed highly by the ancient Greeks. Their favorite legendary heroes were usually people capable of doing things almost or altogether impossible. Atlas was one of these heroes.

He was a second-generation Titan, a brother of Prometheus and cousin of Zeus. When Zeus led a revolt against the cruel dynasty of Titans, Atlas fought on their side. When Zeus won the war, banishing most of the Titans to the Underworld and putting others to various tasks, he gave Atlas the responsibility of holding up the sky. Atlas was condemned to stand near the western end of the earth, close by the Hesperides, and support the sky on his shoulders. Of course, the sky had to be held up or else it would fall.

When King Eurystheus assigned Hercules his twelve "labors," the eleventh of these was to get the golden apples of the Hesperides and bring them to the king. Going for them, Hercules came upon Atlas standing there with the sky on his shoulders. The dreadful hundred-headed serpent, Ladon, guarded the apples. Pretending to be afraid of this monster, Hercules proposed to Atlas that he would hold up the sky for Atlas if Atlas would get the apples for him. Atlas agreed, and while he gathered the apples, Hercules held up the sky.

Having collected the golden fruit, Atlas was at the point of leaving to make the delivery to Eurystheus when Hercules complained that he needed to arrange padding for his shoulders. Atlas consented to resume the sky-holding duty while Hercules did this. Atlas must have been of the gullible sort, or else he didn't know the wily Hercules very well, for as soon as Atlas again had the sky firmly in place on his back, Hercules walked away with the apples. Atlas wasn't left merely holding the bag; he was left holding the whole sky.

And there for a long time he stood. Eventually, though, another traveler dropped by, Perseus. Sometime earlier, Perseus had killed the Gorgon named Medusa, had severed her head, and had carried it around with him ever since. Now, this head, or the face portion of it, had a strange power: Anyone who looked at it was instantly turned into stone.

Perseus had used the head effectively on various occasions, converting adversaries into stone statues. On this occasion, Atlas became the victim; he made the mistake of looking upon the late Medusa's dead face, and some have said that the Atlas Mountains in northwest Africa are the result.

So much for Atlas, but his name lives on not only to denote a mountain but all sorts of other things that are supposed to be strong or rugged. Atlas and his old enemy, Hercules, have at last gotten together—in linguistic usage—as the two top "strongmen" of all time. (See also CLEAN THE AUGEAN STABLES.)

Strength of Hercules The strength of Hercules, a Herculean task, and all the labors of Hercules are phrases commonly heard, and in obvious reference to the person who bore this name. He was the most popular of the Greek mythological figures. Actually, his name was Heracles, but we usually call him by his Roman or Latin name, Hercules. By whatever name known, he was an almost invincible champion of physical prowess and clever shenanigans.

He began life as an object of controversy, son of the high god Zeus and a mortal woman of Thebes named Alcmena. Alcmena had a husband, of course, but this was of small consequence to Zeus who, after all, was a god, and gods could usually do pretty much as they pleased. Besides, Alcmena's husband was out of town at the time Zeus decided to spend a night with her. About nine months afterward, Hercules was born, along with a twin brother, Iphicles.

There was a complication, however. Zeus had a wife, Hera, and she did not look kindly upon her husband's affair with Alcmena. Out of spite, she sent two huge poisonous snakes to kill the twin boys when they were less than a year old. But Hercules awakened, grasped the neck of a snake in each hand, and choked them to death. From this first triumph, he went on to many victories, although through all of it the resentful Hera set herself against him, doing everything possible to bring him down.

Believing it would make him immortal, Hercules bound himself in a twelve-year servitude to King Eurystheus of Mycenae. Hoping to get rid of Hercules, Eurystheus assigned him twelve most difficult tasks or "labors," each believed absolutely impossible to achieve. Instead of getting himself killed in the process, as Eurystheus hoped, Hercules successfully completed all the tasks.

In the very first of these, he not only killed the Nemean lion, which was supposed to have killed him, but he also made for himself a garment of its skin that he wore for the eleven remaining ventures.

When Hercules was still alive after completing the first eleven of his tasks, Eurystheus was probably thinking: What does it take to finish off this fellow? Anyway, for assignment number twelve, he sent Hercules to hell. That is, he sent him to the Underworld, to the dark kingdom of Pluto, from which no traveler had ever returned. The task to be performed there was indeed a difficult one. Pluto had a dog named Cerberus, a watchdog, and this dog had three heads, all with watchful eyes and snarling mouths and teeth that were razor sharp. Hercules was required to steal this dog and bring him back to Mycenae. Now, as everyone knows, nobody likes to have his watchdog stolen, and Pluto likewise. But Hercules did it!

One of his most notable achievements, though, was not one of the twelve. It happened in the happy land of Thessaly where the good King Admetus fell ill and worsened until he was about to die. Earlier, the Fates, who managed such matters, had promised to spare him if someone else would die in his place. Nobody could be found, however, who was willing to do this. The rich said they had too much to live for, and the poor claimed that life was about all they had. The young chose not to give up the many years remaining for them, and the old said their few years were too precious to give up.

The people needed their king; and knowing this, the beautiful Queen Alcestis gave herself to die in her husband's place. Having prepared herself for death, she lay in mortal pain. Death had come out of Hades to take her away, and Hercules, on one of his many journeys, arrived just in time to see Death carrying off the spirit of the stricken queen. He accosted Death at the palace gate, seized him in his mighty arms, and wrestled him to the victory. Death was compelled to drop the queen's spirit and hasten empty-handed back to Hades.

Pluck a spirit from the hands of Death—one who can do this, it would seem, would be able to do almost anything. Looking at the man's record, it's no great surprise that we talk about the power of a Hercules or about a Herculean task. (See also CLEAN THE AUGEAN STABLES.)

Strength of Samson   If a man is strong, we may say he has the strength of Samson, or a man of much strength may be known simply as a Samson. According to the story, this Samson fellow was the main character in a somewhat pathetic melodrama played out in the Middle East more than 3,000 years ago, and reported in connection with the history of the Hebrew people.

It was a time when the Israelites and the Philistines shared the land of Canaan, the Philistines being the overlords and the Israelites the underlings. Samson was an Israelite. Even before his birth, he was consecrated by his mother to be a Nazarite, meaning that he must never drink alcohol, have his hair cut, or do anything that might defile his body.

When Samson grew to manhood, he fell in love with a Philistine girl. In compliance with Philistine custom, he went to her home for the week-long festivities preceding their marriage. It was a rowdy, raucous occasion, attended by his best man and thirty other young men. During the revelries, Samson posed a riddle to the men, making a wager that they would be unable to solve it within the seven days, with the payoff to be thirty men's garments of fine quality. By finagling the help of Samson's girlfriend, the men did, on the seventh day, come up with the solution. Samson told them, "Had you not plowed with my heifer, you would not have solved my riddle." Nevertheless, Samson was obligated to provide thirty fine garments, which he didn't have. No problem at all for Samson, though: He promptly went down to the nearby town of Askalon, killed thirty Philistine men, and took the clothes from their bodies.

While Samson was away doing this, his girlfriend's father gave the girl in marriage to another fellow; to be specific, he gave her to Samson's best man. Understandably, Samson was furious, his anger not so understandably directed toward Philistines in general. To get even, he caught 300 live foxes, hitched them tail-to-tail in 150 teams of two, fastened a burning torch between each pair, and released the whole pack. Their tails ablaze, these terrified creatures ran helter skelter throughout the countryside, setting afire all the Philistine grain fields, vineyards, and orchards.

Learning that Samson had done this because of what his girlfriend's father had done, the Philistines then put the torch to that family home, burning to death the girl, her father, and the entire household. Now more angry than ever, Samson made a general slaughter of the Philistines in the whole area. Then he went into retreat at Etam.

The Philistines, in retaliation, made a major raid against Israel at Lehi, letting it be known they were doing this because of what Samson had done to them. So, Samson's fellow Israelites, quite willing to sacrifice their strong man to save themselves, bound him in two new ropes and turned him over to the Philistines. Upon seeing the huge number of his captors, Samson became enraged and, with a single mighty flexing of muscle, broke the ropes that bound him. He then seized the nearby jawbone of a dead ass, and with this weapon killed 1,000 of the Philistines.

A short while afterward, in Gaza, Samson was spending the night in a prostitute's house when word got out that he was there. Philistines surrounded the place, preparing to take him when morning came. But at midnight, Samson arose, went to the city gates, lifted them off their hinges, and carried them nearly forty miles to a hilltop just outside Hebron.

Rather strong, this fellow, right? Yes. But most men have their weaknesses, and Samson had his—women. Meeting one named Delilah, a Philistine, he let her con him into confessing himself a Nazarite, one whose hair must never be cut. It followed quickly then that while Samson slept, his head on Delilah's lap, the Philistines gave him a haircut, a very expensive one, for it took away every ounce of his enormous strength. The Philistines then gouged out his eyes and put him to grinding grain at their mill in Gaza.

After some time, during which Samson's hair was all the while growing, the Philistines held a great celebration in the temple of Dagon, their god. Remembering their famous prisoner at Gaza's mill, they brought Samson in for the sport of mocking him.

While there, although sightless, Samson was able to locate the two huge pillars on which the temple's roof structure rested. Pretending to lean against these for support, he suddenly encircled them with his arms, and gave one powerful tug, dislodging the pillars from their places. As the pillars fell, so did the roof, and the whole structure came down. Together with many Philistine lords and ladies, there that day beneath that mound of stones and bricks, Samson died—and so the melodrama ends.

Sword of Damocles   "Uneasy lies the head that wears a crown." As Shakespeare tells it, these words were spoken by King Henry IV one midnight as he paced his palace floor. He was commenting on the perils and hazards that plague one in a high position.

Another ruler who keenly felt the precariousness of high office was Dionysius the Elder, who for nearly forty years in the fourth century B.C. was the tyrant of Syracuse. Syracuse was a mostly Greek city on the island of Sicily, and in those days a tyrant, while an absolute ruler, was not necessarily an evil one. Dionysius, in fact, was a rather good one.

One of the courtiers who attended him was much impressed by the trappings of his office, but had given little consideration to the responsibilities of it. This man's name was Damocles. Inclined to flattery, Damocles persistently praised Dionysius, speaking enviously of his privilege and power, extravagantly extolling the secure and luxurious lifestyle of kings.

The shrewd old tyrant at last grew weary of the frothy mouthings of Damocles, and decided to give him an object lesson in realism. Accordingly, he invited Damocles to a fine banquet. At the appointed time, all were assembled and in place at the great table, Damocles in the place of honor.

Early in the festivities, Damocles happened to glance upward, to discover directly above his head a heavy sword, point downward, suspended by a single horsehair. There he was, poor fellow, surrounded by all the notables of the realm, too scared to dine and too proud to run. For him, the remainder of that evening was torture. The slightest stirring of air could break that hair, or a little passing of time might do it just as well. Total torment—it must have been the longest banquet at which Damocles ever sat.

After-dinner speeches come in all categories, from utterly boring to highly exciting, and the speech made by Dionysius that evening must be classified among the more exciting. He made his point: how tentative is a ruler's power; how uncertain the outcome of any venture; how great the danger that is always present; all is not felicity, carefree, with contentment unsullied; there is always the specter of impending calamity; the heavy burdens borne by the man at the top may not be always seen by the casual observer, but they are present.

We still talk about the sword of Damocles. When we speak of some impending doom, we like to say that the sword of Damocles hangs over our heads. Or we may say that the threatened onset of some disaster hangs by a hair.

— T —

Take the Low Road   The Scots were always loyal and home-loving people, with a passionate affection for their lochs and hills and highlands; when unavoidably away, they yearned to be home again. Tradition and folkways were strong among them. It was a common folk belief that if any Scotsman should die outside of Scotland, his spirit would immediately find its way home by means of an underground passage.

For about 400 years, from the twelfth through the sixteenth centuries, the Scots were embroiled in complicated, bloody conflict with the English. In one skirmish, two young Scots were captured by the English and imprisoned together in Carlisle Castle in northern England.

It was an intolerable ordeal to be held against their wills in a foreign land. But, worse yet, one was deemed guilty of spying and was sentenced to die at dawn the following day. That night in that jail cell, so tradition says, that young man wrote a hauntingly beautiful song, and the next day he was killed. The other lad was eventually released, and he returned to Scotland with that song.

The song is "Loch Lomond," and it has been loved and sung ever since. In it the condemned soldier speaks to his companion prisoner. Longing heartbrokenly for his beloved homeland, he says:

By yon bonnie banks, and by yon bonnie braes,
Where the sun shines bright on Loch Lomond,
Where me and my true love were ever wont to gae,
On the bonnie, bonnie banks of Loch Lomon'—
Oh! ye'll take the high-road and I'll take the low-road,
And I'll be in Scotland afore ye,
But me and my true love will never meet again
On the bonnie, bonnie banks of Loch Lomand.

The young Scot found a certain consolation in the knowledge that he would soon be home again. His companion would have to trudge wearily many long, difficult miles; but not so for him—by that underground way, his return would be magic and swift. No, he would never meet the girl he loved, nor stand by that shining blue lake; but somewhere unseen, his spirit would be free in Scotland. The young singer is saying the low-road is a good road for it is the road that leads home.

And for those who fondly hold the faith that dying is not ending, but is really a way of going on, to die is to take the low road home.

Tantalize   To tantalize is to present something desirable and then withhold it. It's a sure-fire technique for producing misery, especially when prolonged.

The technique was devised and first used by the gods who figured so prominently in the mythology of primitive Greece. In those days, so the story goes, there lived a man whose name was Tantalos. Actually, he himself was some sort of demigod, a mix of the human and the divine. He was rich and powerful, and the gods welcomed him in their society.

After a while, though, they concluded that he had betrayed them. The "bill of particulars" against him charged him with divulging the secrets of the gods to humans, stealing the ambrosia of the gods and giving it to humans, and on one occasion, killing his own son, cooking the flesh, and serving it at a banquet to see if the gods would know what they were eating. (They did, incidentally.)

For all these crimes, Tantalos was condemned to the Underworld. But merely to incarcerate him was not deemed sufficient punishment, so the gods contrived a diabolic means of compounding his agony.

He was forced to stand in water up to his neck and under a tree's branch that bore luscious fruit; but whenever he stooped to drink, the water would recede, and every time he reached for fruit, the limb would spring away. Thus, in the presence of water, Tantalos was forever thirsty, and in the presence of food, always hungry. In this way, the Olympian gods designed a strategy for making misery, and its first and most famous victim gave that strategy his name.

Thirty Pieces of Silver   For nearly three years Judas had been a follower and disciple of Jesus. He served as treasurer of the small band of fellow followers who traveled with their master. With the others, he had received from Jesus the exhilarating hope of good things to come—justice, peace, and freedom. At length, though, it appeared the good things were a long time coming and Judas grew tired of waiting, perhaps giving up hope they would ever come at all.

For reasons and with feelings nobody has ever fully understood, Judas turned against Jesus. Going to Jesus' enemies, he offered his services to them—for a price, apparently. They gave him thirty pieces of silver to lead them by night to where Jesus was and to identify him for them.

Jesus was arrested, and following the arrest the awful enormity of his despicable act came upon Judas with a force unbearable. In panic, he raced back to the men who had paid him, saying, "I have sinned; I have betrayed innocent blood." Their reply was cold, callous, and cruel: "What is that to us? You see to it." In utter desperation, Judas flung those thirty coins on the floor and ran. Somewhere he found a rope and hanged himself.

Today, the phrase "thirty pieces of silver" is used as a synonym for a bribe. And the money used to inflict injury upon another is known as blood money. (See also JUDAS' KISS.)

Titanic   Why do we say that something big is titanic? Because the ancient Greeks, out of a fertile imagination and an urgent need to explain things, created a series of oft-repeated stories featuring a race of mighty beings called Titans. As the stories were told by Hesiod and others, in the beginning there was nothing, a void, Chaos. Then the Earth took shape, and Chaos was divided into two parts, the part under the earth and the part above the earth.

The part above was Uranus and the earth itself was Gaea. These two, the Earth and the Heavens, mated, and of their union twelve children were born, six males and six females. These were the Titans. They intermarried and became the parents of many children. There was, for example, Hyperion, who married his sister Theia, and of their union were born the sun and the moon.

The youngest of the Titans was Cronus, who mated with his sister Rhea, and they became the parents of Zeus, Hades, and Poseidon. Later, Zeus became the high god of Heavens, Hades ruled the Underworld, and Poseidon oversaw the Sea. Thus the Titans gave birth to the gods.

They were, however, a rather lawless and undisciplined lot. Finally, Zeus, somewhat more genteel than most, rebelled and went to war against them. He and his forces fought from Mount Olympus and they from Mount Othrys. The long, mammoth conflict was a battle before which the whole universe trembled. Zeus won and threw most of the Titans into the Underworld, and the others submitted to his authority.

Early in the twentieth century when the British-based White Star Line began to build the largest and fastest oceangoing vessel in the world, it was decided to name it the *Titanic*. A well-chosen name, one would think, but as the Titans of old were at last subdued by Zeus, the *Titanic* proved no match for the ice-strewn waters of the North Atlantic on April 15, 1912. The Titans were monstrous and mighty, but not invincible.

Tom Sawyer   *See* Whitewash a Fence.

Tortoise and the Hare   *See* Hare and the Tortoise.

Trojan Horse   The Trojan war was fought over a woman, Helen. One wonders if she was worth the fighting, but two mighty armies fought, and the struggle lasted for ten long years.

Helen was the wife of Menelaus, ruler of the Grecian city of Sparta, and Troy lay eastward across the Aegean Sea from Greece. A swashbuckler named Paris came over from Troy, persuaded Helen to leave her husband, and took her away with him to his home. Paris' parents,

Priam and Hecuba, were the king and queen of Troy, and with them Paris and his stolen mistress found safe haven.

But the several city-states of the Greek federation rallied to the support of the gravely offended Menelaus, and a huge army was assembled to cross the sea and bring Helen home. Agamemnon, king of Mycenae, was put in command, and among the soldiers were such stalwarts as Odysseus, Achilles, and Menelaus himself.

When the Greeks had anchored their ships in the harbor at Troy, Odysseus and Menelaus entered the city demanding the surrender of Helen. This demand rejected, the battle ensued. The harbor was blockaded and the city surrounded.

The Greek attempt was to breach the city walls or break down the gates in a massive frontal assault. But for more than nine years the city stood. The Trojans were a courageous fighting force, fighting, of course, for the very survival of their city. Obviously, Helen could have stopped the war at any time; all she had to do was cross the lines some dark night and go back to her husband who was camped out there somewhere. Most Trojans had come to despise the woman, and, no doubt, would have been glad to see her go; but this she did not do.

The inspiration of the Trojans, as well as their most heroic warrior, was Prince Hector, the more noble brother of the infamous Paris. In the ninth year, Hector was killed by Achilles, and most Greeks believed his death would bring the immediate surrender of Troy, but it did not. Reinforcements came from the outside, among them the Amazons, a valiant army of female warriors.

The war went on, the Greeks finally concluding that their only way of winning was to resort to some kind of trickery. It was Odysseus who came up with the idea of a huge wooden horse. The plan was brilliantly conceived, having some rather sophisticated pyschological aspects.

The Greeks pretended to withdraw; most of the army boarded the ships and sailed for a place of concealment behind a nearby island. Others, on the plain before Troy, artfully constructed the gigantic horse, hollow inside, and with a door so cleverly disguised that it could not be seen from the outside. Into this piece of craftsmanship the Greeks put some of their best fighting men and closed the door. Then the remainder of the army withdrew.

With the dawning of the next day, the people of Troy looked out upon an empty field. The Greeks were gone! The war was over! Or so the Trojans thought, this being precisely what the Greeks wanted them to think. Shouting and singing with joy, the citizens and soldiers of Troy rushed out onto the field. In amazement, they gathered around the wooden horse, marveling at its majesty and wondering what it might mean.

About this time there appeared in their midst a disheveled and badly battered little man in the garments of a Greek. He told the Trojans that when the Greeks withdrew he had been abandoned and left stranded through the malice of Odysseus and others. The Trojans promised to spare his life if only he would tell them the truth about that horse: Why was it there and what did it mean?

The Greek was actually a part of the plot. His name was Sinon, and like an accomplished dramatist, he played out his act. He told the Trojans that the horse was a special offering to the goddess Athena, that it had been left on the field so long occupied by the Greeks to assure the favor of the goddess wherever the army moved from there. He declared that it was made large so the Trojans would be unable to move it into their city, and thus obtain the favor of the goddess for themselves.

Believing the story, the Trojans naturally were determined to have that thing inside their city walls. So, with a massive and mighty effort, they dragged it in. That night Sinon opened its secret door and the Grecian warriors came out. They opened the city gates, and before dawn, the armies of Greece were inside the walls.

The Trojan War was over. Menelaus took "fair Helen" home to Sparta—but whether to live happily ever after appears doubtful. What raw military power could not do, subterfuge and trickery had done. What could not be destroyed from without was at length destroyed from within. And still we speak often of a Trojan horse, meaning a hidden danger within. It means the acceptance of something that is outwardly appealing, but is actually about to do great harm.

Sometimes also we say, "Beware of Greeks bearing gifts." This is said as a warning against those who would give insincerely and with ulterior motive, who would give in order to get. It was Roman poet Virgil in the first century B.C. who first made this application of Homer's ancient story. (See also AMAZON; ODYSSEUS.)

True as Tell's Arrow   Traditionally, the Swiss have been a rugged, independent, and freedom-loving people. In the thirteenth century, the emperor of Austria claimed their land as a part of his empire and sent a man named Gessler to rule there. Wishing to stand well with his emperor, he ruled with iron hand in an oppressive and dictatorial manner. To make the people feel the constant pressure of his power, he placed the ducal cap of Austria atop a pole in the public square of Altorf and issued orders requiring all citizens to pause and bow when passing it.

Into the town square one day came a tall, strong young man leading his small son by the hand. He was William Tell, a man whose skills with a bow and arrow were unmatched in all of Switzerland. Passing the ducal cap that day, Tell didn't bow before it; he didn't even halt or hesitate—he simply walked by. Gessler's spies instantly reported this disrespect to their chief, who immediately ordered Tell brought to him.

Gessler said, "They tell me you shoot well. Instead of punishing you, I'm going to give you a chance to show me just how well you shoot. Have your son stand yonder a hundred paces off; place an apple on his head; and you stand here and pierce that apple with an arrow from your quiver."

It was a devilish design on Gessler's part. Tell's friends who were present turned pale with fear. But, looking Gessler squarely in the eye, Tell carefully withdrew two arrows from his quiver. "Go yonder," he said gently to his son, and some of Gessler's men walked with the boy, counting the paces, one hundred altogether.

With some measure of compassion, they turned the lad's back to his father. Firmly and strongly, Tell called out, "Face this way, son," and the boy quickly turned, stood straight and still, an apple on his head.

Tell tested the tension of his bow, fixed an arrow in its place, took aim, and fired. The apple split into two parts and fell to the ground, and a great shout went up from the people. But Gessler, pretending to be unimpressed, said in a surly voice to the bowman, "You were not very sure of your first shot, were you? I saw you place a second arrow in your belt."

Tell flashed back, "That arrow was for you, tyrant, had I missed my first shot." "Seize him!" Gessler cried. As the soldiers rushed forward, so did the people in overwhelming numbers. In the confusion, Tell took his son and escaped into the mountains. Some say he shot and killed Gessler before he fled, and others say he did so somewhere in the mountains a little later. In either case, history records that Austria gave the Swiss virtual independence in 1299 and finally withdrew all occupying forces in 1308.

To say that anything or anyone is as true as Tell's arrow, or as swift, or as straight is to recognize the very highest level of integrity or performance.

Tweedledum and Tweedledee   *See* JABBERWOOKY.

– U –

Ugly Duckling   From the fertile imagination of Hans Christian Andersen comes the tale of the ugly duckling. It was summertime in the country when a mother duck, sitting on her nest, observed that one egg failed to hatch when the others did. Her duck friends advised her to abandon it; but patiently she sat there, giving that one egg the warmth of her body, until several days later the shell finally popped open.

But what a disappointment! Her newborn was big and ugly and not at all like her other children. A friend pronounced it a turkey, but it could swim like a duck, and turkeys can't do that.

Growing up was hard for the new hatchling. In the barnyard the poor creature was cruelly abused by everyone. The ducks pecked at him, the chickens beat him with their wings, and the girl who tended the animals kicked him with her feet.

Eventually learning how to fly, he flapped his way over the fence and kept on flying as long as he could. At last he found a flock of wild ducks, who thought him strange, but agreed to let him stay with them provided he wouldn't marry one of their family.

Two young wild geese appeared and invited him to fly with them as their "bird of passage." But the invitation was a trick, for hunters with guns and big dogs lay in wait. The duckling barely escaped with his life and was then caught in a terrible storm. Taking refuge in an old cottage occupied by an aged woman, her cat, and a chicken, the duckling was ridiculed unmercifully because he could neither lay eggs nor arch his back or purr.

It was mutually agreed that he should leave this place, so he went away into the autumn chill and found a small lake that was good for swimming—and he loved swimming. Soon a flock of swans came by, flying south, and the duckling thought they were the most beautiful creatures he had ever seen. Oh, to be like them, he thought! But they flew away, leaving him alone on the lake.

As the days and nights grew colder and colder, ice formed everywhere along the water's edge and gradually closed around him. Unable by his paddling to keep the water from freezing, one night when he was totally exhausted, it froze tight around his body.

There the following morning a peasant found him, chopped away the ice, and carried him home to his wife and children. When the children tried to play with him, he thought they meant to do him harm and, frightened, he fluttered about the house, making a general mess of everything, and then escaped through the open doorway.

For the duckling, it was a hard winter. When spring at last came, he discovered that he could fly well, better than he had ever believed possible, and that he loved flying more than he had ever believed he would. So, flying a long way, he came to a beautiful garden where apple trees were in bloom and a lake of clear, smooth water glistened in the sun.

Here he glided down and came softly to rest. Soon, three graceful white swans swam out from among the rushes, and the ugly duckling was strangely moved by their beauty. And he loved them. He thought, "I must swim to them, and I will let them kill me if they wish."

As he bowed his head, expecting their murderous strokes to fall on his neck, he suddenly saw his reflection in the water. He was like those wonderful birds! He was a swan! Having never known what he was until now, a great wave of happiness swept over him.

The other swans gathered around, caressed him, and bowed their heads before him. Then children came to throw food into the water. One of them exclaimed, "See, there's a new one; a new swan has come, and he's the most beautiful of all."

Here the story comes to its happy ending, but telling it is incomplete without the addition of this one sentence from the story as Andersen

wrote it: "To be born in a duck's nest, in a farmyard, is of no consequence to a bird if it is hatched from a swan's egg."

As an expression sometimes appearing in our speech, an ugly duckling is one whose potential exceeds his appearance, one who seems
to be a misfit, or one who, while scorned by those around him, may
have in him the stuff of greatness.

Uncle Tom   Uncle Tom and Aunt Chloe were married slaves on the
plantation of Mr. Shelby in Kentucky. In financial straits, Mr. Shelby
found it necessary to sell Tom to a slave dealer from New Orleans.
Mr. Shelby's son George, a good friend of Tom's, vowed that he would
someday buy him back. Many slaves were running away at this time,
by the underground railroad going north; but Tom accepted his fate
obediently, believing that somehow there was a hidden wisdom in all
that was happening to him.

Taken south by Haley (the slave trader) aboard a Mississippi
steamer, Tom was able to save the life of another passenger, Eva, a
semi-invalid daughter of Augustine St. Clare. In appreciation, Mr. St.
Clare bought Tom. Tom's new owner was a good, well-meaning
planter, ambivalent about slavery, good to his slaves, but not a good
businessman or manager.

Tom and Little Eva became devoted friends. Just before she died,
she obtained her father's promise to free all his slaves, but before he
could fulfill that promise he was killed while attempting to stop a
fight between two men.

Mr. St. Clare's wife was of a different temperament, having no interest at all in giving freedom to anyone. Putting Tom on the auction
block, she sold him to Simon Legree, a plantation owner who was a
heavy drinker, mean, cruel, and generally a brute devoid of any redeeming virtue. He kept a pack of dogs to hunt down any slave
attempting escape. Patiently, Tom bore Legree's abuses without a
whimper. Legree was especially abusive of Tom because of his many
efforts to assist and show kindness to his fellow slaves.

One day while picking cotton, Tom helped fill the basket of a slave
woman who was ill. Seeing this act of generosity, Legree became
violently angry—perhaps because Tom's kindness was so totally con-
trary to his own nature. In utter spitefulness, Legree ordered Tom to

flog the woman he had just helped. Tom refused, and then Legree flogged him into unconsciousness.

Two of Legree's women slaves, Cassy and Emmeline, were determined to escape. Misleading him into the belief that they were somewhere in a nearby swamp, they actually were temporarily hidden in the attic of his house. Suspecting Tom knew something of their whereabouts, Legree beat him brutally until the old man could neither stand nor speak.

Two days later, George Shelby arrived to buy Tom and take him home to Kentucky. But the old man was dying. George threatened to have Legree tried for murder; Legree responded with mockery, and George flattened him. Before returning to Kentucky, George helped Cassy and Emmeline escape.

There is much more, of course, to Harriet Beecher Stowe's story of "Life among the Lowly," *Uncle Tom's Cabin.* Several subplots run parallel with the main one. When the story appeared in 1852, it came as an igniting spark to fire the national conscience in regard to slavery. Almost instantly, Simon Legree became archetypical of the worst of slave ownership. Very quickly, too, this man's name entered our language as another name for any man who is abusive of others, callous, cruel, and unfeeling.

A century after the publication of Mrs. Stowe's novel, another name emerged from it and fitted itself rather significantly into our language, Uncle Tom. During the long struggle of African-Americans for equality and citizenship, a black man who accepted white domination without resistance came to be known by some as an Uncle Tom.

Up Salt River   Salt River flows into the Ohio not many miles below Louisville, Kentucky. In pioneer days, pirates who harassed Ohio River traffic often took their booty up Salt River to a secret place of concealment. When anything in the area was stolen or mysteriously disappeared, it was commonly said that the missing thing had probably gone up Salt River.

A more pointed instance of going up that river, however, occurred in 1832 when Henry Clay ran against Andrew Jackson for the presidency of the United States. As the anecdote goes, once when Clay was scheduled to make a campaign speech in Louisville, he hired a boatman to row him upstream to the place of his appointment. The boatman, being strongly inclined to favor Jackson, made a convenient "mistake" at the confluence of the two rivers, rowing up Salt River instead of the Ohio and causing the candidate to miss his engagement in Louisville.

During the remainder of the campaign, this anecdote was often told and retold, and when Clay suffered an overwhelming defeat, the story was well remembered. Because Clay had failed to reach a goal and had been sidelined, it was virtually inevitable that people would jokingly say, "Clay went up Salt River."

The expression has been in use from then until now, as a way of saying that a person has met defeat or that an effort has failed.

Uriah Heep   One who is forever calling attention to his or her humility may be derisively identified as a Uriah Heep. It is Uriah Heepish to boast of one's humility.

A creation of Charles Dickens in the story of *David Copperfield* (1850), Uriah Heep is one of the best defined characters in literature and one of the most obnoxious. Always professing to be "an 'umble man," he is in reality a hypocritical sneak. Using his vaunted humility as a cover-up, he schemes to filch something from almost everyone in his reach.

Mr. Wickfield, a good man, is an attorney at Canterbury and the father of Agnes, a young woman of finest qualities and impeccable character. Uriah Heep is Mr. Wickfield's clerk; Heep's only close relative is his mother, who is as deceitful and conniving as he is. Concealing his true character, Heep cleverly manipulates Wickfield, worming his way into a full partnership and surreptitiously assuming more and more authority. Taking advantage of Wickfield's failing health, Heep manages to get control of his estate and believes Agnes will be compelled to enter into marriage with him.

Young Copperfield has lived in the Wickfield home while a student at Canterbury and has since maintained a close friendship with the family. He intensely dislikes and strongly distrusts Heep. His suspicions are deepened when it becomes apparent that Heep and his mother are doing everything possible to interfere in the developing relationship between Copperfield and Agnes.

Wilkins Micawber, who overdramatizes everything and who is always in debt, is employed as confidential secretary to Heep. It is observed soon afterward that Micawber is secretive, withdrawn, and troubled in some way. Actually, Micawber's problem is that, as Heep's secretary, he has accumulated massive evidence of his employer's dishonesty, and is perplexed about what to do with it.

As is normal for him, Micawber is in financial straits and knows that squealing on Heep will cost him what little security he has. All his life he has been a perennial believer that something will turn up, and now that this job has turned up, he is hesitant to destroy it. Neither can he bear the thought of working any longer for Heep.

Eventually, after consulting Copperfield's friend David Traddles, a lawyer, Micawber dramatically confronts Heep with damning accusations and the evidence to support them. The scene is at Wickfield's, and the drama is played out in the presence of Copperfield, Wickfield, Traddles, Agnes, Copperfield's great aunt Betsy, and Heep's conniving mother, who urges her son to plead humility to the end.

Stripped of his pretense, Heep is revealed as without a redeeming virtue. By every underhanded trick and deception, he has persistently robbed Mr. Wickfield, and he is now proved responsible for Miss Betsy's loss of her fortune. Plainly guilty of thievery by every imaginable kind of trick, he is forced to make restitution.

Neither Mr. Wickfield nor Miss Betsy press charges against him, and the sniveling culprit leaves Canterbury, goes elsewhere in England, and becomes involved again in similar perfidies. He is eventually sent to prison for forgery. With the financial assistance of Copperfield's aunt, Micawber and his family emigrate to Australia, where he hopes something will turn up. And, yes, Copperfield eventually marries Agnes.

Utopia   Erasmus called Sir Thomas More "A Man for All Seasons," as did Robert Bolt in 1960 in his memorable play by the same title. Statesman, churchman, philosopher, author, and (since 1935) saint, More was a sixteenth-century giant. Daring to cross wills with Henry VIII, he was executed on Tower Hill, London, in 1535. Mounting the scaffold, he jokingly said to the attendant, "See me safe up; as for coming down, let me shift for myself." Seriously, he spoke to all present, "I die the king's good servant, but God's first."

In 1516 he provided humanity with a classic springboard for discussion, his book *Utopia*. He invented the word, composing it from the Greek negative *ou* and *topos*, meaning "place," or the English *utopia*, meaning "no place," "nowhere."

The story he tells is of a visit to Antwerp to see his friend Peter Giles. Here he meets an acquaintance of Giles, a mysterious fellow, widely traveled apparently, named Raphael Mythloday. From the Greek, his name means "one who talks nonsense." And talk the man does, persistently, and passionately, of his travels about the world, notably in the land of Utopia.

Utopia is a crescent-shaped island kingdom somewhere in the west. The kingdom is unique among all nations of the world. The government is people oriented; each group of thirty families elects an annual ruler, each ten groups elects a member of the realm's council, and this council elects a prince who becomes the chief ruler for his lifetime. The council meets every third day, but no decision is ever made on the day an issue is raised; time is taken to think about it.

In Utopia, the working day is six hours long. Everyone works and each person is required to work at least two years on a farm. All property is commonly owned, and no person ever desires to have more than the others. The citizens want their state to be financially strong, for it is Utopian policy to pay off an enemy rather than fight him, and therefore they need a great deal of money. They wish their enemies to have the resources to fight so they may kill off one another, leaving the Utopians unscathed.

The Utopians' finest jewelry is given to their children to play with. Gold and silver are despised and used to make such items as chamber pots. There is no capital punishment; the severest punishment one can get is to be sentenced to slavery. Violence and vice have been eliminated; gambling is unknown. Labor is looked upon as a recreational activity.

Such are conditions in the land of Utopia. The name has become symbolic for the ideal state, the perfect society, therefore the unattainable. To speak of an idea as utopian is to declare it visionary, impractical, and something that may be dreamed about but never realized.

– V –

Vandals   These were a people known to history for a period of about 1,000 years, but significantly for only about 130. They are known to have inhabited the Oder River valley as early as the fifth century B.C., but for 800 or 900 years they made no important impact on the continent of Europe.

Then shortly after A.D. 400, they began to move, and for the next century they were the terror of two continents. Then they disappeared. They made no contribution to culture or knowledge. They left no monuments, no art, and no literature. They left only their name and a trail of ruin. They were the Vandals.

In the year 406 they invaded Gaul (France); in 409 they crossed the Pyrenees into Spain. Here they quickly developed a seagoing capability, and in 429 crossed the Mediterranean into Africa. North Africa was controlled by Rome, but the Vandals defeated the Roman general Boniface, and ten years later took North Africa's most important city, Carthage.

Having already migrated from Eastern to Western Europe in just thirty-three years, these people had fought their way through two strong nations, built a naval fleet, crossed a sea, and established themselves on the opposite shore. And this was not merely an army on the move; it was a whole nation of men, women, and children.

In North Africa, and operating out of Carthage, the Vandals soon controlled the Mediterranean Sea, plundering ships and making excursions into Sicily, Italy, and other nearby areas. In 455, just sixteen years after taking Carthage, the Vandal armies again crossed the Mediterranean, this time conquering and sacking the city of Rome. For two weeks they prowled the streets, looting, burning, and killing; when they left, little of value remained.

Firmly entrenched at Carthage, the Vandals maintained themselves for the next twenty-two years as a pernicious thorn in the flesh of the whole Mediterranean world. Then in 477 their King Gaiseric died, and their power began abruptly to decline. It wasn't, however, until sixty-six years later that the final blow fell upon them.

It was in 533 that Emperor Justinian I of the Byzantine Empire sent his armies westward from the Dardanelles. With little resistance, the Carthagean defense collapsed, and as of that date the Vandals ceased forever to exist as a nation. The residue of Vandal people drifted away and was in the course of time absorbed and lost in other cultures and among other people. Gradually, Carthage became a ruin; a few of its ancient stones may be seen today near the modern city of Tunis.

But the name Vandal lives on. Vandalism is the deliberate and wanton damaging or destruction of someone else's property.

Vanity Fair *See* Slough of Despond.

— W —

Wash Your Hands Pontius Pilate was in a difficult position, a weak man in a hard place at a bad time. The Romans, having assumed control of Judea and the surrounding area in 63 b.c., had been represented there by a series of governors, of whom Pilate was the fifth. Whenever one country is taken over and occupied by the armies of another, there are inevitable tensions, and this was especially true of Rome's occupation of the volatile Palestinian area.

It was Pilate's lot to be governor there when Jesus lived. While the common people heard Jesus gladly, his teachings quickly aroused a fervent hostility among priests and upper-class groups of the Jewish population. At length, they conspired to have him arrested, bringing him before the authorities for judgment.

Jesus was brought first by night to Caiaphas, the high priest at Jerusalem, who was himself one of the conspirators. Here, numerous witnesses spoke deceitfully or falsely concerning Jesus, their various testimonies often contradictory. At last, Caiaphas asked Jesus, "Are you the Christ, the Son of the blessed God?" Jesus answered, "I am."

This was seen as blasphemy, and Jesus was promptly at daybreak taken away in bonds to Pontius Pilate for sentencing, the high priest himself having no authority to pronounce the sentence of death. Appealing to Pilate's Roman loyalty, the priests told him that Jesus had forbidden the paying of taxes to Rome and had claimed that he was a king, therefore a rival of Caesar.

Examining Jesus, Pilate found no support for these accusations and, in effect, declaring that he wanted nothing to do with the matter, said to the priests, "Take this Jesus and judge him by your own law." This they declined to do. Learning then that Jesus was from Galilee, a small province to the north and knowing that Herod, the primary administrator of that province, was at that time visiting in Jerusalem, Pilate sent Jesus to this Jewish tetrarch.

Herod at first was glad to see Jesus, for he had long wished to meet him; but under pressure of Jesus' accusers, he was soon taking part in the general harassment and humiliation of his fellow Galilean. Refusing, however, to pass judgment on Jesus, he sent him back to Pilate.

When Jesus appeared before the Roman governor this second time, Pilate somewhat impatiently said to the mob that brought him, "As I told you before, I find no fault in this man." Then Pilate made a diplomatic proposal to the accusers of Jesus. He said to them something like this: Because it is your custom at this festival time to release one prisoner as an exercise in forgiveness, I will choose Jesus as the one to release, and will let him go free.

By this time, the priests and lawyers had incited the people into a raging fury against Jesus, and now these people shouted, "No! Don't release Jesus. Release Barabbas!" Barabbas was a notorious criminal, guilty of robbery, sedition, and murder. But rather than release Jesus, the mob chose him. Pilate asked, "If I release Barabbas, what then shall I do with Jesus?" The answer came as a well-orchestrated and vicious scream, "Let him be crucified!"

Pilate, unwilling to agree but afraid not to, called for a basin of water and there before the assembled crowd he made an elaborate show of washing his hands, saying, "I am innocent of the blood of this good man; you see to it!" And they did.

But by his dramatic disclaimer, Pontius Pilate created a figure of language used freely in many tongues from then until now. Wishing to pull away and disassociate from something, we often say, "I wash my hands of that." To wash one's hands of something is to disclaim responsibility for it.

Wear Your Heart on Your Sleeve To wear your heart on your sleeve is to let your feelings show. The expression originates with Shakespeare, in Act I of *Othello*.

Othello is a professional naval officer, a commander, serving at Venice, Italy. He has recently married Desdemona, a lady of impeccable character who is completely faithful to her husband. Iago is an officer under Othello's command, and perhaps the most consummate villain ever to appear on the Shakespearean stage.

When Othello makes Cassio his chief lieutenant, Iago is bitterly resentful, feeling the position should have been his. So he sets out to ruin both Othello and Cassio. He uses a gullible young man named Roderigo to carry out his foul scheme.

In conversation with Roderigo, Iago confesses frankly, even proudly, that he is a deceptive sort of fellow and that he serves Othello for his own selfish reasons—not out of "love or duty, but for my own particular end," he says. Somewhat boastfully, he confides, "I am not what I am," asserting that he will not permit his outward actions to reveal his inward feelings. If I do that, he says, "I wear my heart on my sleeve for daws to peck at." Daws are small black birds, and Iago does not wish to have birds pecking at his heart.

It is, of course, against the background of chivalry that Iago makes his speech about the sleeve and the heart. A common practice among knights was that a man wear on his sleeve some token from his lady, a "pledge" it was called, perhaps her kerchief or scarf. This he wore as a signal that his heart belonged to her and to her only. Iago is of no mind to display his misshapen and calloused heart.

His intentions thus disguised, Iago launches a vicious campaign of character assassination. By trickery, he has Cassio ousted from his position in Othello's navy. He then contrives to create the appearance of something improper between Cassio and Othello's wife. Totally trustful of Iago, and believing the lie, Othello strangles Desdemona to death.

Iago, however, has a wife whose integrity is far superior to that of her husband. Becoming aware of his dastardly schemes, she reveals all this to Othello. Realizing the horrible wrong he has committed in the murder of his wife, he then commits suicide. For all these and other similar acts of perfidy, Iago is condemned to punishment by torture.

Weave a Penelope Shroud In its primitive form, the old Greek legend of Odysseus and Penelope is one of the more moving tales of mythology. For it we are indebted mostly to Homer and *The Odyssey*.

Odysseus and Penelope were the king and queen of Ithaca, a devoted couple ruling a peaceful land. Then came the Trojan War, and Odysseus was forced to join the armies of Agamemnon in the ten-year siege of Troy. When at last the city fell, it took another ten years for Odysseus to reach home. During the war he had angered Poseidon, god of the sea, and the vindictive god made his homeward voyage as difficult as possible.

Thus, Odysseus was away from his home and his wife for a total of twenty years. Through all those years, Penelope hopefully and faithfully awaited his return, always believing that one day he would come home. But with the war long over, many believed Odysseus must be dead.

Somewhat like a flock of vultures, suitors gathered around Queen Penelope, vying and sometimes conspiring with one another for her hand in marriage. Mostly they were a gang of con men seeking the wealth and power of a kingdom. Penelope resisted them with every stratagem she could devise, still refusing to give up her hope that her beloved Odysseus would come home.

In due course, however, she was forced by circumstances to relent a little. She let it be known that she would select a new husband from among her suitors, but that she would do this only after she had completed a task she had undertaken. She was weaving a burial shroud for her father-in-law; she declared she must finish this, and that then she would choose among the men.

From then on, week after week, month after month, Penelope spent her days working on that shroud. This was done openly for all to see. What most people did not know, however, was that most of what she wove by day she secretly unraveled by night, postponing the fateful day as long as possible.

Her strategy worked well; before the shroud was finished, her long-absent husband returned. At first in disguise, he inspected the state of affairs in his palace and kingdom, moved by the deep devotion of his wife and angered by the scheming shenanigans of her suitors. Having fully informed himself of the situation, he then flew into that bunch of scoundrels like a stormwind in a field of chaff. With the aid of his son and two others, the entire lot met a bloody end.

Because of this story, an interesting expression long ago found its way into our speech: weave a shroud of Penelope or weave a Penelope shroud. It is to pursue a course that goes on and on and intentionally is never finished: a make-work situation in which the activity is prolonged to postpone or avoid what will happen when it is concluded. It's a strategy for delaying an unwelcome event. (See also ODYSSEY.)

What Will Mrs. Grundy Say? The play, *Speed the Plough*, by Thomas Morton, was written in 1778. First produced in London around 1800, it was popular for several years and then quickly faded from the literary scene.

Farmer Thomas Ashfield is a country rustic, but a kind, good man, given to homespun philosophies. His feelings and thoughts always seem to be too profound for his limited vocabulary. Dame Ashfield is as good at heart as her husband, but of simpler mind and utterly obsessed with an apprehension of Mrs. Grundy. As for Mrs. Grundy, she never appears in the play, and nothing is revealed of her except that Dame Ashfield is forever seeing everything in the light of what Mrs. Grundy will think of it or say about it. Her presence often felt, she is obviously a woman of whom the farmer's wife stands in awe and whose opinions are highly held.

When Nelly, the former servant of the Ashfields, marries gentry in the person of Sir Abel Handy, Dame Ashfield's comment to her husband is typical: "I wonder, Tummas, what Mrs. Grundy will say?" At the prospects of their much-adored daughter's forthcoming marriage to Sir Abel's son, her first thought is her usual one: "What will Mrs. Grundy say then?" The patient, plodding "Tummas" Ashfield is weary of all this Mrs. Grundy business, adjuring his unheeding spouse: "Be quiet, woolye? Always dinging Dame Grundy into my ears—what will Mrs. Grundy say? What will Mrs. Grundy think—Cans't thee be quiet, let ur alone, and behave thyzel pratty?"

Ashfield's ears were not the last to have Mrs. Grundy dinged into them; it has been happening for nearly two centuries now, for the woman's name has become a paradigm for all who in a judgmental or censorious manner would monitor the lives of others.

Speed the Plough is somewhat more than the comedy it is billed as being. There is intrigue, mystery, suspense—and surprise, no villain but a clash of cultures—and, in keeping with the title, in the end the simple virtues win.

Whitewash a Fence   In front of the house where Tom Sawyer and Aunt Polly lived was a board fence nine feet high and thirty yards long. Aunt Polly gave Tom a bucket of whitewash and a brush and sent him out one summer morning to whitewash that fence. Tom's heart wasn't in it; he'd rather go swimming or do any one of several other interesting things.

After a couple of brush strokes, unenthusiastically delivered, Jim came by with Aunt Polly's water bucket on an urgent mission to the town pump. Tom tried to persuade Jim to do his work for him, but Jim resisted. Tom even tried bribery, going so far as to offer marbles and a look at his sore toe. Just as Jim was at the point of yielding, Aunt Polly came out and squelched the whole deal.

After a couple of swipes with the brush, Tom was again utterly bored and sat down in despair. All the other boys would soon be passing on their way to the swimming hole and other attractions. They would poke fun at Tom for having to work on that fence; Tom knew that. And Tom didn't have enough treasures to bribe any of them; he also knew that.

As he sat there, an idea suddenly struck him. In the excitement of keen anticipation, he leaped up, seized the brush, and "went tranquilly to work."

A little later, when Ben Rogers came by, Tom maintained the appearance of being utterly engrossed in his whitewashing. He actually was able to affect a genuine enjoyment of it. When Ben began to taunt him about having to work, Tom was able to convey the impression that he would much prefer the privilege of wielding a whitewash brush than to go swimming anytime: "Does a boy get a chance to whitewash a fence every day?"

After some reflective silence, Ben said, "Let me whitewash a little." Tom pretended hesitation, protesting that Aunt Polly was "very particular" about having a good job done, that she would entrust it only to one who could do it well. When Ben offered the remainder of the apple he was eating, Tom relented, gave Ben the brush, and sat down to munch the apple while Ben worked.

Then came Billy Fisher who was willing to give up a "kite in good repair" for the chance to whitewash for a little while. Johnny Miller gave a dead rat with a string for swinging it. Soon Tom had boys waiting in line to surrender their treasures for the privilege of participating in this rare enterprise. By midafternoon the fence job was finished, Tom was rich in treasures, and he had scarcely worked at all.

This episode is from *The Adventures of Tom Sawyer* written by Mark Twain in 1876. The tale provides us with a convenient and picturesque way of concisely expressing a somewhat subtle idea. To pull a Tom Sawyer is to trick someone into believing an unwelcome and burdensome task or situation is really a privilege to be enjoyed. "Don't expect me to whitewash your fence" may be an appropriate response when some disagreeable chore is made out to be exciting, rewarding, or otherwise attractive.

Winged Sandals of Hermes   In all the transporting of children to and from this and that, racing about on business errands, keeping social and service engagements, a harried parent may say, "I need the winged sandals of Hermes." Many busy people, caught in the helter-skelter of modern living, might wish for some kind of flying shoes. Well, Hermes had them.

Hermes was a kind of intermediate-grade god in the Olympian pantheon. He came from pretty good stock, his father being Zeus, the high god of the heavens, and his much older brother, Apollo, was already an important deity when Hermes was born. But Hermes really didn't need his auspicious ancestry to make him notable; on his own, he was precocious in the extreme.

On the day of his birth, he sneaked out of his bed and went on a binge of vigorous and adventurous activity. First, he made sandals, equipping them with wings that could take him almost anywhere in almost no time at all. Among other significant doings, he invented a musical instrument called the lyre. Among his more mischievous activities, he stole fifty of Apollo's cattle, driving them away backward to confuse the trail. He sacrificially butchered two of the cattle, nailing their hides to a rock, and enclosed the remainder of the herd in a cave.

He then crept back to his crib and covered himself with his baby blanket. Apollo, realizing his cattle had been stolen, and suspecting his baby brother, confronted him with the charge. Hermes pointed out that he was only a day-old baby and interested, so he said, only in his mother's milk. Zeus, however, knew the truth about Apollo's cattle and ordered Hermes to restore them.

When Apollo and Hermes went to retrieve the cattle, Apollo observed the two skins where Hermes had nailed them to the rock, saying to Hermes, "What about those two?" Hermes replied. "Oh, those? I sacrificed them to the twelve gods." Apollo said, "I know of only eleven gods. Who is the twelfth?" To which Hermes blithely replied, "I am!" And he meant it.

From then on, Hermes used his winged sandals a lot. He was almost everywhere and into almost everything. He was a sort of messenger god who ran errands for the others, a trouble-shooter type, and a bit of a swashbuckler. On his various missions, he sometimes succeeded and sometimes failed. When Zeus sent him to wrest a critical secret from the impaled Prometheus, he failed. However, when Zeus sent him to slay the hundred-eyed Argus who was guarding Io, he succeeded.

The mischievous bent with which he started stayed with him generally throughout his colorful career. Among the gods, he was something of a maverick. Never the self-effacing type, he was usually out to get what he could for himself from any situation. Hermes has never been accused of laziness. Those winged sandals—he wore them well.

Wisdom of Solomon   When speaking of superior wisdom, we are likely to make reference to the wisdom of Solomon. Why Solomon? Why not Socrates, or Nostradamus, or some other noted intellectual? Perhaps it's because Solomon is unique in being the only person ever to ask God specifically for wisdom and the only person ever to be specifically granted it. Also, no person ever used wisdom more productively or, on occasion, abused it more outrageously.

Solomon, son of David, was the king of Israel for about forty years. His older brother Adonijah was actually first in line for the throne, but David preferred Solomon because Solomon was the son of his favorite wife, Bathsheba. On his deathbed, David gave his blessing to Solomon and charged him with these dramatic words: "Be strong, and show yourself a man."

One of Solomon's first kingly acts was to make a pilgrimage from Jerusalem to Gibeon. Here there was a high altar where David had often worshiped, and Solomon wished to do as his father had done. While at Gibeon, in a dream state of some sort, Solomon had a critical conversation with Jehovah, the God of Israel. By night, Jehovah came to the new king with this question: "What shall I give you?"

Solomon's prudent answer was to profess that, in the face of his great task he was like a little child, so he asked for an understanding mind and the ability to discern between good and evil. Being much pleased that Solomon had not asked for wealth or long life, Jehovah said, "I do now give you a wise and discerning mind, and I give you also what you have not asked, both riches and honor."

Soon thereafter, Solomon's gift of wisdom was put to the test. Two prostitutes who lived in the same house came to Solomon asking that he settle a dispute between them. Both had given birth to babies, three days apart, and one of the babies had died. One woman accused the other, testifying: "This woman rolled over on her baby in the night and killed it. Then, while I slept, she brought her dead baby and laid it in my bosom, taking my live child as her own. Next morning, finding the dead baby beside me, I looked at it carefully, and quickly saw that this dead baby was hers, not mine. I want my live baby back!"

The dispute raged, each woman shouting at the other: "The dead child is yours; the live child is mine!" Solomon was called upon to make a judgment. One woman was lying—but which one? The polygraph hadn't been invented yet, but Solomon came up with a lie detector test better than the polygraph. His test was based on his knowledge of human nature and a mother's feeling for her child.

He ordered his servants, "Bring me a sword," and the sword was brought. Then, in the presence of the women, he commanded, "Divide the living child in two, and give half to the one and half to the other." Instantly, one of the women screamed, "Oh, no, no, my lord, give her the child; don't kill it." And to that woman Solomon gave the baby, knowing that she was its mother.

It was this episode that, more than any other, gave Solomon his reputation for superior wisdom. His subjects stood in awe of him, and his reputation has outlived him, surviving now for almost 3,000 years.

Wolf in Sheep's Clothing Skillful and voracious predators, wolves like to prey on sheep; legs-o'-lamb seem to suit their palates perfectly. They will stalk a flock for hours, or even days, looking for a chance to make a kill and then a quick getaway. Flocks are usually well guarded, and for the wolf, the sheep-killing business is both difficult and risky.

Aesop, the famous fabler, tells us that once there was a sort of nonconformist wolf who decided there was an easier way to catch sheep. Being a rather lazy rascal, as well as a deceptive one, he clothed himself in the wool-covered skin of a sheep and joined the flock. By night, when none were looking, he could creep up on an isolated lamb, silently cut its throat with his razor-sharp fangs, and have a midnight snack. The next day, the lamb's absence would be blamed on marauding wolves who had sneaked up in the dark and done this dastardly killing.

This program worked out very well for the wolf for a few days and nights. Then, one evening, guests came to the shepherd's house, and for their dinner he needed a sheep from among his flock. Hurrying to the sheepfold, he beheaded the first one he came upon—the wolf.

That was the end of him, but not of his story; in our language it lives on. A wolf in sheep's clothing is a deceitful person, who for the purpose of doing harm or gaining advantage, poses as being what he or she is not.

Work Like a Trojan   The expression to work like a Trojan has long been common among English-speaking people. Many, no doubt, have used it without much knowledge of a Trojan or his work. More recently, therefore, the expression has suffered corruption, mutating, for instance, into "swear" like a Trojan or "drink" like one. The Trojans deserve better than this.

Most of what we know of them comes from Homer's legend of the Trojan War. They are portrayed as an heroic and courageous people. Their city, Troy, was one of the great trade centers of the ancient world, strategically located on the Asiatic side of the Aegean Sea. Their king was Priam, an aged and honorable man. His son, Paris, though, lacking most of his father's finer qualities, was the black sheep of the royal family.

Paris went over to the Greek city of Sparta where Menelaus was king, seduced Helen, the king's wife, and took her away to Troy. Priam probably should have told Paris to take his stolen woman and go elsewhere; but he was, apparently, a father first and a king second. So Paris and Helen remained in Troy. The Grecian city-states united under King Agamemnon, assembled a powerful army, sailed across the Aegean, blockaded Troy's harbor, and laid siege to the city. Their purpose was to rescue Helen, and that siege lasted ten years.

For that full decade the Trojans labored to save their city. Paris was not held in highest esteem, and in time Helen sank to the low level of being despised by most Trojans. But they were a patriotic people, and loyal to their king.

For those ten long years they watched their ramparts day and night. They struggled with the awesome problems of providing themselves food, fuel, clothing, and other necessities. Their women and children joined in the struggle. Heroically, they fought off every assault. Some of their people were among the noblest of all time, for example, Hector.

After more than nine dreary years, the Greeks at last concluded there was no hope of defeating the Trojans. The Trojan resolve and industry were just too great. As a last resort, Odysseus devised a scheme to trick them. The trick was the famed wooden horse that hid Greek soldiers and brought them within the city walls to destroy the Trojans. (See also TROJAN HORSE.)

—X Y Z—

Xerxes' Tears   One sheds the tears of Xerxes when grieving openly about the unfortunate consequences of doing something that one intends to do regardless.

Ten years earlier, Xerxes' father, Darius I, had suffered humiliating defeat by the Greeks at Marathon. Now, in 480 B.C., yielding to pressure from vindictive advisors, Xerxes led 360,000 of his Persians on a mission of revenge. As tradition has it, on seeing his assembled army, the king wept at the realization that many of his men would never return.

He had good reason to weep. Nevertheless, the mighty force crossed the Hellespont with about 800 ships. At first, the Persians were somewhat successful. They wiped out Leonidas and his three hundred at Thermopylae in mid-August and occupied the city of Athens on September 21—but not for long. Eight days later, the entire Persian fleet was destroyed at Salamis, and the king retreated to Persepolis.

However, he left an army of occupation. A few months afterward, though, this army was also done in by the Greeks, and the surviving Persians returned to Persia.

Xerxes never again attempted a conquest of Greece. His power in decline, be became preoccupied with petty affairs and eventually was murdered by a member of his court.

Key-Word Index

Numerals indicate pages on which stories begin.